PRAISE FOR TOM RUSSELL

"Tom Russell is Johnny Cash, Jim Harrison and Charles Bukowski rolled into one. I feel a great affinity with Tom Russell's songs, for he is writing out of the wounded heart of America."
Lawrence Ferlinghetti

"The best songwriter of my generation...raises and sets the bar for contemporary singer-songwriters. "
Mike Regenstreif, *Montreal Gazette*

"Tom Russell is an original, a brilliant songwriter with a restless curiosity and an almost violent imagination."
Annie Proulx

"I so admire his work. It's fine craft, and posey, none of which dwarfs its embracing humanity and urgings."
Van Dyke Parks

"Tom Russell is the last great American voice."
Ken Bruen

"...surgical songwriting skills..."
The New Yorker

"The most powerful voice on the contemporary folk circuit..."
Boston Globe

"Tom Russell is the most original songwriter out there... I think of Tom Russell as the musical equivalent of Cormac McCarthy."
Professor Allen Josephs

"One of the best singer-songwriters of our time."
The Washington Post

"A master storyteller..."
Chicago Sun Times

"Tom Russell is the last wandering Beat...a prolific and venerable artist writing the best songs of his career....impeccably written."
San Francisco Chronicle

"To my mind, Tom is a contemporary exemplar of a long tradition of composing songs of the soul of the sort Schubert was really the first to write. And, man, by my lights, he is worthy to be compared with him... I have been profoundly affected."
Dr. Kenneth Ring

"Russell is our finest writer/criminologist/poet/taxi driver/painter."
USA Today

"The greatest living country songwriter...he's written songs that capture the essence of America. A trait that can only be matched by the country's greatest novelists...."
John Swenson, *Rolling Stone*

"The lyrics are jewels."
Robert Hunter
Grateful Dead Lyricist

"Tom Russell's songs saved my life."
Dave Alvin

"Tom Russell writes a song that comes right at you and evokes a mood of being there...bloodcurdling."
Ramblin' Jack Elliott

"Tom Russell writes better songs than most anyone about anything he wants to write about...they affect me like wonderful novels."
Buck Ramsey

"Russell's work summons the spirit of Walt Whitman's *Leaves of Grass* and Howard Zinn's *A People's History of the United States*. Russell's reach is both wide and deep...."
Charles Young, *The Atlantic*

"How great is Tom Russell? Isn't he tremendous? Always the best. I'd like to quit my job and travel with him....if the money can be worked out."
David Letterman

"Tom Russell has made a career of writing poetry from the plain, by turning hardscrabble, inelegant lyrical ruminations into some of the most probing songs in contemporary folk music."
The Hartford Courant

"Russell's *The Man From God Know's Where* should be required listening for every student of American History. One of the most important folk records ever recorded."
John Lomax III

"When Joe Ely sang me 'Gallo del Cielo,' I said...who the hell wrote that? Great song."
Bruce Springsteen
(in a letter to Tom Russell)

"Joe did a hell of a song tonight...A Tom Russell song. It's about a fighting rooster. It's called 'Gallo del Cielo.' It's good. And I'm hard to impress."
Bob Dylan
In Clarence Clemmons's *Big Man*

"With his burnished voice and mastery of Americana song craft, Tom Russell takes his place alongside Dave Alvin, Guy Clark, Kris Kristofferson, the late John Stewart and other like-minded folk artists who can find the perfect phrase and deliver it with smoky, understated eloquence."
J. Fusilli
The Wall Street Journal

120 SONGS TOM RUSSELL

Montana
2012

120 SONGS

Copyright © 2012 by Thomas George Russell

ISBN-13: 978-0-9828601-7-5

Manufactured in the United States of America

All rights reserved. With the exception of short excerpts used for promotional, review, or academic purposes, no portion of this work may be reproduced or distributed in any print or electronic form without the written permission of the publisher.

Published in the United States by

Bangtail Press
P. O. Box 11262
Bozeman, MT 59719
www.bangtailpress.com

All woodcut illustrations by Tom Russell.
Woodcut photos by Brian Kanof.
Cover photograph by Eric Temple.

*To Nadine and Izzy,
Tallulah, Patrick, and Molly*

TABLE OF CONTENTS

Acknowledgments	xv
Introduction	1
Notes on Song Introductions and Guitar Chords	19

CHAPTER ONE
Early Songs: The Vancouver/Austin Years

The End of the Trail	22
Cropduster	24
Alkali	26
Zane Grey	28
Joshua Tree	30
Rayburn Crane	32

CHAPTER TWO
The New York/Oslo Years

Saint Olav's Gate	36
Canadian Whiskey	38
Spanish Burgundy	40
U.S. Steel	42
The Road to Bayamon	44
Blue Wing	46
Veteran's Day	48
Walkin' on the Moon	50
Outbound Plane	52
Oil Field Girls	54
Beyond the Blues	56
Chinatown in the Rain	58
The Biggest Border Town in the World	61
Mineral Wells	63
Chocolate Cigarettes	65
The Cuban Sandwich	68
Nazareth to Bethlehem	70
Jack Johnson	72
Hong Kong Boy	74
The Heart	76
Saint Lily of the Mohawks	78

CHAPTER THREE
Gallo del Cielo

Gallo del Cielo	83

CHAPTER FOUR
New York to the San Joaquin

Haley's Comet	90
La Goulue	92
Amelia's Railroad Flat	95
Hurricane Season	98
Winnipeg	100
The Evangeline Hotel	102
Manzanar	104
Box of Visions	106
Blood Oranges	108
The Angel of Lyon	110
The Eyes of Roberto Duran	112
They're Closin' Sunny's Diner	114
Sparrow of Swansea	116
Wings of a Blackbird	118
Denver Wind	120
Ten Cent Lemonade	122
Home before Dark	124
Half Moon Boulevard	126
Billy Collins	128
The Rose of the San Joaquin	130
Hand Carved Heart	132
What do you Want	134
Out in California	136
Between the Cracks	138

CHAPTER FIVE
Cowboy Songs

Navajo Rug	142
The Sky Above, The Mud Below	144
The Banks of the Musselshell	148
Hallie Lonnigan	151
Claude Dallas	153
Roanie	156

Tonight We Ride	159
All This Way for the Short Ride	162
Bucking Horse Moon	164
Bacon Rind and Chief Seattle	166
The Ballad of Edward Abbey	168
Little Blue Horse	170
The Basque	172
The Heart of a Bucking Horse	174

CHAPTER SIX
The Man from God Knows Where

The Man From God Knows Where	178
Patrick Russell	180
The Outcast	182
Ambrose Larsen	184
The Dreamin'	186
Acres of Corn	188
Sitting Bull in Venice	190
When Irish Girls Grow Up	192
Throwin' Horseshoes At The Moon	194
The Outcast (Revisited)	196
Love Abides	198

CHAPTER SEVEN
The Border Years

Touch of Evil	202
Down the Rio Grande	204
When Sinatra Played Juarez	208
Where the Dream Begins	210
California Snow	213
What Work Is	215
The Kid From Spavinaw	218
The Boy Who Cried Wolf	220
Muhammad Ali	222
Racehorse Haynes	224
Isaac Lewis	226
Grapevine	229
Woodrow	231
The Pugilist at Fifty-Nine	234
Beautiful Trouble	236

Four Chambered Heart	239
Stealing Electricity	242
The Sound of One Heart Breaking	244
Ash Wednesday	246
It Goes Away	248
Old Heart	250
The Death of Jimmy Martin	252

CHAPTER EIGHT
Blood and Candle Smoke
Mesabi

East of Woodstock, West of Viet Nam	256
Santa Ana Wind	258
Nina Simone	261
Finding You	263
Criminology	264
Crosses of San Carlos	266
Mississippi River Runnin' Backwards	268
The Most Dangerous Woman in America	270
Don't Look Down	272
Guadalupe	274
Mesabi	276
Farewell Never Never Land	278
The Lonesome Death of Ukulele Ike	282
Sterling Hayden	284
Furious Love	286
Roll the Credits, Johnny	288
The Road to Nowhere	290
Heart within a Heart	292
And God Created Border Towns	294
Goodnight, Juarez	296
Saint Francis	298

APPENDIX A
Co-Write Information — *301*

APPENDIX B
Tom Russell Discography — *303*

APPENDIX C
Title Index — *305*

ACKNOWLEDGMENTS

I would like to thank Peter O'Brien, Steve Toner, Mike Regenstreiff, and John Yuelkenbeck for their fine and enduring interest in my songs over the years. Peter and Steve have done quite a bit of compiling lyrics. Corky and Bill at www.villagerecords.com have always been supportive and keep the records available to the public. Alec Wightman has been a good friend and always provides sage legal advice. He has also been a huge supporter of the music. Allen Jones has done an incredible job editing this work and is also a very fine American writer. Thanks also to the musical support of Thad Beckman. My wife Nadine has remained the inspiration for many of the later songs and keeps me young in spirit so I can do the work.

Finally, the co-writers themselves have taught me an enormous amount about the craft, particularly Ian and Sylvia Tyson, and also Katy Moffatt, Nanci Griffith, Dave Alvin, Peter Case, Bob Neuwirth, Alan Rhody, Greg Trooper, Andrew Hardin, Gretchen Peters, Steve Young, and Paul Zarzyski.

Mil gracias.
TR

WOODY GUTHRIE
Woodcut by Tom Russell
2012

INTRODUCTION

MIDNIGHT IN THE TOWER OF SONG

"It's called songwriting. It has to do with melody and rhythm. Then after that, anything goes. You make everything yours."
Bob Dylan
Rolling Stone

Songs travel. They come out of the whorehouses, bars, and churches and fly away on the tongues of the rakes and rambling boys. They mutate, shift gears, add another chorus and sail across the seven seas. The old songs come from the folk, but are never buried with the folk. The good songs endure. They *gather ye round* an audience and spin the lyrical news of the day. They amuse or hurt, divert and stop time for a holy moment. They pretend to be art, and sometimes succeed. With a snicker. They suck us in, slap us around, kick us in the belly and heart, and then push us back out into the world with a memory we'll never purge from our blood. The *good* songs. They tell us subliminal things about love we knew but wouldn't admit. Songs. They are the weapons of the fortune teller, the rogue, the Don Juan, the cowboy, the troubadour, songstress, minstrel, Bard, opera singer, and shoeshine boy. They are the melodic pitch of every Molly Malone hawking mussels in the marketplace. They beguile us with their sing-song rhyme and tinkle-down melodies, yet they are imbued with truer feel for human history, poetry, emotion, and cold hard facts of life, then a thousand dusty tomes from social scientists, poets, politicians, theologians, and academic historians. Songs travel.

That's why I was attracted to the trade.

Let me tell you a story. That's the way it always begins, heh? Move a little closer here. Gather ye round. A *story*—by way of introduction to this war bag filled with many of the songs I've written. I was on a train a few months ago. We called it a songwriter train. Songwriters and *fans* of song. We travelled from Los Angeles and Portland, round trip. Antique cars and a dome liner. Rolling back south through the lush agricultural valley of Central California, I was admiring the Steinbeckian landscape—which was coastline on one side of the train, and fields filled with harvesting machines and Mexican workers on the other. Dozens and dozens of workers. It all seems postcard colorful when you're not the laborer in the vineyard. You're safe inside a train. Humming old songs and sipping red wine.

Then the train jerked hard, jumped, and came to a slow halt in the middle of the fields. Time stopped. We'd hit a car. A man had backed up, by mistake, over the tracks, in front of the oncoming train. He was thrown out of the car, into the field. Right outside our window. His young child was lying a few yards away from him. That division between the secure world inside and the broken landscape outside was erased. A woman came running alongside the train with her arms stretched out in grief. *The dying man's wife*. He'd been driving in the car to pick her up from the harvest work. Our train window drowned her screaming. But that made it worse. Two worlds melting into one. One long silent cry.

A woman passenger in our train group was a doctor. She jumped off and ran to the man and child, but there was nothing she could do. The father was dead. The child would not make it. The mother was lying in the field weeping. People were holding her down, trying to soothe her. Another relative, maybe the brother of the dead man, walked back beside the train. Crying and flailing his arms. The prosaic Steinbeck landscape had transformed into a medieval, living-life study by Goya or Brueghel. Only this was in real time. Pain. Agony. The crushed car. The bodies beneath blankets. The wife face down in the dirt. And then the farming backdrop. Out beyond the bodies the work was still going on in the fields. The big harvesting machine moved down the rows. *Relentlessly.*

When the doctor got back aboard, tears in her eyes, she said, "Nothing I could do." And then she thought for a moment and blurted out, "This is just like a Woody Guthrie song..." A few of us nodded our heads in agreement. Nobody could speak. Nobody had to. There was grief and confusion and songs ringing around in our heads. Woody Guthrie songs. Songs we hadn't thought of in years. In *Plane Wreck at Los Gatos*, Guthrie wrote, "Is this the best way we can grow our big orchards?... / To fall like dry leaves to rot on my topsoil? / And be called by no name except deportees?"

He nailed it down. His hard poetry echoed around the train car and out the door and into those fields. Then his words circled back and strangled us with the truth.

The train sat there for hours. The ambulances arrived. The harvesting continued. The *light sparkling wine* tasted bitter that afternoon. *Altered.* The grapes were tainted with blood and pain and hard poetry. Tragedy in real time. Woody's songs certainly didn't solve anything out in the fields, or raise up the dead. But his words helped make sense of it all.

Woody had said he was always searching for *a voice*. A voice he didn't hear on the stage, screen, radio, records, jukebox, or in magazines and newspapers. A language all his own. A voice that untangled the words that he felt in his belly and heart. When I looked out on that field and whispered fragments of his lyrics I realized that Woody found his voice, sure enough, and it wasn't a socialist voice, a communist voice, male or female voice, a white or black voice, or a Mexican voice. It was a *human* voice. A truthful human voice, in song, that carried with it the force of entering your heart when you most needed it.

Songs travel. And arrive.

II
THE RAVAGES OF IMPOSSIBLE NECESSITY

> "Woody Guthrie created his own morality, fashioning his precepts and convictions out of the raw stuff of his own vital existence, and those included love, and grief, and blood, and work…and the ravages of impossible necessity, courage and sweat and incessant trouble."
> Grover Lewis
> *Splendor in the Short Grass:*
> *The Grover Lewis Reader*

Incessant trouble. Grief and blood and love. The *journey*. There's a ceramic statue in my library of a man holding a guitar. A troubadour. It's three feet high. A one-off piece of art created by one of Woody Guthrie's nieces. It's the William Oliver Award from the first Woody Guthrie Song Festival in 1974. The brass plaque on the statue's base quotes Woody: "All you can write is what you see." Amen to that, or so I thought in 1974. I won the award for one of my first songs: "Here's Your Indian Mr. White Man." Looking back I don't consider that song a profound classic, by any means, but it came from a sincere place at the time. It was *a start*. A few lines:

> *Here's your Indian, Mr. Whiteman, drunk as well you know*
> *Take him to your mission, dress him up in welfare clothes*
> *Then turn him out on Main Street with a food stamp in his hand,*
> *Let him search the piss-soaked gutters for his reservation land*

Well, okay. A bit overwrought. Angry. Preachy. *Young.* This wasn't "Plane Wreck at Los Gatos." Or "The Ballad of Ira Hayes." But it was what I saw at the time. Or what I *thought* I saw. I was just beginning. The poetry was lacking. The voodoo. The jab, the uppercut, the dance. The knockout. The hidden element.

The man who presented me with the award (over the phone) was Earl Robinson who co-wrote the classic topical song, "I Dreamed I Saw Joe Hill Last Night." I was honored. I was living in Vancouver, Canada, and Earl called me from down in Seattle and said he'd bring the statue up. He asked what tribe I was in. I told him I wasn't in *any* tribe. Never claimed to be. I was a white man playing music in hootchie-koochie joints on skid row. He seemed confused and disappointed. I suppose they'd wanted a Native American poster child. Well, they'd misunderstood.

Earl suddenly changed his mind and said they'd *mail me* the statue. That was it. First song, first award, first indication that there were categories and communities and a skewered politicized view, from the outside, that art was aimed at specific groups by specific writers, and we'd better pick a group, join a club, and buy a uniform and state our type of music. Folk. Protest. Country. Jazz. Blues? What have you there in your song bag, kid? Who are you? What type of music do you play? Which side are you on? Killer questions that demean the reach for higher art. *The lie that life was black and white.* So sayeth the bard, Bob Dylan. We'll get to Bob in a moment.

That same year, 1974, I won another award, the professional country category of the first American Song Festival (both these song contests are long gone) for my second song, "The End of the Trail." I was on a roll. I was writing songs about Native People because I was working in skid row bars frequented by North Coast Indians, and I witnessed a lion's share of poverty, drunken agony, drug dealings, and violent crime. The Natives in Canada weren't getting the raw deal Indians got in America—but the lives I saw were rough enough.

I was an armchair criminologist with a master's degree and a Martin guitar, fresh off the boat from a year of teaching in Nigeria during the Biafran

War. I had walked away from the academic trade before they snuffed out my creative chops, art visions, and musical daydreams. I wanted to write songs. I'd wanted to write songs since I was a ten year old kid with an autoharp and a cheap banjo. I'd wanted to write songs since I saw Bob Dylan sing "Desolation Row" at the Hollywood Bowl, right after he'd written it. Now I was finally ready.

I believed, fully, in the concept *of paying one's dues*. It was the law of the streets. So I was playing the dives, starting at the bottom, and had a growing interest and empathy for the Indians along Vancouver's, East Hastings street. I was a big fan of Peter La Farge, who'd written "The Ballad of Ira Hayes" and other songs about Native Americans. I sang "Ira Hayes" most every night. I still sing it. "And then Ira started drinking hard, / Jail was often his home…"

In those joints in Canada I was learning how to survive in front of a microphone. How to reach out for a voice—a *writing* voice, as well as a singing voice. An authentic voice. That fleeting concept Woody Guthrie kept harping about in his notebooks. To be truthful, I was hired in those clubs because I was a good master of ceremonies for burlesque carnival. I had a polished side-show spiel: "And now ladies and gentlemen, here's Spongy the Rubber Girl, *and* Onyx *and* his snake Pharaoh, *and* Big Jimmy the three-hundred-pound female impersonator." It was show time at the end of the world. I relished it.

And country-rock music was the backdrop. Those were the days when country music was still hard-core working-class blues. People drank and fucked around on their wives and *killed people* in those songs. The lines of the songs were fired out of heavy weapons: "I shot a man in Reno just to watch him die!" Or how about, "If you see me coming better step aside, a lot of men didn't, a lot of men died…Sixteen Tons." A hit. Can you imagine? The people who wrote these songs sounded like they'd *been there*. On the street. In the mines and factories and cotton fields. Prison. Death Row. Divorce Court. It was folk music with real blood running through it. We played it behind the topless dancers and sideshow acts. It worked.

For the drinkers in the dives and honkytonks it was all catharsis. Bent over your third drink and hearing George Jones singing "Things Have Gone to Pieces" or "The Selfishness of Man" could divert the personal blues with the *real* blues. You were not alone. The guy in the song was worse off than you were. He'd take your pain. Only cost you a quarter in the jukebox. A cheap three-minute shrink. That was the deal. The music told the truth. There were lines in "The Selfishness of Man," written by Leon Payne, that could lift you off the bar stool. "Little children painting pictures of the birds and apple trees / Oh, why can't the grown up people have the faith of one of these / And to think those tiny fingers might become a killer's hand...."

Swallow that along with your cheap whiskey. The lumberjacks, fishermen, Indians, hookers, and ex cons loved it. Songs about their lives, failures, and violent dreams. Skid row poetry. The songs kept the merry-go-round moving. The painted ponies went up and down on the topless stages. We played eight sets of music on long violent nights. The cheap drinks and warm beer were slammed down onto tables. Drugs were passed underneath. Your clothes stunk of cigarette smoke and stale beer. Bands were fired. Waitresses disappeared. Dancers overdosed or changed clubs. Knives flashed. The drunks were rolled and thrown out in the alley. They piled up behind my car. Shoeless and wasted. "All you can write is what you see," said my Woody Guthrie statue. I was taking notes. *Eyes wide open.*

I was on *the path*. A working musician on an early roll. My first two songs had won major awards. Then I wrote a quick honky-tonk novel that was accepted by one of the top literary agents in the world. I moved to Austin in 1974 and recorded a record with Patricia Hardin. We were about to be signed to a prestige folk label, Vanguard. We'd been reviewed in *Rolling Stone*. These events all happened in those first four years of gigging and writing. Then slowly it slipped out of my hands. I hadn't found my voice. I was trying to run across the high wire before I'd learned how to walk.

I'm able to weigh these matters now, looking back. This book is a catalogue of songs and musings which are mile markers on a long journey towards a more authentic writer's voice. Higher ground. If I hadn't started with "Here's Your Indian, Mr. Whiteman," I could not have reached, "Guadalupe."

Yeah, Woody, *all you can write is what you see*—but also feel, hear, smell, taste, digest, spit out, live, and endure. After that initial cloud of early songs and false hope rolled away—I went back to the honkytonks in Vancouver, Austin, and San Francisco, and eventually found myself in New York, seven years later, driving a taxi. Then one night I picked up Grateful Dead songwriter Robert Hunter, and my life turned back around towards music. But I'm asking myself—what are the earlier roots of this insatiable yen for song? What keeps bringing me back to song and minstrelsy?

It began with blood memory.

DARK WAS THE NIGHT, COLD WAS THE GROUND
Woodcut by Tom Russell
2012

III
THE WINE GLASSES OF DAWN, THE BLOOD MEMORY

"Lightnin' Hopkins, I understood at last, had accomplished in his fashion as much as any man can do. With only one good arm and a splintered toothpick for a bat, he stepped up to the plate and knocked the concrete ball aimed at his head clear out of the largest goddamn park there is."
      Grover Lewis
      Splendor in the Short Grass:
      The Grover Lewis Reader

My mother *rock-a-bye-babied* me in the cradle, and the cradle rocked, and then rolled over and spilled me out on the wooden floors of coffee houses, where I stared up into the face of Sam "Lightnin'" Hopkins, singing about selling wine to an underage Indian girl in Arizona. Yes, indeed. Seemed like before I could crawl I got the *heebie jeebies* and the *blues willies* and the *goose-flesh-tingle* from old songs. And nursery rhymes. And fairy tales. It's all connected up in my blood memory, and I need to go back and rub my soul over these touchstones. I need the healing. I get the profound notion that we've lost our blood memory in this current plugged-in, strip-mall, digital age. We've gone all Facebook emotional. I feel something slipping away.

My mother sang songs she'd heard from *her* mother, and so on, back through the tribe. Back to the Irish minstrel Zosimus—*tap tap tapping* with his blind man's cane through the cobblestone streets of Dublin, 150 years ago. Back to the very Spanish caves at the dawn of time—*when the singer is hoarse and the room is cold, when the wine is crusted on the glasses*—or to borrow from Lorca, "The wine glasses of the dawn are broken, the cry of the guitar begins."

I recall an old poem, "The Pirate Don Durk of Dowdee." My mother recited it when we were very young. It scared the hell out of us. She savored the words and hit on the alliteration and dark rhymes. This pirate was bad to the bone. His conscience was black as a bat and crooked as a squash.

> *It's true he was wicked as wicked could be,*
> *His sins they outnumbered a hundred and three,*
> *But oh, he was perfectly gorgeous to see,*
> *The Pirate Don Durk of Dowdee.*

She sang another song about a man name of Johnny Roebeck, who invented a sausage machine. Johnny was a freakish individual, a sociopath who lived way out in the forest and ground-up the neighbor's cats and dogs for sausage. One day Johnny fell into his own machine and his wife ground *him* into sausage. My mom acted it out. She *relished* it. Scared the living hell out of a four-year-old kid. Prepared us for the meat grinder of life and spoiled my appetite for sausages. But her recitations stoked my thirst for mystery and rhyme and dark humor. The taste for words which clang together and pull you inside the story. In concocting literature and song there is the sound of words; the sound of words hitting against words; and the sound of silence between words. James Joyce said that. My mother proved it.

Sir James Barrie, the author of *Peter Pan*, praised his mother's songs and fairytales for developing in him "the trend toward the whimsical, the wistful and the mystic." Amen. Later, when I was old enough, my mother gave me a thesaurus so I might look up words to go into the stories I was making up. Roget first published it in 1852. A desk companion for those wishing to improve their creative use of the lingo. A word finder. God created the word for us to deliver a message. The poet and songwriter and novelist were the "messenger angels." Sayeth my mother. Forty years later I sat across from the master songwriter, Ian Tyson. He had a thesaurus and a dictionary and a road atlas in front of him. He was writing songs. He looked up and said, "I fell in love with the English language at the age of fifty."

I still use the thesaurus my mom gave me. She wrote my name inside. I look into it now to see her handwriting. Her mark on my blood memory. She later helped me write a short story which garnered an A+ in my tenth grade English class. We sent it off to men's magazines, but, alas, they said there wasn't enough sex in it. My mother taught me narrative, rhyme, appreciation of literature, and the craving for wild stories and dark lyrics. She taught me to love music. She had a great album collection and her kid brother was a concert pianist.

It's a short ride from "The Pirate Don Durk of Dowdee" to Lightnin' Hopkins staring down at me with black wrap-around shades and whiskey breath, singing about going to jail for selling wine to an underage Indian girl. *Frightening*. Criminal. *Bad ass*. "Poor Lightnin'," as he called himself, sang from a place deep inside our blood memory. A dark place where the secret password was a bottle neck sliding down the strings of an open-tuned guitar.

In Native American culture, the blood memory is the ancestral connection to language, song, spirituality, and tribal teaching. If you lose the blood memory of your people's language, you've lost your center. (To paraphrase Paul Hendrickson.) The notion of blood memory reminds me of the idea of songlines—the notion that Australian aboriginals *sing up* their ancestral ground as they walk across it. When an aboriginal crosses a river bed, there's a song which goes with crossing that river. There's a song for rock formations and ant hills and old trees. The landscape is an ancient opera, waiting to be sung up as you waltz through it all. A song painting.

Bruce Chatwin spoke of all this in his work *Songlines*. My songlines lead back through Los Angeles streets, to Iowa and Missouri farm towns, on back to the roads near Templemore, Ireland, and the harbor in Bergen, Norway, and further and further back and to the caves of ancient Spain. Songs travel. The wine glasses of dawn are broken.

Hand me down my guitar.

Songs. I taste them like blood in my mouth. Song is my true language. My *lingo*. A form of rhyming prayer. My blood memory is riddled with lullabies, nursery rhymes, fairy tales, Irish ballads, folksongs, Broadway musicals, cowboy songs, Hawaiian music, Mexican *corridos, cante hondo,* flamenco wails, blues, Native American chants, Chopin piano pieces (played by my uncle), pop songs and rock songs, and on and on. Songs are prayers which open a crack in the void to get to the heart of the secret, eh? This may sound like philosophical hogwash, but what the hell, it's *my* hogwash. And it's the truth. Songs have taught me more of the deep essential mysteries than school, politics and religion. Songs *are* my politics and religion.

Somewhere along the road I picked up the guitar, a 1946 Martin D-18 purchased for $150 in 1966, in a pawn shop in San Luis Obispo, California. It was beat-up and scratched with pick marks and sweat stains. Somebody had played the hell out of it. It was a wild harp, all right. Scarred from the battle. It looked like Lightnin' Hopkins's guitar—that "splintered toothpick for a bat," the one he used to step up to the plate of life and knock "the concrete ball aimed at his head clear out of the largest goddamn park there is." Old guitars have absorbed the heat and smoke and teardrops of every room they've been played in. There are ghosts in the Rosewood cracks. "Wood never dies," as Leonard Cohen said.

I learned three chords and the way out of town. Like Woody, Dylan, Hank, and Homer. I had a fanatic heart.

IV
STOLEN MOMENTS AND FANATIC HEARTS

"I consider myself a poet first and a musician second. I live like a poet and I'll die like a poet."
Bob Dylan
Highway 61, Hulton Archive

My older sister, Nan, walked into my room one day and threw a brochure on my desk. It was a folded glossy pamphlet from an agency in New York which booked young Bob Dylan. The year was 1963, or thereabouts. The brochure held Dylan's long poetic/biographic piece, *My Life in a Stolen Moment*. My sister was thinking of booking Dylan for a charity concert at her college. Hence the brochure from the booker. My eye found a couple of random lines. "I rode freight trains for kicks / An' got beat up for laughs…" She decided to book Louis Armstrong instead. Louis was a bigger draw at the time. No problem, Nan. Louis was great. But I kept the Dylan booklet, reading it over and over.

Man, this kid Dylan had done it all. He'd worked the carnivals. Ridden in boxcars like Woody Guthrie. Danced with Indians. Got jailed for armed robbery and held for a murder rap. *Dig it*. I bought his story, hook, line and sinker. That same day my sister also gave me Lawrence Ferlinghetti's, *A Coney Island of the Mind*. A big day for young Tom. Bob Dylan and The Beats! *The answer*. The map which pointed of town. I took this trove of literature into my room and poured over it as I listened to music. I'd stop for a moment and hold up my album covers up and stare into the faces of folk singers while their songs played. They were talking to *me*, this kid holed up in his room. Then I'd go back and read Dylan's stories and the Beat poetry books. Weeks and months. Years. A lifetime. I'm still at it.

In that poem Dylan talked all about how he'd run away from his home in Hibbing, Minnesota a lot of times and he'd "been caught and brought back

11

all but once." It was a long way from my life in Los Angeles. School. Catholic mass. Baseball and donuts. Then we found out that Dylan, wanting to be like his idol Woody Guthrie, had made some of that stuff up. *Most* of it. Including his name. People began booing. And they booed for the next fifty years. Didn't seem to bother Bob Dylan.

Myself, I thought Dylan's reinvention made him *even cooler*. America was the New World wasn't it? Perfect for reinvention. That was art, man. He was writing the great songs, wasn't he? And what about Ramblin' Jack Elliott? What a cool name that was! Why should I care if Jack came from Ocean Parkway in Brooklyn and his name was Elliott Charles Adnopoz? He ran off with the rodeo and never came back. That's the shit, all right. That's what I wanted. But this Bob Dylan kid. I never got over it. Tom Waits has said that when he saw the young Bob Dylan in concert he was amazed at what Dylan was doing, with no props at all—only a guitar, a stool, and a glass of water.

Fifty years later, last week as I write this, the President awarded America's top civilian honor to Bob Dylan and eleven other folks, whom he described as his *heroes*. The President stated, "What sets these men and women apart is the incredible impact they have had on so many people—not in short, blinding bursts, but steadily, over the course of a lifetime." Then he said of Bob Dylan, "There is not a bigger giant in the history of American music." I'd subscribe to that thought. Dylan's work certainly changed my life when I was a kid.

My road as a songwriter has been a little different. There's a lot yet to learn. Flannery O'Conner said that you've got to "chop a path through the wilderness of your own soul." She also said, "You have to push as hard as the age which pushes against you." And Van Gogh shrieked, "Art? That is the action to create a path through an invisible iron wall that seems to be situated between what we feel and what we can do. How should we go through this wall? It is useless to hit strongly, we have to sap this wall and go through it with a file, slowly and, in my opinion, with great patience."

I've learned patience. I'm still trying to make it through the invisible iron wall.

Back in the year 1963, you must understand, I was in a Catholic High School in the middle of downtown Los Angeles. Secretly reading Allen Ginsberg's *Howl* and playing defensive right end on a championship football team. The team was rated second in the nation. I got to play in the Rose Bowl Stadium and also the Coliseum. High school championships. I was a pretty good athlete on a team full of *great* athletes, but my head wasn't truly wrapped around knocking people down. I was an artist, you see. *In my head.* I was with young Bobby Dylan, dancing with the Indians in Gallup, New Mexico. I was with Jack Kerouac, when he looked out his college dormitory window one snowy New York afternoon, listening to Beethoven, and decided that he wasn't going to football practice that day. *Or ever again.* He was going to be an artist.

In that fated year 1963, Bob Dylan understood he wasn't Woody Guthrie. He had to find his own voice. Dave Van Ronk has said Dylan idolized Guthrie, but at least Bobby actually had the heart to go out and *visit* Woody, see the real person on a regular basis. He had to take two different buses out to the mental hospital where Guthrie was dying of Huntington's Disease. In meeting his idol, Dylan realized he had to move on and create his own voice.

One hundred years ago or more, Emile Zola declared that artists had to give more of themselves. Zola claimed a mandate for modern art: Nothing will be fulfilled until someone, somewhere finds inside himself an art at once liberal and poetic, real and symbolic, personal and enchanted.

Dylan accomplished this.

In creating the modern lyric, Dylan, in one swoop, realized he was not Woody or Hank. He had absorbed these influences and then left them behind. He read everything from French Symbolist poetry to Civil War history, soaked up traditional folk, country, blues, and the dark poetics of Kurt Weill and Bertholt Brecht, swallowed whole the tomes of Beat literature, joined the folk music club and destroyed it with an electric guitar, and climbed higher.

Dylan's new art was evidenced in three collections of songs which together are the high water mark of American music-poetry. *Bringing it All Back Home, Highway 61 Revisited*, and *Blonde on Blonde*. The three records were created within a period of eighteen months. Counting outtakes, it's probably sixty or seventy songs! In one-and-a-half years. You might compare this to Van Gogh, in his final year, painting over three hundred works of great art. I sat in the Hollywood Bowl in 1965 listening to Dylan sing "Desolation Row." And that was it. I was going to be a songwriter. That was the only job that made sense.

I snuck into a lot of shows as a teenager. If I didn't have the bread for a ticket, I found a way in. I became an accomplished folk gate crasher. I had to satisfy that yen of hearing live music. I honed my skills. I walked into exits backwards, muttering about a "lost wallet." I climbed fire escapes. I carried people's guitar cases. I acted like I knew what I was doing. I had to hear the songs. I had a fanatic heart.

My first full Bob Dylan concert was the Santa Monica Civic Auditorium, 1963 or '64. I snuck in with my friend Tom Boyle. I was in the parking lot when a Western Union guy pulled up and said he had a telegram for Bob Dylan. I said I'd deliver it. I grabbed it and we walked through security and right *into* Dylan's dressing room and gave it to young Bob. He thanked me. ("Thanks, man.") We walked out of the stage door and sat in the audience. Grinning.

After the concert we found Dylan sitting in a station wagon in the parking lot, waiting for his tour manager to get the money for the show. He was thirsty, and asked us where the nearest liquor store was. We said, "Follow us." We drove down Santa Monica Boulevard with the Dylan entourage behind us. At one of the stoplights, Dylan got out and danced around our car. *Completely around*. Like a whirling, laughing dervish. Like one of those toy clowns that pop out of a jack-in-the-box. We couldn't believe it. Dylan was dancing around our car. It was beyond our comprehension. What did it mean? Now I'd like to think that the dance was a blessing from Bob. Aimed at my heart. *Good luck, kid, I hope you make it*. He danced around the car, sure enough. Then the light changed and he drove off.

Into history.

My greatest gate crashing achievement was to sneak into the Hollywood Bowl with the Beatles in 1964, posing as a security guard. I was a hefty footballer back then, dressed in a Madras jacket, and when I saw their limo approaching the front gates I jumped in front, barking orders, and led the limo through five security gates to the backstage entrance. I opened the limo door and led John Lennon and boys up to the stage. John thanked me. I took my place at the edge of the stage and watched the show.

Finally someone next to me said, "Who are you, man?" It was the reporter from the now defunct *L.A. Herald Examiner*. I concocted an on-the-spot story that I was Tom Berman, son of Stan Berman, a New York cab driver who'd snuck into John F. Kennedy's inaugural box, and also snuck onto the stage at the Academy Awards. The *Herald Examiner* printed my story on the front page the next day: "Son of the World's Greatest Gate Crasher: A Chip Off the Old Block." None of my friends believed me, because I used the name Tom Berman. But my sister, Nan, did. John Lennon did. I had a fanatic heart, I'm telling you. I had to *hear the music*.

I began frequenting coffeehouses, college concerts, and folk clubs—like The Ash Grove on Melrose Boulevard in Hollywood. Sometimes I even paid to get in. I saw Ramblin' Jack Elliott jump off the stage and walk around the tables, playing guitar right in my face, three inches away! I could feel the wind coming off his flat pick. I saw Mississippi John Hurt, Lightnin' Hopkins, Mance Lipscomb, Doc Watson, The Kingston Trio, Bud and Travis, and Ian and Sylvia. I was usually in the first row. Flesh and blood and folk music. I *loved* Ian and Sylvia. They were bigger than life. The best folk group ever. Later I was honored to write songs with both of them, and Ramblin' Jack and Ian were my best men at my wedding in Elko, Nevada. Songs pull you into these fantastic situations. All you have to do is hold on.

And Dylan? Capitol Records later ran a contest on naming the Bob Dylan painting on the cover of The Band's first record, "Music from Big Pink." I named Bob's painting "Crayon Amnesia," and won the contest. They sent me a bright pink Honda motorcycle. I exchanged it for a black one and strapped my guitar on the back.

I could rattle on forever about my early immersion into the world of song. The years flew by—then it was me looking down from the stage. Two sets, four sets, eight sets, ten thousand—honkytonks, Italian bars, Norwegian concert halls...I woke up thirty years later, staring at the crimson mountains of El Paso. I'd written almost a thousand songs. They rolled around in my head and inside my blood memory, making the often brutal road of touring, broken romance, and occasional madness worth the journey.

Resurrection and revelation were hidden in those songs. The keys to survival. Salvation in three-quarter time.

IV
THE WILD HARP TAKEN UP, THE BATTLE JOINED

The minstrel boy to the war is gone,
In the ranks of death ye will find him;
His father's sword he hath girded on,
And his wild harp slung behind him;
Thomas Moore
1779 to 1852

I still feel like Dylan Thomas on his twenty-fourth birthday. Engaged in poetry and music. Still wrapped up in the journey. To quote that Welsh bard, "By the light of the meat-eating sun... / In the final direction of the elementary town / I advance for as long as forever is." Hand me down my wild harp. The minstrel boy to the war is gone, and he ain't never comin' back, ma. *Advancing for as long as forever is...towards the next song. Guitar and thesaurus in hand.*

I feel an urge to end this essay in the manner of Hemingway in his masterful last chapter to *Death in the Afternoon*. In a grand flow of epic writing, he details all that he has left out of the book. Sayeth Hemingway: "If I could have made this enough of a book it would have everything in it...The change in the country as you come down out of the mountains and into Valencia in the dusk on the train holding a rooster for a woman who was bringing it to her sister...what else should it contain about a country that you love so much? If this had been enough of a book..." Then Hemingway proceeds to name a hundred things he left out. Beautifully written.

Song is that country that I love too much. In trying to spit out an introduction to this collection, and say *everything*, my wife calmly informed me that I was going crazy, and what was worthwhile was in the songs themselves.

And yet—if I could have made this enough of an essay it would have had that afternoon in a writing cabin in the Canadian Rockies, where I sat across from the master, Ian Tyson, as he pondered quotes by Alfred Lord Tennyson on the vagaries of love. This introduction should have that wonderful moment on stage singing "Paradise" with John Prine, when I looked back around at his stage table and saw photos of his wife and kids. The photos were John's inspiration and charged his joy at being alive.

And what about singing next to Merle Haggard? And, on another stage in Switzerland, having Johnny Cash sing the verse of "Peace in the Valley" into my ear? Then next morning at breakfast, Johnny is telling me he liked my work and would record my songs. And he *did*. This essay should have the feel in my throat when Johnny Cash turned to me across a crowded parking lot, thirty yards off, and raised his hand up toward me and waved goodbye. "Keep writing them, Tom," he yelled. "Keep writing them."

I never saw him again.

What about breakfast in San Francisco with Lawrence Ferlinghetti as he sketched my portrait on a napkin with ink and iced tea? Or breakfast in New York with Doug Sahm when he patiently explained to the waitress how to make Texas corned beef hash. And we talked songs all day. Or dinner at Dave Van Ronk's apartment and that magic glass pitcher with an ice shaft down the center, which held a half gallon of white wine, and we drank it all and then another one, as he commanded his lovely wife to play us this song or that song on the record player. And if this was enough of an essay it would have Ramblin' Jack Elliott waking me up in the middle of the night to sing me "The Wild Colonial Boy," because he'd forgotten it earlier and remembered it in his dream.

Yes this introduction could have had all that. And more.

I should have put in those wonderful moments when a song knocked me to my knees and tore out my heart—hearing Finbar Furey sing "The Greenfield of France" on the jukebox in a pub in York, England, when I was in despair and the poetry in my work eluded me. Hearing and feeling the pain of Johnny Rodriguez, his hit-song career long over, singing his guts out in a honky-tonk down the road from my hacienda—singing to thirty people. Tearing the songs up. Nailing them. Ripping his throat and guts out, as the waiters were passing by with plates of carne asada tacos and nobody was listening. You should have been there.

I could have told about backstage at *The David Letterman Show*, with the fresh cookies and sandwiches and the photos of Bob Dylan and James Brown on the dressing room wall. Finally, and most importantly, it would detail that night in a honky-tonk in Switzerland when my future wife walked in with her mother, and told me they were good friends of Doug Sahm and Augie Meyers, and I looked at her and declared, "I'm going to marry you." And I did. In Venice, Italy, we were engaged, and for a ring I used a piece of fried calamari.

Yes, if this had been enough of an essay...

Two weeks ago I was feeling off my game, walking through the medieval city of Bern, Switzerland. I was daydreaming and dazed. I walked around a corner and there was a fifty-year-old American guy busking, with his guitar case open and his wild harp strapped across his shoulders. And he was brilliant. He'd been busking in train stations and parks and public streets for thirty years. A humble minstrel with a great gift of singing from his heart.

My soul was taken back to why I got into this deal, and why I advance and write songs *for as long as forever is*...Because the mystery and the magic can knock you down at any moment. We wait for those moments. "Life is on the wire," said the great wire walker Karl Wallenda, "the rest is waiting." The songs have taken me up on the wire.

But let's get to those songs now.

"We've seen it all go and we'll watch it go again," wrote Papa Hemingway in that last chapter I mentioned above. "The great thing is to last and get your work done and see and hear and learn and understand, and write when there is something that you know, and not before, and not too damn much after." Amen, Papa.

"All you can write is what you see," said Woody Guthrie. Amen again.

Yes. Songs travel. And they arrive. I hope you enjoy these songs as much as I've had composing and singing them. We'll see you down that long troubadour road. *I'll sing you a song*, to quote Edith Piaf, *and then afterward I might pass the hat.*

Adios.

Tom Russell
El Paso, Texas
July, 2012

A Note on Song Introductions

Songs shouldn't need explication from the writer. We'll leave that to the music critics. And the hidden mystery. I've tried to add a few details on when, and under what conditions, they were written. *Background color.* When asked to write why and when he wrote "Just Like A Woman," Bob Dylan replied, "I was in a motel in Kansas City. It was Thanksgiving. I was invited for dinner somewhere. I stayed in the motel and wrote this." Indeed.

A Note on Guitar Chords

This is an inexact science. I've tried to use the chord positions I used on the recordings, and keep it simple. I've mentioned the keys, and when I've used the capo on the guitar. The chords are arranged in lines that should correspond to the lines of lyrics on the opposite page. Beyond that you'd have to hear where the changes fall. I didn't want to clutter the lyrics with chord letters. I'd recommend listening to the recordings a few times, for a feel of when the chords change, and follow along with the chord lines printed here. Also, many of these songs exist on *YouTube,* on the internet. I've tried to mention on which records the individual songs appear. All of my records are available from www.tomrussell.com.

Good luck! I always appreciate anyone who takes the time to learn a song of mine. It's an honor.

THE BUNKER IN BROOKLYN
Woodcut by Tom Russell
2012

CHAPTER ONE

EARLY SONGS: THE VANCOUVER/AUSTIN YEARS

THE END OF THE TRAIL

> *When Columbus got off the boat, he asked us who we were. We said we're the Human Beings, we're the People. Conceptually the Europeans didn't understand that…we went from being Indians to pagans to savages to hostiles to militants to activists to Native Americans. It's five hundred years later and they still can't see us. We are still invisible.*
> John Trudell

I'd always been drawn to the giant James Earl Fraser statue which now stands in the Cowboy Hall of Fame. *The End of the Trail*. It was sculpted for the Panama-Pacific National Exhibition in 1915. It depicts an Indian on a pony—horse and rider bent forward in weariness. Fraser also sculpted the Indian head and buffalo figures on the buffalo nickel. This song was written in 1974. The first verse tells of Shakopee and Medicine Bottle—Dakota Indians hung in 1865 for their part in the Dakota wars. The second verse documents the death, by police, of a Canadian Chilocotin Indian named Fred Quilt. It happened when I was living in Vancouver.

I was influenced a great deal by the Indian-related songs of Peter La Farge—especially his "The Ballad of Ira Hayes." Johnny Cash recorded an entire record of Peter's songs called *Bitter Tears*. "The End of the Trail" won the professional country division in the first American Song Festival, 1974. Five thousand bucks. Big money then. It was part of an ABC TV special. They flew us all to New York. My song, on the TV show, was sung by the Hager Twins (from Buck Owens's *Hee Haw* show.) A rather weird experience that was…they wanted to change the tribal names 'cause they couldn't pronounce them. I refused. My first foray into the music business left a bitter aftertaste. I went out and got "The End of the Trail" statue image tattooed on my left leg. Back when only death row inmates and sailors had tattoos. My first song.

My version appears on the record *Hardin & Russell: The Early Years*. The Hagers' version appears on an L.P. on Buddha records, *Winners*.

CHORDS

Key of D.

Verse
D-F#m-G-D
D-G-D-G-D
D-F#m-G-D
D-G-D-G-D

Chorus
D-F#m-G-D
D-G-D-G-D
D-G-D

THE END OF THE TRAIL

Shakopee and Medicine Bottle
Hangin' in the Minnesota sun
One last stand for their Indian land
Now their race on earth is run

    Mama pack up your medicine bag
    Wrap with a prairie dog tail
    We're headed for the land where the buffalo graze
    And they call it the end of the trail

Freddie Quilt was Chilocotin
He was known to drink his wine
He fell one night by the side of the road
But he didn't commit any crime

Mounted police stomped on his back
They hauled him into town
If Fred Quilt's doin' any drinkin these days
He's doin' it underground
Six feet underground

    So mama pack up your medicine bag...

CROPDUSTER

"Some of them crop-duster pilots get rich, if they live long enough..."
                                                  North by Northwest
                                        Screenplay by Ernest Lehman

"Soon it got dusk, a grapy dusk, a purple dusk over tangerine groves and long melon fields; the sun the color of pressed grapes, slashed with burgundy red, the fields the color of love and Spanish mysteries."
                                                      Jack Kerouac
                                                      On the Road

This was inspired by a crop duster pilot in a small, Central California town where my brother used to ranch. The pilot would buzz the plane low over my brother's house as a joke. *To scatter the horses.* Maybe the pilot had a grudge. Maybe it all had to do with a woman? I recall my brother took a shot at the guy once with a rifle. But he didn't bring the plane down. There's a bit of poetic license being scattered around here—I doubt whether there were any Puerto Rican ladies working in those fields below. I guess *Puerto Rican* fit the melody better than *Mexican*. Boy, I liked to sing about those beautiful brown legs. Cabbage Rows? Dew? It all seems like sexual innuendo. I must have needed love that season. This scenery is right out of Leonard Gardner's great California novel, *Fat City*. Or maybe John Fante's, *The Brotherhood of the Grape*. Or Steinbeck's *East of Eden*.

    "Cropduster" is on the record *Heart on a Sleeve* as well as *Beyond St. Olav's Gate* and *Veteran's Day: The Tom Russell Anthology*.

CHORDS

Key of C. Capo up on fifth fret in G chord formations.

Verse	*Chorus*
G-D-G	C-Em-Am-G
C-G-D	C-Em-G-D
Am-D-G Em	Am-D-Am-D
Am-C-D	Am-C-D-G

CROPDUSTER

I love to see those Puerto Rican ladies
Standin' in the carrot fields at dawn
With their short-handled hoes, and their legs so brown and slender
Singin' out the verses to a Puerto Rican song

    But I'm flying too close to the ground again
    Looks like I'm gonna lay her down again, in a field of grapes
    Let 'em harvest my blood right off the vine, turn it into some exotic wine
    Cabernet Sauvignon Cropduster '49…Cropduster

I love to see those cabbage rows at sunrise
Sunlight reflectin' on the dew
I love the smell of onions in the evening
Tomato fields against the sky of blue

    But I'm flyin' too close to the ground again…

ALKALI

"I would not sacrifice a single living mesquite tree for any book ever written. One square mile of living desert is worth a hundred 'great books'—and one brave deed is worth a thousand."

                              Edward Abbey
                              Postcards from Ed

I wrote this in Austin, Texas, around 1974. I'd moved there from Vancouver, B.C. This was in the early days of the Austin scene: Willie Nelson, Guy Clark, Townes Van Zandt, Doug Sahm, Jerry Jeff Walker, Joe Ely, Butch Hancock, and others were hanging out in the small cafés and honkytonks. You heard great Texas-based songs on the radio. I formed a duo with a fine singer/piano player named Patricia Hardin. She's gone on to do well in the classical world, but back then we had a special sort of desert-mystic-folk sound going. We drove back and forth across the deserts of California and Arizona and Texas. I was always drawn to that raw and spare geography— and the cactus and agaves and mesquites. I was fascinated by towns like Gila Bend and Death Valley and Barstow. And the folks who'd ended up there.

    This song was on my first record with Patricia Hardin, *Ring of Bone*, and was also re-recorded for *The Road to Bayamon*, on Rounder, and *Songs of the West* on Hightone. It was also one of my first song covers, by Bill Staines.

CHORDS

Key of C.

Verse
C-Dm-F-G-C
C-Dm-F-G-C
Am-Em-F-G-C
Am-Em-D-G

Chorus
Dm-F-G-C

ALKALI

Alkali, here's mud in your eye, lost in the desert twenty-five years or more
Whiskey streams and your goldfield dreams, Lady Luck won't let you dark her door
Yeah, they tell me you are a ghost of a man, and, yes, I believe it's true
They say you had a woman once, but she turned her back on you

    You old gold minin' hobo, dry well desert rat, Alkali

Alkali, put the bacon on to fry, the sun's comin' up
    and the mule's waitin' for his grain
Just a one room shack by the Santa Fe track, an old lick of earth
    screamin' for a drop of rain
And there's a time for work and a time for play, and a time for lyin' down
And the road might lead to the rainbow's end, or a dusty old desert town

    You old gold minin' hobo, dry well desert rat, Alkali

Alkali, there's a buzzard in the sky, he's a-countin' his chances
    on pickin' your skinflint bones
So raise your hand, throw a curse on the land, they're gonna find you one day
    lyin' 'neath an unmarked stone
And the desert is a lonely place, for a man to lose his head
They tell me you start to talkin' to yourself, you might as well be dead

    You old gold minin' hobo, dry well desert rat, Alkali

ZANE GREY

Look back at our struggle for freedom,
Trace our present day's strength to its source;
And you'll find that man's pathway to glory
Is strewn with the bones of the horse.
                                    Author Unknown

"The wind of heaven is that which blows between
a horse's ears."
                                    Arabian Proverb

Zane was an old Texas cow pony, named after the western author Zane Grey. He probably came out of the old Los Angeles Horse and Mule Auction in the 1950s, and ended up in the San Fernando Valley on one of those movie-dude ranches. Riding kids around for a dollar an hour. I grew up around that scene in the 1950s, and my brother Pat rode bulls out there in the valley. We bought old horses at the auction. I wrote "Zane Grey" around the same time as "Alkali" (early 1970s). Those two songs won a New Folk Award at the Kerrville Folk Festival in 1974. Zane appears on the first Hardin and Russell record, *Ring of Bone*, which was re-released as *Hardin & Russell: The Early Years*. It's also on the record, *Cowboy Real*. "Zane Grey" was also covered by Bill Staines, and a group from Canada, The Garrison Brothers, and that was a hell of a cover. Back then I was thrilled to have anybody sing my songs. I still am.

CHORDS

Key of G.

Verse   *Chorus*
G-D   G-C
C-G   G-D
G-D   Em-C-G
C-G   G-D-Em-D

ZANE GREY

Time's when old Zane could run,
Fast as any horse in the Texas sun
But that was back in '51,
Too many trails ago

    And it's get up, Zane, the ground's too cold,
    Get up Zane, I know you're gettin' old
    Got the whoopin' cough, and a swayback fold
    And it's get up old Zane Grey

They shipped him up North, it was early one spring
And auctioned him off to a rental string
Ten long years in a dusty ole' ring
Dreamin' of his Texas home

    And it's get up, Zane...

A sorrel-red hide all covered with flour
You could ride old Zane for a dollar an hour
Outlaw trails by the water tower
Till Zane couldn't run no more

    And it's get up, Zane...

Gonna end out your days in the back ranch grass
Swattin' the flies as the mares run past
A broke down trot is about as fast
As ole' Zane Grey can move

    And it's get up Zane...

JOSHUA TREE

O Israel, thy prophets are like the foxes in the desert.
Ezekiel 13:4

Gram Parsons died in a Joshua Tree, California, motel in 1973. Drugs and alcohol. Gram used to like to go out into the desert and snort coke with folks like Keith Richards. The Joshua Trees, named by the Mormon settlers, are mystical trees, especially when seen against those desert sundowns. A year or so after Gram died I found the spot where Phil Kaufman and another guy torched Gram's body and coffin at Cap Rock, in Joshua Tree National Monument (as per Gram's wishes). They acted as funeral directors and stole the body from L.A. International Airport. I don't want to sound macabre, but I picked up a few pieces of charred coffin, or bone, and carried it in my cowboy hat band for a few years. I was a fan. I'd seen Gram as far back at 1967 working with the Burrito Brothers in L.A. He crossed country music over to rock people, and rock music over to country people. I liked his guts and style. He had a deep understanding and reverence for real country music. You could hear it in the crack in his voice. *Passion.* But let's not forget Steve Young, who's still with us, was also making his first records at that time, and helped invent what they used to call country rock. Now, after a hundred permutations, it's called Americana. The song appears on the *Hardin & Russell: The Early Years* record, *The Road to Bayamon* on Rounder, and *Veteran's Day: The Tom Russell Anthology* on Shout! Factory.

CHORDS

Key of G.

Verse
G-D-C-D-C-G
Em-Am-D
G-D-C-D-C-G
Em-Am-D

Chorus
Am-D-G-Em
Am-D-G-Em
C-G-B-Em
D-C-G-C-Am-D-Em

JOSHUA TREE

No one knows the age of those trees on White Tank Mountain
They're timeless as a legend, they'll hold you in their spell
And 'neath those ageless roots, they say, there rolls a secret fountain
Fed by ancient waters, from hidden, mystic wells

The lizards resting wisely near the rocks of White Tank Mountain
Keep one eye on the desert and one eye on the sea
The lizards tell the story of a man who drank the fountain
And left his ashes blowin' across the sands of Joshua Tree

> And some called him a holy man and some called him insane
> Might have been his alibi as he put the crowds to shame
> And some called him a seer, flyin' blind and soarin' free
> Like a bird above the fault line, in the land of the Joshua Tree

So if you climb the rocks along the road to White Tank Mountain
You might hear a song blow by you with his ashes in the breeze
The song is just as sacred as the waters in the fountain
And its message is as ageless as the roots of a Joshua Tree

> And some call him a holy man…

RAYBURN CRANE

> *"...and I swims in the Tagus all across at once, and I rides on an ass or a mule, and swears Portuguese, and have got a diarrhea and bites from the mosquitoes. But what of that? Comfort must not be expected by folks that go a pleasuring."*
> Lord Byron
> Lisbon, July 16, 1809

Rayburn Crane was a mule packer out of Mineral Springs, California, up in Sequoia National Park. We used to rent cabins up there when I was a kid. My brother ran off to the mountains when he was sixteen and learned how to pack horses and mules from this man. In my brother Pat's words:

> *Rayburn Crane was an old man that came from Missouri every year to work up in the Sierras. He's the first guy that told me about seeing a real black panther up in the Sierras... He was in his seventies. A real horseman. A real mule man. He taught me how to tie the diamond hitch and balance the packs.*

Walt Disney tried to buy Mineral Springs at one point but I don't think the deal went through. A snow avalanche took most of the cabins away about thirty years ago. And mules? Lately I've come to know the cowboy poet and mule man Ross Knox, who packed mules into the Grand Canyon. I wrote about him in an essay in *Ranch & Reata* magazine. The song appears on the Rounder record, *Cowboy Real*, and the Hightone Record, *Song of the West*.

CHORDS

Key of A, capo up on second fret, played in G chord formations.

Verse
G
C-G
G-Em
A-D
G
C-G
C-G-Em
D-G

Chorus
B-Em-C
G-D-G

RAYBURN CRANE

Well, Rayburn Crane he rode these mountains
Like the streams he rode 'em through
Through the Farewell Gap and the Franklin Lakes
And up North to Chagupa Plateau
With the government men and the hunters and the dudes
And the leaders of the business world
Yeah, Rayburn Crane was a packhorse man
And a mighty good hand with a mule

    Rayburn Crane—Rayburn Crane
    The mountains and the valleys and the trees
    Remember your name

He rode forty-five years through the mountains and the valleys
Just a-pullin' them strings of mules
And the ropes and the chaps and the halters and the saddles
These were Rayburn's tools
Sittin' down at night by the firelight talkin'
And a-pullin' at the whiskers on his chin
Didn't need no music when Rayburn went to talkin'
'Bout the mountains and the packhorse men

    Rayburn Crane...

Then the business men they bought these mountains
For a big time ski resort
And ol' Rayburn he went down to die
In a Three Rivers' trailer court
Now the canvas-flapjack-cook-tent moans
With the bushes and the trees in the wind
'Cause there ain't no place in a ski resort
For a mule skinnin' packhorse man

    Rayburn Crane...

NEW YORK
Woodcut by Tom Russell
2012

CHAPTER TWO
THE NEW YORK/OSLO YEARS

SAINT OLAV'S GATE

"From my rotting body, flowers shall grow and I am in them and that is eternity."
                                                    Edvard Munch

I wrote this in 1982 in the old Edvard Munch Hotel (now gone) in Oslo, Norway. It was near the street Saint Olav's Gate, pronounced *ga-ta* in Norwegian. In the early 1980s guitarist Andrew Hardin and myself played seven nights a week, for two months at a time, in the folk bars and honkytonks of Oslo. An old vaudevillian agent from the U.K. found us the job. Oslo! Those were indeed wild, bohemian times. I know a lot of singers from that era have passed on to the big beer and hashish garden in the sky. *Party time. Full time.* The girls were very pretty, I must say, and the beer was strong. This was the old Oslo of coffee shops and beer gardens and book stores and buskers plying their trade in the town square. We started our career there in the old Scotsman bar, and every night was warfare. Drunks would climb up on stage and we'd kick them off and they'd keep flying back for more. I miss it all. There was smoke and passion.

This is mainly a drinking song, and it's been recorded by Nanci Griffith, Doug Sahm, and a lot of English, Irish, and Canadian musicians and buskers. Bless 'em all. It appears on my records *Heart on a Sleeve, The Long Way Around, The Wounded Heart of America* (Doug Sahm version), and *Veteran's Day: The Tom Russell Anthology*. Nanci Griffith sings harmony with me. Nanci's version is on her record *The Last of the True Believers*, and Lyle Lovett is singing harmony. Doug Sahm's version is also on his record, *Get A Life*.

CHORDS

Waltz. Key of C. Capo on the 5th fret played in G chord positions.

Verse
G-Am
D-G
G-C rundown to Am
D-G

Chorus
Same as verse

SAINT OLAV'S GATE

Drinkin' black market vodka in the back of the Scotsman's Saloon
Then its red meat and whiskey, like a coyote drunk on the moon
Outside in Oslo the buskers all sing the same tune
"Waltzing Matilda" while the bagpipes play old "Clair de Lune"

She was a lady, she came down from Bergen, she said
She spoke a little English, we laughed and drank whiskey instead
And in the morning I found it, a rose and a note on my plate
"Meet me at midnight on the corner of Saint Olav's Gate"

   So here's to the ladies you love and you don't see again
   The night is warm whiskey, the morning's a cold, bitter wind
   And the blue-eyed Madonna leaves town, while a drunken man waits
   Standing alone in the shadows of Saint Olav's Gate

CANADIAN WHISKEY

"There is no bad whiskey. There are only some whiskeys that aren't as good as others."
                                    Raymond Chandler

I knew a woman in Prince George, British Columbia, who loved Canadian Club whiskey. And beautiful she was. We were drinking whiskey and watching TV the night Picasso died. That's all I remember, Lord. The liner notes to my first solo record, *Heart on a Sleeve,* indicate that *Canadian Whiskey* was recorded in the spring of 1982, in Oslo, Norway. The notes state, "This recording owes to the financial assistance of a Scottish gentleman I know only as George. George is an oil rig inspector who commutes to the North African desert from Oslo." I remember George sitting at the bar in the old Gamle Cristiana. He never said much. But he helped finance my first solo record. Richie Bull, a banjo player from the early English band, The Coursel Flyers (which included Albert Lee), produced the sessions. I heard Ritchie now operates a skin diving school in Bristol. The first verse originally spoke of "the hills of Prince Rupert" (British Columbia), where I worked month-long gigs in the honkytonks, back in the early 1970s. Knife and gun cabarets. The song has been recorded, in duet form, with Nanci Griffith and Ian Tyson, on one of Nanci's *Other Voices, Other Rooms* records. My version appears on *Heart on a Sleeve.*

CHORDS

Waltz. Key of A.

Verse
A-C#m-D-A
D-A-Bm-E
A-C#m-D-A
D-A-E-A

Chorus
A-E-D-A
D-A-Bm-E
A-E-D-A
D-A-E-A

CANADIAN WHISKEY

In the hills of Montana, there's a timber wolf howlin'
The rangers are prowlin', for a woman alone
She'd run away, from an Indian lover
He'll never recover, she turned him to stone

    She drank Canadian Whiskey, pure blended whiskey
    She drank it like wine
    Her eyes were the color of Canadian Whiskey, pure blended whiskey
    So light brown and fine

Twenty years later, I heard of a woman
She's living alone, up by Yellowstone Creek
And old Trapper John, brings her cases of whiskey
Canadian Whiskey, says she never will speak

    She drank Canadian Whiskey…

SPANISH BURGUNDY

"The Greeks didn't call wine the blood of the gods for no reason at all...."
                          Charles Bukowski
                          In a letter to Tom Russell

Give me a good glass of Rioja, or even a cheap glass of *sangria*. I'm a lover of Spanish wine and culture. I wrote "Spanish Burgundy" one night in a cabin up in the Canadian Rockies near Ian Tyson's ranch. We used to hang out there, long afternoons, and co-write songs back in the 1980s. Songwriting graduate school. Tyson is a master. One night Ian left me there to write and he drove back to his ranch. I imbibed in a bottle of Spanish wine and wrote this song. That's the way I choose to remember it. I may have been to Barcelona once or twice by that time, and certainly found it to be a poetic city—with the Gaudi architecture and *La Rambla* and the *paella* cafés along the harbor. One night I enjoyed a fine seafood *paella* in a waterfront café, and as I was about to leave, the waiter *plonked* down a bottle of frozen rum or brandy or something, and bought me a final drink on the house. When the sun came up the next morning I wondered how I found my way back to my pensione. That last sip was all I recalled. This song appears on *Poor Man's Dream* and *The Long Way Around*.

CHORDS

Key of C, capo on the 5th fret in G chord positions.
Finger picked.

Verse	*Chorus*
G-C-G	G-C
G-D	G-C
G-C-D-G	C
G-D	D-G

SPANISH BURGUNDY

Barcelona is a woman's town, there are women everywhere
Barcelona is a woman's eyes and raven gypsy hair
I got drunk in Barcelona, then she walked away from me
My tears ran down a bottle of Spanish Burgundy

    And I drank until I slept
    And I slept until I dreamed
    In every dream her lips did taste
    Of Spanish Burgundy

There was once a gypsy saying, it may come from Catalan,
'*First the man he takes the drink, then the drink it takes the man*'
It may lead you to destruction or a love that's meant to be
But beware the Barcelona girls and the Spanish Burgundy

    And we drink until we sleep…

So I will join the old men, down in the sad café
The sun goes up, the sun goes down, shadows cross our face
As we sing of how it might have been, and how it used to be
And the moon shines through a bottle of Spanish Burgundy

    And we drink until we sleep…

U.S. STEEL

"One cannot walk through an assembly factory and not feel that one is in Hell."
  W. H. Auden

The sound of this song is a hammer hitting a piece of steel. One-armed men and desolate working class bars. Pittsburgh! The Heart of America. Thirty years ago. Three rivers crossing under iron bridges, near closed-down factories. We used to play Pittsburgh quite a lot with the Tom Russell Band, thanks to a supporter who owned Jerry's Vinyl Records. The song speaks of the last lunch before the closing of the U.S. Steel factory in Homestead, Pennsylvania. I'd read about Hess's bar being one of the joints where steelworkers hung out. I went looking for Hess's one night and found it. It was closed, but a one-arm gas station attendant down the road told me a fella could *get his butt whipped pretty good in Hess's*. Quote. Unquote. This song has been used quite a few times in documentaries on Pittsburgh, and this can be seen in our documentary, *Don't Look Down*. The song appears on the albums *The Road to Bayamon*, *The Long Way Around*, and *Veteran's Day: The Tom Russell Anthology*.

CHORDS

Key of A. Make it sound like Johnny Cash's first record.

Verse
A-E-A
A-E-A
D-A-D-A
D-C#m-Bm-E
E-A

Chorus
A-D-A-D-A
D-A-E-A
D-A-D-A
D-C#m-Bm-E
E-A

U.S. STEEL

Homestead, Pennsylvania, the home of U.S. Steel
And the men down at the Homestead Works, are sharin' one last meal
Sauerkraut and kielbasa, a dozen beers or more
A hundred years of pourin' slab, now they're closin' down the doors
This mill won't run no more

There's a silence in the valley, a silence in the streets
A silence every night here, upon these cold white sheets
Where my wife stares out the window, with a long and lonely stare
She says, "You killed yourself for thirty years, and no one seems to care…

    "You made their railroad rails and bridges, you ran their drivin' wheel
    And the towers of their Empire State, are lined with Homestead steel
    The Monongahela Valley no longer hears the roar
    There's cottonwood and sumac weed inside the slab mill door
    This mill won't run no more."

So me, I'll sit in Hess's bar, and drink my life away
God bless the second mortgage, and the unemployment pay
And my ex-boss, Mr. Goodwin, he keeps a shakin' my one good hand
He says, "Son, its men like me and you, who built the Promised Land."

    "We made their railroad rails and bridges…."

THE ROAD TO BAYAMON

"Democracy is the art and science of running the circus from the monkey cage."
H.L. Mencken

"When you're born you get a ticket to the freak show. When you're born in America, you get a front row seat."
George Carlin

In 1981 an old friend of mine named Marc Feldman got me a gig as an urban cowboy singer in his father's Puerto Rican carnival. The backup band was a thirteen-piece, French-Canadian disco band named Fussy Cussy. When we did the Urban Cowboy routine we were known as *Tom Russell y Sus Nightriders*. Can you imagine? The job lasted two months. My Martin D-18 guitar has a bullet hole in the back from that particular gig. Long story. Short song. Good and bad memories.

Our tent was right next to the tent of *El Hombre de Goma*, The Rubber Man. Freaks galore. It was the largest carnival Midway ever assembled, and eventually it ended in torrential rains and violence. I took a duffel bag filled with one thousand one dollar bills back home to Brooklyn. Gypsy, who appears in the first verse, was a rather large woman who told me insider carny stories about ride jockeys, pimps, killers and possum belly queens—the lowest level of carnival whores, who enacted their trade in the possum belly, or tool cabinets, underneath semi-trucks.

Gypsy put me on her *Astro Ride* one night and pulled the throttle back, and the thing took off whirling—over, under, sideways, and down. I've never been the same. The best version of the song might be by the Finnish band Engels, Marx, Freud, and Jung. They recorded it in Finnish and changed the Puerto Rican carnival to a Finnish disco. Go figure. My version appears on *The Road to Bayamon* and *The Long Way Around*.

CHORDS

Key of C.

Verse
C-G-C
C-G-C
F-C-F-C
F-C-C-G

Chorus
C-F-C-G
C-F-G-C

THE ROAD TO BAYAMON

All you possum-belly queens, get outta here, Gypsy's out for blood tonight
She's got "love" and "hate" tattooed on her fists, she's drunk and she's ready to fight
She used to run a little shot and beer joint, now she's a jockey on the Astro Ride
She took me for a whirl one night, man, it messed me up inside

    Ai-yi-yi, ah the rain, how long can this rain go on?
    There's nothin' sadder than the carnival, on the road to Bayamon

In a parking lot down in old San Juan, out on the road to Bayamon
We set up the tents and the alibi joints, and the freak show from Leon
We had French Canadian racketeers, and rednecks from down south
And the Puerto Rican pistol boys, with boa constrictor mouths

    Ay-yi-yi, ah the rain…

Then the wire walker started drinkin' hard, the payroll check never came
And somebody stole the little two-headed calf, and the midway drowned in a rain
Yeah, it rained through the month of April, and the first two weeks of May
And all across the Island, I could hear the children sing

    Ai-yi-yi, ah the rain…

BLUE WING

This song saved my life one afternoon in Edmonton Maximum Security Prison when the show wasn't going over very well. "Blue Wing" warmed up the boys and I was able to make it out alive. Recently we polled our fan base, asking what people's favorite song was, and "Blue Wing" won the poll. I've run into sailor's wives in England who have blue wing tattooed on their arms or legs. Ex-convicts from the British Columbia Penitentiary told me, face to face, how much they appreciate the song. The color, detail, and emotional elements of this story were influenced by my early days in the bars of Vancouver, B.C. But Little Willie John? The great songwriter Otis Blackwell visited my *bunker,* when I lived in Brooklyn, and told me how he wrote "Fever" with Little Willie John. Otis mentioned that Willie died in prison. Somehow, in my mind, Little Willie meets a Native American salmon fisherman and they concoct a dream song. I wrote the song in Ian Tyson's writing cabin in the Canadian Rockies.

Dave Alvin did a killer version (probably the *best* version) of this song on his *King of California* record. Dave took my version, which was originally a country treatment, and turned it back around into a more Woody Guthrie, folk feel. Then I started doing it like Dave. Dave said the song saved his life one time when he was trying to write songs in Nashville. Johnny Cash once told me, over breakfast in Switzerland, how much he admired the song. He wanted to record it. I've heard that it exists in his archives somewhere. Later he recorded my song "Veteran's Day." Tracy Grammer does a fine version of "Blue Wing" on an EP titled *Book of Sparrows*, and my version appears on *Poor Man's Dream*, *The Long Way Around*, and *Veteran's Day: The Tom Russell Anthology*.

CHORDS

Key of C. Capo on the 5th fret, in G chord positions. Finger picked.

Verse	*Chorus*
G	G-C
G-Am	G-D
Am	G-C
D-G	G-D
	Em

BLUE WING

He had a blue wing tattooed on his shoulder
Well, it might have been a bluebird, I don't know
But he'd get stone drunk, and talk about Alaska
The salmon boats and forty-five below

He said he got that blue wing up in Walla Walla
Where his cell mate there was Little Willie John
And Willie, he was once a great blues singer
And Wing and Willie wrote 'em up a song

   (They said)
   "It's dark in here, can't see the sky,
   But I look at this blue wing and I close my eyes
   And I fly away, beyond these walls
   Up above the clouds, where the rain don't fall
   On a poor man's dream"

They paroled Blue Wing in August, 1963
He moved north, pickin' apples, to the town of Wenatchee
But winter finally caught him, in a rundown trailer park
On the south side of Seattle, where the days grow grey and dark

And he drank and he dreamt a vision, of when the salmon still ran free
And his father's fathers crossed, that wild ole' Bering Sea
And the land belonged to everyone, and there were old songs yet to sing
Now it's narrowed down to a cheap hotel, and a tattooed prison wing

   "It's dark in here, can't see the sky…"

Well, he drank his way to L.A., and that's where he died
But no one knew his Christian name, and there was no one there to cry
But I dreamt there was a funeral, a preacher and an old pine box
And halfway through the sermon, *Blue Wing* began to talk

   He said, "It's dark in here, can't see the sky…"

VETERAN'S DAY

"When I record somebody else's song, I have to make it my own or it doesn't feel right. I'll say to myself, I wrote this and he doesn't know it!"

Johnny Cash

I lived in Brooklyn during the 1980s and early 1990s, in a rough part of town that hadn't been gentrified yet, whatever that means. The white families with 1.3 babies hadn't moved in and opened the absinthe and wine bars. The Cuban sandwich joints still melded together with the dollar-a-slice pizza joints, voodoo stores, and the Puerto Rican milkshake palaces. There was a Veterans of Foreign Wars club there, above a storefront church, and I used to go in occasionally and have a beer with a guy named Billy. Behind the bar were photos of Brooklyn kids who didn't come back from World War Two or Viet Nam. I heard a lot of stories in there, and put the song together from different angles. Some of the VFW guys were always hoping some of their buddies were missing in action, instead of gone forever.

Johnny Cash recorded a great version on a record called *Boom Chicka Boom*, and his version also appears on a record of my covers, *The Wounded Heart of America: Tom Russell Songs*. Johnny changed a few words, but what the hell. I was deeply honored. He also threw in a little rap at the end of his version. "Let's bring all of 'em home..." I had the pleasure of talking with him on a few occasions about the song. He was one of a kind.

My recorded version appears on the records *Poor Man's Dream*, *The Long Way Around*, and *Veteran's Day: The Tom Russell Anthology*.

CHORDS

Key of A. I play the song with a sort of Johnny Cash, Sun Records feel.

Verse	*Chorus*
A-E	D-A
E-A	A-C#m-Bm-E
A-E	A-D-Dm
E-A	A-E-A

VETERAN'S DAY

I used to hang out down at the local VFW hall
I was starin' at the photographs up on the wall
Of all the boys in the neighborhood who died back in World War Two
And the hand-lettered sign said, "Remember our Jimmy McGrew"

Well, Jimmy went away back in 1965
There's a lot of men here think Jimmy McGrew's still alive
They carved his name on a stone down in Washington D.C.
But his brother says, "That stone don't mean a damn thing to me."

> It's Veteran's Day and the skies are grey
> Leave your uniforms home, boys, there ain't gonna be a parade
> But we'll fill up a glass for ones who didn't make it through
> And leave a light in the window tonight for Jimmy McGrew

There's a hot rain fallin' on the backstreets of Saigon
And there's a white man runnin' down the alley with his *Mama San*
But Lord, his eyes are cloudy and his arms are black and blue
And he's a-hangin' by a thread and he looks like our Jimmy McGrew

> It's Veteran's Day and the skies are grey…

WALKIN' ON THE MOON

My young love said to me,
My mother won't mind
And my father won't slight you
For your lack of kind.
And she laid her hand on me
And this she did say:
It will not be long, Love,
Till our wedding day.
   "She Moved Through the Fair"
   Traditional Irish Ballad

I co-wrote at least thirty songs with Katy Moffatt. Mostly in the 1980s and 1990s. There's a bunch of good ones and I'd encourage anyone to seek out Katy's records. *Walkin' on the Moon* was the most known of our co-writes, and the most covered. Janie Fricke did a powerful version, as did Sylvia Tyson. Eliza Gilkyson recorded one for a collection of my songs, *The Wounded Heart of America*. Katy is a great singer and has a fine sense of melody, and co-writing with a strong musician always pulls you in different melodic directions. Widens the musical boundaries. This is a sweet little song and it's always been popular with audiences. My recorded versions appear on *Poor Man's Dream* and *The Long Way Around* (with Katy Moffatt).

CHORDS

Key of D. Capo on 2nd fret, played in C chord positions.

Verse	*Chorus*
C-F-G-C	C-F-C-G
F-G-C	F-G-C
C-F-G-C	C-F-C-G
C-G	F-G-C

WALKIN' ON THE MOON

The lights of the town were just shuttin' down
The sun was fresh on the rise
I met Mama at the door, she'd been walkin' the floor
She said, "Boy, you got stars in your eyes."

    "Mama, I was walkin' on the moon last night
    And two lovin' arms held me tight
    As the stars danced around so bright
    I was walkin' on the moon last night."

Mama she did weep, "Boy, you've been walkin' in your sleep
You can't keep your feet on the ground
It's not always what it seems, young love might be a dream
And some angels fly high just to fall down."

    "Mama, I was walkin' on the moon last night…"

Now the lights of the town are glowin' yellow brown
The moon is beginning to rise
I left Mama at the door—I said, "Don't worry anymore
I've seen Daddy put those same stars in your eyes.

    "And I'll be walkin' on the moon tonight.…"

Co-written with Katy Moffatt

OUTBOUND PLANE

"Tom Russell and I wrote this song at my kitchen table when I first moved to Nashville. Back then I couldn't even afford a fan to put in my window...and it gets hot in Nashville in the summer."

Nanci Griffith

Sometime in the late 1980s I was in Nashville and my old friend Nanci Griffith offered to let me sleep on her couch. I'd known Nanci since she was eighteen. By then Nanci was well on her way as a folk and country music heroine. She walked into the front room one day with a set of lyrics she told me *needed work*. It was "Outbound Plane." I think I helped polish up the chorus and changed a few lines in the verses. Don't really recall how it all went down, but we finished it quickly and Nanci recorded it on her next record. Suzy Bogguss released a version in 1991, on a record named *Aces*, and her version became a top ten country hit. The song has since entered into the wonderful world of *Muzak* and *Karaoke*. I have an ASCAP award that states "Outbound Plane" was one of the most radio-played songs of the 1990s.

My version appears on, *Poor Man's Dream*, *The Long Way Around* (with Nanci Griffith), and *Veteran's Day: The Tom Russell Anthology*.

CHORDS:

Key of G. A galloping beat, and G chord that rolls round and round.

Verse	*Chorus*	*Bridge*
G-D-C-D	C	C-Bm
G-D-C-D	Bm	Am-D
G-D-C-D	Am-D	G-D-C-D
G-D-C-D	G-D-C-D	C-D-G
	C-D-G	

OUTBOUND PLANE

Don't want to be standing here with this ticket for that outbound plane
Yeah, I've been here before, hey, somehow this don't feel the same
Talk is cheap and we could talk all night long
You may never figure out where our love's gone wrong

    Yeah I don't wanna be standin' here
    And I don't wanna be talkin' here
    And I don't really care who's to blame
    If love won't fly on its own free will
    It's gonna catch that outbound plane

Old people say love's not forever anymore
Young people walk away from love, alone to pace the floor
Hey, young or old I say that love is still the same
You can walk away from love but you'll fall head and heels again

    And I don't wanna be standin' here...

    Two lonely hearts in this airport knowin'
    Neither heart knows which way the other heart's goin'
    If love won't fly on its own free will
    It's gonna catch that outbound plane

That frown you're wearing, that's your halo turned upside down
Where's the laughter we once shared back in the lost and found?
These broken wings are gonna leave me here to stand my ground
You can have that ticket for that lonely plane that's headed out

    And I don't wanna be standin' here...

Co-written with Nanci Griffith

OIL FIELD GIRLS

Civilization is drugs, alcohol, engines of war, prostitution, machines and machine slaves, low wages, bad food, bad taste, prisons, reformatories, lunatic asylums, divorce…electric chairs, guillotines…famine, disease, gangsters, money barons, horse racing, fashion shows, poodle dogs, chow dogs, Siamese cats, condoms, syphilis, gonorrhea, insanity, neuroses, etc., etc.…

                          Henry Miller

There's a 1940 painting by Texas artist Jerry Bywaters titled "Oil Field Girls." It pictures two healthy looking women hitchhiking through an oil field. Prostitutes, I would guess. They're all dolled-up, and one of them is wearing a short skirt with red cowboy boots. Waiting for the next truck driver. Something out of the opening to that Jack Nicholson film, *Five Easy Pieces*. This is a drinking song, sung by a drifter leaving the oil fields. I must have written this after driving through those oil towns in California, near the Cuyama Valley, where my sister-in-law has a ranch. Though I don't think anyone there would have been drinking "Old Peculiar" ale. I just liked the name. There are towns out there, near Bakersfield, where rusty oil wells stand motionless in the heat and dust. Like conceptual art. The wells dried up. The hookers have left town. A demo of this song might appear on a coming "rarities" record.

CHORDS:

Key of G.

Verse
G-Am
Am-C-D
D-Bm-Em
C-D

OIL FIELD GIRLS

Those oil field girls all taste of whiskey
Their thoughts are free, their clothes are torn
They walk the Strip like painted shadows
Cursing the night when man was born

There's one named Frida and one named Angel
There's the Rose of Hatred and The Ragtime Gal
All legs and heart, bright lips in the moonlight
Young men will die at the turn of a curl

I'm packing my bags, I'm shipping out on a freighter
I'll lick my wounds in a far off world
One hand on my heart, one hand on a bottle
Just a drunkard's dream of the oil field girls

Here's a round for the priest, here's a round for the beggar
Here's a round for the rogues all over this world
But I'll drink me a case of Old Peculiar
'Fore I raise me a glass to the oil field girls

Those oil field girls all taste of whiskey…

BEYOND THE BLUES

"I do not play no rock and roll, y'all...I just play the straight 'natchul blues."

Mississippi Fred McDowell

I was hanging out with Peter Case in Santa Monica, must have been the late 1980s, early 1990s. He had this title rolling around in his head and we gave it a shot. Peter is well steeped in the blues and he brings blues passion and tone to a lot of his material. When we were almost finished with the song, in walked Bob Neuwirth. Neuwirth offered advice on some of the lines and we three finished the song. Neuwirth is a fine writer and painter and was known early on for his work with Bob Dylan. He's since released some cool records. I've co-written other songs with both Peter and Bob. In his version of "Beyond the Blues," Peter sings a different line for, "When you're walkin' in circles with holes in your shoes." He sings, "When you know in your heart, there's no way out but through." I like that just as well, because it's the *truth*. The soundman at The Bottom Line in New York called me up once, in the mid-nineties, and said Bruce Springsteen was singing this song at his sound check. He never recorded it. Bob Neuwirth's version appears on his record *Look Up*. Peter Case's versions appear on *Six Pack of Love*, *Travellin' Light*, and *A Case for Case*. Hayes Carll also does a version on *A Case for Case*. My versions appear on *Hurricane Season*, *The Long Way Around* (with Jimmie Dale Gilmore), and *Veteran's Day: The Tom Russell Anthology*.

CHORDS

I play it in "E." Capo on the 2nd fret, playing in the D chord positions. The capo is across every string *except* the low E string (a trick I learned from Guy Clark) which gives you the drop "D" effect without re-tuning.

Verse
D-G-D
D-G-D
D-G
D-A-G
D

Chorus
D-G-D
D-A-D
D-G-D
D-A-G
D

BEYOND THE BLUES

Old man on the corner, singin' my life
And he's playin' his guitar with a rusty old knife
And every line that he's singin' rhymes with the truth
And a promise of something beyond the blues
Beyond the blues

Well, you and me, darlin', took the long way around
Through the wide open country and the heart attack towns
To every fork in the road where we've all got to choose
Between darkness and light, out beyond the blues
Beyond the blues

> Beyond the shadows, beyond the rain
> Beyond the darkness and all the pain
> When you're walkin' in circles with holes in your shoes
> Love is the road that leads out beyond the blues
> Beyond the blues

Old man on the corner, he's been gone for years
And the guitar and the knife blade are rusty with tears
But there's a song that he left us, we'll never lose
About love that will carry us beyond the blues
Beyond the blues

> Beyond the shadows, beyond the rain…

Co-written with Peter Case and Bob Neuwirth

CHINATOWN IN THE RAIN

"Poor Mexico, so far from God, so close to the United States."

Attributed to Porfirio Diaz

"Anything can happen here amigo. Even the cockroaches have wings."

Jackie Sprague

This is the product of a night of drinking vodka in my storefront bunker in Brooklyn in the late 1980s—toying around with an old TEAC reel-to-reel tape recorder and an electric guitar and some cheap Chinese chorus effects. I think I wrote the song "Hurricane Season" the same night. *Scary.* This song is a twisted recollection of a trip I took down to the Yucatan peninsula of Mexico back in the 1980s. I believe there was a lot of rum and coke involved. *Cuba libre!* Jackie Sprague was based on one of these weird expatriates you meet in third world countries, exiles who can never go home again and have a twisted view of survival. Scam artists. Failed poets and matadors. Living on their wits, or money from a rich aunt.

The old Pullman trains were still running through Mexico back then and you could meet bona fide characters onboard. The song has echoes of William S. Burroughs, Graham Greene, and B. Traven. Something out of *The Treasure of the Sierra Madre*, or maybe *Under the Volcano,* or Tennessee Williams's *Night of the Iguana,* starring Richard Burton. Maybe a little of the song "Sonora's Death Row" by Kevin "Blackie" Farrell. All of that and more. Near the end I allude to my life in "the bunker" I was living in…I could hear Spanish voices threatening each other all night. There were no windows, so I had to imagine what was going down out there on the street. Violent hallucinations. Ghetto blasters and guns.

The demo of that frightening night, and the only version I know of, appears on a rare CD, *Museum of Memories*. Good luck.

CHORDS

I'd suggest two shots of vodka for starters, then take off finger picking in the Key of C, doing a sort-of talking blues *rondo*, with *Beat* overtones. You're on your own. I wish I could have had Chet Baker backing me up that night…or Art Pepper.

CHINATOWN IN THE RAIN

I met Jackie Sprague down in Mexico
On a night train to the Yucatan
Jackie moved like a spider
So we called him *puppet man*
He was on his way to Juarez
To see the Juarez Medical School
They had Zapata's eyes there
Down in the basement dark and cool

Jackie told me about the Tarahumara
The Indians who run all day and night
Me, I couldn't get a word in edgewise
As that Pullman ran through the night
At sunrise we pulled into Palenque
Took a beat-up taxi into town
Watched two shoeshine boys beat each other senseless
While *campesinos* gathered round

Jackie said, "Anything can happen here, amigo
Even the cockroaches have wings."
The café danced like a marionette
Waiting for somebody to cut Jackie's strings

    And the moon came up like it always does
    A few *Cuba libres* ease the strain
    And Jackie sang a song he said he'd written
    One he called 'Chinatown in the Rain'
    And I closed my eyes and I thought
    Of that Chinese fish joint on the Bowery
    Where you and I ate mussels soaked with wine
    Yeah, but what does that have to do with my current problem?
    God, what rum and coke does to your mind…

CONTINUED

Well, this room I'm in ain't got no windows
But I can hear wild voices out on the street
Spanish talk, moans, and babies wailing
The down and out not admitting their defeat
And the rain beats down here in late August
And I keep hummin' Jackie's goddamn song
Yeah, I can still see his face when they locked him away
He said, "Amigo, they ain't gonna hold old Jackie long."

But now I hear 'em hammering the gallows
In harmony with Jackie as he sings
And tomorrow he'll be dancing from a cheap hemp rope
And somebody's finally gonna cut Jackie's puppet strings

    And the moon will come up like it always does
    A few *Cuba libres* would ease the strain
    I'll sing the song "The Great Pretender"
    And a tune Jackie wrote called "Chinatown in the Rain"
    And I'll close my eyes and dream
    Of that Chinese fish joint on the Bowery
    Where you and I ate mussels soaked with wine
    Hey, but what does that have to do
    With my current legal problems?
    God, what rum and coke does to your mind
    "Chinatown in the Rain"
    "Lady of Spain…"

THE BIGGEST BORDER TOWN IN THE WORLD

> *"New York is my Lourdes, where I go for spiritual refreshment...a place where you're least likely to be bitten by a wild goat."*
>
> Brendan Behan

Here's an amusing little look at New York City in the early, and still edgy, 1980s. I was hanging around The Village and got to know Bob Neuwirth, the painter, songwriter, and former Dylan protégé. Bob had this idea for a realistic and amusing song on surviving in New York: you could get by if you understood that it was just a big border town full of muggers, thieves, pimps, hustlers, and con men...and kept your money and knife in your boot, etc. Sorta like how you'd act in Juarez, Mexico. Back then this was a fairly true picture of New York. I had escaped a few rather hairy situations late at night by acting crazier than the man pursuing me. Three Card Monte games were in evidence on many street corners. The game involved a cardboard box and three cards. It was *fixed*. Fats Kaplin once explained to me how this particular con game works. You have to have several shills or stoolies, and keep an eye out for the cops. It's a great way to get hundreds of dollars off Japanese tourists.

I like all the name-dropping we got away with in the song: *Thomas Wolfe, Jackson Pollock, Hank Williams, Jimmie Rodgers*...what the hell. But there's an underlying reality here that resonates: Lots of Hindus *do* sell you magazines, and most of the taxis are now operated by men from the Middle East, and corner stores are run by Koreans...it's the great melting pot.

This appears on one of Neuwirth's records, *99 Monkeys,* and on *Museum of Memories*.

CHORDS

Key of C.

Verse
C-Dm
F-G
C-Dm
F-C

Chorus
C-Dm-C
F-C-G
F-C-E-F
C-G
F-G-C

THE BIGGEST BORDER TOWN IN THE WORLD

Well, it ain't exactly the way that you read about
The streets aren't all that hard to walk at nights
Keep your money in your boots and your business to yourself
Keep your head down when you see the flashing lights

Well, once you made your way across the river
And line up for your own slice of the pie
Watch your back becomes a way of thinkin'
Making a killing becomes a way of life

    You can throw away your money on Three Card Monte
    And dance at Roseland with the Haitian girls
    Our lady of the subways will sing for you tonight
    In the biggest border town in the world
    In the biggest border town in the world

Hindus selling magazines, Koreans hawking fruit
Taxi drivers all the way from Jamaica and Beirut
Names are changing faster than money's changing hands
Some things never change at all in the city of one night stands

"Only the dead know Brooklyn," I heard Hank Williams say
Or was it Dylan Thomas that night he drank it all away?
No, it was Thomas Wolfe, the old Carolina Kid
As Jackson Pollock danced a jig across the Brooklyn Bridge

    You can throw away your money…

I heard the Singing Brakeman draw his painful breath
He sang one last "'Blue Yodel" then he coughed himself to death
Weary pilgrims travel miles and miles to be alone
The city never sleeps, my friend, but it'll turn your tears to stone

    And you can throw away your money…

CO-WRITTEN WITH BOB NEUWIRTH

MINERAL WELLS

> Joe: *You're Norma Desmond. You used to be in silent pictures. You used to be big.*
> Norma: *I am big. It's the pictures that got small.*
> Sunset Boulevard
> *Directed by Billy Wilder*

Back in the 1970s we used to drive through the little town of Mineral Wells, Texas, on our way to Fort Worth or Dallas. I was always fascinated by the big art-deco hotel that rose up out of the flat cow country. It seemed out of place. *The Baker Hotel*. Closed for years. The mineral springs, which the hotel was famous for, had dried up. The fountain of youth stopped flowing. There was a hotel down the street, The Crazy Water, which was still operating—as an old folks home. I concocted this story about an obese film buff and an actress (right out of *Sunset Boulevard*) who go in search of the fountain of youth—in Mineral Wells. This also reminds me of Betty Davis in *What Ever Happened to Baby Jane?* I sang this for Doug Sahm one night in a dressing room in New York, and he laughed his ass off. Sylvia Tyson and I also worked up an outline of a film treatment, but nothing came of it. This appears on *The Long Way Around* as a duet with Katy Moffat. The Norwegian singer Tine Valand recorded a duet version with Guy Clark.

CHORDS

Waltz in B Flat. Capo on 3rd fret in G chord positions.

Verse
G
G-D
D-G
G
G-C
C-G
D-G

Chorus
C-D
C-D
C-G
Am-D-C-G

MINERAL WELLS

She was living in a Cadillac, bedded down in the back seat
On a back street of the Hollywood Hills
With a shoe box museum of memories, old photos and medical bills
She'd once been a great actress, in two dozen movies
Played Shakespeare on the great London stage
Before three husbands, six kids, and bad breaks
Of fifty-eight odd years of age

Him they called Fat Boy, he wore grey overalls
And he clocked in at four hundred pounds
With a passion for food, and old film magazines
He'd once been a top critic downtown
He'd seen all her movies, he worshipped her face, heard her story and took her on in
Though she bore no resemblance to the star he adored
The film's over, boy, real life begins

    She told him of a fountain of youth, in the hot Texas earth
    It'll heal and renew us, it's somewhere west of Fort Worth
    She'd met Errol Flynn there, in The Crazy Water Hotel
    And they'd danced down the street, in the moonlight of old Mineral Wells

So they boarded a Greyhound in search of the fountain,
Fat Boy and the aging film queen
Through the great painted desert and on across Texas—Amarillo, Plainview, Abilene
They got off in Fort Worth for a fresh cup of coffee,
Caught the local to old Mineral Wells
And it dropped them in front of that boarded up palace,
The Crazy Water Hotel

Disillusioned they found a cheap room off the highway
Drank vodka from a Styrofoam cup
There'd be no healing return to the past, the fountain of youth had dried up
So the critic and the film star, held hands and drank vodka
As the great Texas sun rose and fell
And drunk but still dreaming, they waltzed down the street
In the moonlight of old Mineral Wells

    And he told her of a fountain of youth...

CHOCOLATE CIGARETTES

"Singing is a way of escaping. It's another world. I'm no longer on earth."
                                                Edith Piaf

"Tell me what you'd like to hear me sing. I'll sing whatever you like, after which I'll take up a collection, if you don't mind."
                                                Edith Piaf

*I*t's an Edith Piaf night, tonight, as I put her records on…I suppose there were some nights in my writing bunker in New York that I sat around drinking and listening to old Edith Piaf records. Had to be. *The Little Sparrow*. Weep for me. The French Hank Williams. I can't speak French, but I love hearing love songs in that language. They'll tear you up. As I write this I'm listening to the French version of the show *Les Misérables*. I wrote "Chocolate Cigarettes" with Sylvia Tyson around 1990. I co-produced Sylvia's solo record *Gypsy Cadillac* and this was one of five of our co-writes on the record. Sylvia's version is on her record, *Gypsy Cadillac,* my version appears on *Hurricane Season*, and Barrence Whitfield does a soulful recording of this on a record we did together titled, *Hillbilly Voodoo*.

CHORDS

Key of C. Capo up on 5th fret, played in G chord positions.

Verse	*Chorus*
G	C-G
Am	C-D
D	C-D-G-C
G-D-G	Am-D
(same form again)	Am-D

CHOCOLATE CIGARETTES

Edith Piaf was the Little Sparrow
She flew high above the Paris streets
Saint of the bars and bistros
Chanteuse of a tear-stained sheet
She sang for the drunks and sailor boys
Who'd sunk as low as low can get
I read she kicked a three-pack habit once
On chocolate cigarettes

    She didn't have a smoke
    Though she wanted one
    Didn't take a drink
    Though it hurt her some
    She stared across the River Seine
    Hummin' "No Regrets"
    Pullin' on a chocolate cigarette

Oh, those chocolate cigarettes
I've seen 'em in my youth
Right beside the *Hershey Bars*
The Almond Joys, the *Baby Ruths*
I kicked a three-pack habit once
I won a hundred dollar bet
With the help of chewin' gum
And chocolate cigarettes

    And I didn't have a smoke
    Though I wanted one
    I didn't take a drink
    Though it hurt me some
    I thought of Little Sparrow
    Hummin' "No Regrets"
    Pullin' on a chocolate cigarette

It's an Edith Piaf night tonight
As I put her records on
All that smoky passion
In every line of every song
Old love affairs and wasteful habits
We'll all survive them yet
Memories drown in coffee grounds
And chocolate cigarettes

    She didn't have a smoke…

Co-written with Sylvia Tyson

THE CUBAN SANDWICH

A Cuban sandwich is made with slices of mojo-flavored roasted pork butt, mild, smoked ham, Gouda or Swiss cheese, pickles and mustard. Everyone also agrees Cuban bread is paramount and can never be replaced with crusty French bread. (Ask anyone who's tried that and you may not hear an opinion, since the roof of their mouth is probably still bleeding)...the sandwich is slathered in butter and pressed to perfection.

                                              Betty Cortina

This song sounds right out of a Charles Willeford novel: sex, violence, recipes, food, prison, Latinos, and Murphy beds. The action here takes place along Flatbush Avenue in Brooklyn, where I used to eat at a place called *El Castillo de Jagua*. Cuban-Dominican food. The pick of the menu was the Cuban sandwich. One of those would probably kill me now. Great slabs of ham, pork, melted Swiss cheese, and pickles. Mooney's Irish Bar was up the street, and also another place called The Castle of Milkshakes, which featured illegal cockfights in the basement. Yes, folks, the *old* New York. Bring in *Weegee* to take the photos on this one. Barrence Whitfield and I recorded it on the record *Hillbilly Voodoo*, and there's a great live version from the Edmonton Folk Festival with Barrence and me and the Festival Band, featuring the guitar work of Amos Garrett. That's on *Wounded Heart of America: Tom Russell Songs*.

CHORDS

Key of Dm, sort of talkin' bluesy.

Verse	*Chorus*
Dm-G	F-C
A-Dm	G-Bflat
Dm-G	F-C
A-Dm	A-Dm

THE CUBAN SANDWICH

Well Johnny looks in the icebox, shaking his head
His woman lies sleeping in their Murphy bed
He leaves a note on the table says, "Babe, I'm off to get fed…
I'm thinkin' about a Cuban sandwich."

He throws a nickel to the corner boy for watchin' his car
He drives down to The Castle of the Jaguar
The waitress leans over, he can see her powder blue bra
He says, "Baby give me a Cuban sandwich."

    It's got two kinds of pig meat—ham and roast pork
    And a slice of white cheese in the shape of New York
    So throw on a pickle and pick up your fork
    Say *El Cubano,* that's a Cuban sandwich

Now a masked man runs out of Mooney's Irish Bar
Two cops pull up inside an unmarked car
A shotgun breaks the window of The Castle of the Jaguar
Raining glass down on Johnny's Cuban sandwich

So Johnny picks up his plate and runs out into the street
He knocks the masked man off of his feet
He rubs the sandwich in his face says, "Time for a tough guy to eat…
Hope you like glass on your Cuban sandwich."

    It's got two kinds of pig meat…

Next day the headlines of the *New York Post*
Say, "Hero stops hoodlum, with a Hero roll"
But the waitress down at the Jaguar says, "That wasn't so…
That wasn't a Hero, that was a Cuban sandwich."

So out at Riker's Island now behind iron bars
Some scumbag named Cesar sits lickin' his scars
His cellmate says, "Man you look like you been through a shotgun war"
Cesar says, "That wasn't a shotgun, that was a Cuban sandwich."

    It's got two kinds of pig meat…

NAZARETH TO BETHLEHEM

When Joseph was an old man,
An old man was he,
He married Virgin Mary
The Queen of Galilee.
He married Virgin Mary
The Queen of Galilee
                         The Cherry Tree Carol

Katy Moffatt and I wrote this in New York back in 1990. We used to record in a rugged little brownstone studio, owned by a guy named Hank Bones, overlooking Prospect Park. Katy recorded quite a few of her records there. I have no recollection of writing this except that I liked the concept of a Christmas *road song*. Growing up with twelve years of Catholic education, I was pretty familiar with the story. I'm a big fan of anybody born in a stable, and this child grew up to have quite a career. I see Jesus, really, as a major league *troubadour* whose songs and stories stood the test of time. If you don't think Jesus was a songwriter, check out the Gnostic Gospels. Katy recorded this on her album, *Midnight Radio*. I might record it on a Christmas album one of these days.

CHORDS

Recorded in Bb, capo on the 3rd fret, played in G position.

Verse
C-G-D-G
C-G-Am7-D
C-D-G-Em
Am7-Bm-C-D

C-G-D-G
C-G-Am7-D
C-D-G-Em
Am7-Bm-C-D7-G-(Am7/G)

Chorus
D
C-G
D
C-Em-D (D7)
G-D-G
C-G-D-G
Am7-Bm-C-D7-G (Am7/G)

NAZARETH TO BETHLEHEM

Joseph meek and Mary mild
Out on the road with their unborn child
Driven by law of a tax decree
They traveled far from Galilee

Oh, her gentle eyes, his carpenter's hands
They moved as strangers through the land
They found no room at journey's end
Out on the road from Nazareth to Bethlehem

>   And the shepherds on the hillside
>   Raised their heads as they passed by
>   The wise men lay in waiting
>   For a sign up in the sky
>   For the Son of Man was coming
>   Of His Kingdom there would be no end
>   All along the road from Nazareth to Bethlehem

Look up, look up at the Christmas star
The Child is born in a stable dark
Where beasts of the field stare down at Him
Out near the road from Nazareth to Bethlehem

>   And the shepherds came to worship
>   Angels sang on high
>   The wise men led their camels
>   Toward that light up in the sky
>   For Christ is born, praise be to Him
>   Of His Kingdom there will be no end
>   All along the road from Nazareth to Bethlehem

Co-written with Katy Moffatt

JACK JOHNSON

"You don't always have to hold your head higher than your heart."
                                Jack Johnson

Jack Johnson was born in Galveston, Texas. He went on to become, early last century, the first black heavyweight boxing champion of the world, pissing off every redneck and racist sports enthusiast in the country. Everyone was waiting for a White Hope to shut Jack's mouth, but that didn't happen for quite a while. Jack rubbed it in their faces by hanging out with white women and dancing through life with a cigar in his mug. He was a *bad ass* for sure. Muhammad Ali took a few lessons from Jack. I've lately been working on a novel about Juarez and Jack's name crops up all the time in early newspaper articles about his fights at the Juarez racetrack. Jack ended up fighting in exhibitions and private cellars for short money. He died in 1946. I ran across an old Lead Belly song about Jack wanting to sail aboard the Titanic, where the captain said, according to Lead Belly, "Sorry, boy, we ain't haulin' coal." I stole that line for the song. My version appears on the album, *Hurricane Season*, and Barrence Whitfield does a great version on a record we did called *Hillbilly Voodoo*.

CHORDS

Key of G, rocking back and forth a lot from G to C. Rock and Roll.

Verse	Chorus:
G-C-G-C	G-D
G-C-G-C	G-C
G-C-G-C	Bm-Em-Am-C
G-C-G-C	D-G

JACK JOHNSON

He was born in 1890 on the Gulf of Mexico
Fought his way around the world with hand and heart and soul
Hey, trot out all your Great White Hopes, but they'd better bring a gun
Jack Johnson's made of iron, he's *all counter punch and run*

    Yonder comes Jack Johnson
    Like he owns the town
    There's a lot of white Americans
    Like to see a man go down
    Like to see a black man drown

Jack stood on the Titanic pier with a thousand dollar roll
But the Captain said, "Sorry, boy, we ain't haulin' coal."
So Jack danced the Eagle Rock in a tavern on the shore
While the Captain danced his final dance on the Atlantic Ocean floor

    Yonder comes Jack Johnson…

Jack Johnson beat Jim Jefferies, 'til there weren't nothin' left
And every time he'd throw a punch he'd say, "Package for Mr. Jeff!"
Then he ran off with a white girl, man that made 'em mad!
All agreed and all decreed that black man was bad

    Yonder comes Jack Johnson…

Well, I stole a line from Lead Belly, I don't think he'd mind
'Cause Lead Belly and Jack, they were cut from the same vine

    Yonder comes Jack Johnson…

HONG KONG BOY

"The shop owners along Mott Street in Chinatown call him Hong Kong Boy. He is a 20-year-old science major at a college in Queens. Hong Kong Boy stakes out Mott Street—Ghost Shadow territory. Armed with a .357 Magnum revolver that he says he bought for $400 in a Roy Rogers restaurant in Queens..."

New York Times
March 10, 1983

Back to the criminology. I like the fact that Hong Kong Boy bought the gun in a Roy Rogers restaurant. The old West never dies. This has got a sort of Warren Zevon flare to it. This song, written with Greg Trooper, is another product of the New York years. Greg and I lived closed to each other in Brooklyn. A soulful writer.

Hong Kong Boy was a gang character around New York's Chinatown—a member of The Ghost Shadows gang who fought against The Flying Dragons and the Born to Kill. The Born to Kill gang was Vietnamese, It was all about controlling the crime territory. Same as Juarez today. Hired guns, gangs, and cartels. It's ancient. These folks were involved in extortion, kidnapping, murder, drugs, prostitution, illegal gambling, and links to the Italian mob. They were also *all hopped up on ginseng...*

This song appears on *Raw Vision* and *Box of Visions*.

CHORDS

Key of G. Rolling Stones meet Warren Zevon. Pedal to the metal.

Verse
G-C-G
G-D-G
G-C-G
G-D-G
D-C
G-D
D7-G-C
G-D-G

Bridge
C-G
C-G
C-G
G-D
D-G

HONG KONG BOY

There's blood on the streets of Chinatown
A shadow in the night
Now he's standin' in the doorway of the Hoy Hong Lounge
Washed in a neon light
The Flying Shadows are crossing town
Who knows what's in store?
You better stay clear of the Jade Pagoda
Here comes Hong Kong Boy

Jack Mack, the cop in his Irish blues
He's walkin' the Chinese beat
He knows every ghost, every new recruit
Canal to Baxter Street
The Mah Jong kings and opium rings
He's seen it all from Precinct Four
But for a house in Queens and a pension dream
He never sees Hong Kong Boy
He turns his back on Hong Kong Boy

> He'll live and die on Mott Street
> In the shadow of the Tombs
> With Dimple, Jade, and the Night Brigade
> The heavy metal goons, beneath the Chinese moon

He got a thousand dollar gold watch band
And boots made of water snake skin
He got a diamond cross in his left ear
There's no mistaking him
It's four a.m. on Division Street
Dragon Fly will be destroyed
He got a .357, it's under his shirt
They call him Hong Kong Boy
Yeah, *Mister Hong Kong Boy*

> He's all hopped up on ginseng
> He ain't slept in weeks
> He'll shoot at will the Born to Kill
> They're Vietnamese, oh, they're lowly refugees

It's four a.m. on Division Street…

CO-WRITTEN WITH GREG TROOPER

THE HEART

"The way is not in the sky. The way is in the heart."
Buddha

"When you fish for love, bait with your heart, not your brain."
Mark Twain

I wrote this with Greg Trooper in Brooklyn around 1993. Back then Greg was being produced by Springsteen's bass player—Garry Tallent—and since Trooper is also from New Jersey, Greg brought some East coast Springsteen-soul to this one. It's a passionate little rock lullaby. Greg Trooper's version is on the record, *Noises in the Hallway*. The song was covered by Lucy Kaplansky, with Shawn Colin singing backup, on Lucy's record *The Tide*. Sarah Elizabeth Campbell also recorded the song on *Running with You*. A demo of my own version appears on the rarities record *Museum of Memories*. I think Trooper sang harmony on that one. Trooper's still out there making great records. God bless the minstrels of the heart.

CHORDS

Key of D.

Verse	*Chorus*
D-A-D	G-D
D-A-D	G-D
D-A-Bm-G	G-Bm
D-A-D	G-A-D

THE HEART

Go to sleep my darlin'
Lay down upon your bed
May the lines of childhood song
Dance inside your head

When nighttime falls around you
I know you are afraid
The heart will bring you home again
The heart is built that way

> The heart will bring you home again
> It hasn't failed us yet
> The heart will bring you home again
> The heart does not forget

Close your eyes my darlin'
Close your eyes and dream
The world was full of promises
When love was all it seemed

Forget awhile the hard road
That leads us all astray
The heart will bring you home again
The heart is built that way

> The heart will bring you home again…

The sun will rise my darlin'
And light the darkest street
So close your eyes, believe in love
And be safe inside your dream

No one's gonna harm you
Or carry you away
The heart will lead you home again
The heart is built that way

> The heart will bring you home again…

CO-WRITTEN WITH GREG TROOPER

SAINT LILY OF THE MOHAWKS

"What made the Mohawks such superb high steel workers remains something of a mystery. The legends assumed some kind of genetic advantage...but someone suggested it's just a question of dealing with fear."
                                             Kevin Baker

Here's an early lyric I unearthed—written with Sylvia Tyson. Katteri Tekakwitha (1656 to 1680)—known as *Lily of the Mohawks*—was an Algonquin and Iroquois Native American religious lay woman from New France, and an early convert to Roman Catholicism. She died young and is the first Native American woman to be venerated as a saint in the Catholic Church. *Saint Lily of the Mohawks* is the patron saint of the Mohawk high steel workers who have worked on the bridges and skyscrapers in New York City. Mohawks are even working on the new World Trade towers. The song references the collapse of the Quebec Bridge in 1907 when seventy-five steel workers were killed. Thirty-three of the victims were Mohawks. The great New York writer Joseph Mitchell wrote about the Mohawks in the *New Yorker* in an essay called, "The Mohawks in High Steel." It appears in his book, *Up in the Grand Hotel*.

CHORDS

Sylvia Tyson is working on the melody; as of the fall of 2012, no recording exists.

SAINT LILY OF THE MOHAWKS

My name's Naz'reth Diabo, I'm Miles Diabo's son.
My father rode the Wild West shows, I ride a rivet gun.
I fell from off the Quebec Bridge in nineteen-hundred-seven,
Now my spirit walks that silver span that joins the earth and heaven

Five hundred feet above the gorge we danced our high iron dance
The bosses couldn't touch us there, they seemed as small as ants
That day up on the Quebec Bridge we heard the high span moan
The Mohawks fell like autumn leaves and St Lily took us home

> "I'll Fly Away" is the song our children sang, their angels are not mine
> Their songs are not the songs we sang back in the longhouse times
> From Hell Gate Bridge to the Golden Gate my restless spirit wheels
> With Saint Lily of the Mohawks on wings of Lehigh steel
> I'll fly away hey-hey, hey hey, hey hey

Way back in Kahnewake the old men fish for eels
All the young men are in Brooklyn at the Nevins Bar and Grill
Where my ghost sits smoking Red Rose as I gaze out with pride
At the high iron towers and bridges where the Mohawks lived and died

> "I'll Fly Away" is the song…

Co-written with Sylvia Tyson

GALLO DEL CIELO
Woodcut by Tom Russell
2012

CHAPTER THREE
GALLO DEL CIELO

GALLO DEL CIELO

"Gallo del Cielo is the greatest song ever written. It's a classic Greek tragedy set to music with Spanish guitar. Are you freakin' kidding me? When I hear it I don't know whether to go out and kick someone's ass or to sit home and cry. That is the mark of a true classic. Man, who wrote that!?"
    Derek Chiarenza
    Online Comment

"When Joe Ely sang me Gallo del Cielo, I said who the hell wrote that? Great song."
    Bruce Springsteen
    Letter to Tom Russell

"Joe did a hell of a song tonight...A Tom Russell song. It's about a fighting rooster. It's called 'Gallo del Cielo.' It's good. And I'm hard to impress."
    Bob Dylan,
    From Clarence Clemmons's, *Big Man*

If we believe songs are like *our children*, and have to make their own way in the world—well this one-eyed rooster has gone out of the house and down the road and raised its fair share of hell. "Kicked ass," as the man said. I think this is a good spot to tell about the side roads and back alleys *one song* might travel. The providence of the rooster! In that respect *Gallo* deserves a chapter all its own. Of all my songs this one has garnered the most intriguing anecdotes and recorded covers. The song is more famous than I am. *For sure*.

There's a laundry list of stories. Gallo has been mentioned and acknowledged by Bob Dylan and Bruce Springsteen, Robert Hunter of Grateful Dead fame, Jerry Jeff Walker and the President of Mexico. It's been sung around campfires and recorded by dozens of folks including Ian Tyson, Joe Ely, Jason Boland (recently) and a ninety-year-old western legend named Katie Lee...for *starters*. There's a famous cutting horse stallion named Gallo del Cielo and cabins, spas, ranches and backyard chicken operations named after the one-eyed bird. I'm sure there are pit bulls, pet alligators, and private airplanes.

Two truck drivers have written me long, passionate letters about how the song changed their lives one dark night—out on the lost highway, as they tuned into some small radio station. I think of all the anecdotes, those letters move me the most. Songs have changed my life and I'm honored that a song like this can *move* people at odd moments. I'm just happy, in this age, that folks would listen to such a long, detailed saga.

Where the hell did it come from? A seven-minute, eleven-verse epic about a mythical fighting rooster? A *corrido* in English? Most of it fell down on me in a two hour span of writing. I wrote it in 1978 in a garage in Mountain View, California. I had color wheels and ideas rolling around in my mind. Shards of background material. I'd been down to the Tarahumara country in Mexico and heard a few Pancho Villa stories, but nothing like this. The plot came out of the blue. A *sky song*, as Townes Van Zandt might term it—songs that fall out of the sky. Like the rooster. But hell, I'm so drawn to the country Gallo came out of: the frontier, the border, the Rio Grande, Northern Mexico…that songs seem to emerge from the ether and the historical soil and the passionate heart of the people.

I think there's a little Marty Robbins "El Paso" flavor in this one, and a nod to Mexican border *corridos* I heard as a kid. Add a few cockfight scenes from the novelist Nathaniel West, and off we go. Cockfighting used to be legal in New Mexico, just up the road from our hacienda, but I've never seen one there. I saw a few fights in Puerto Rico when I was working a carnival on the road to Bayamon. Never became an *aficionado*. But I loved that Steinbeckian landscape and atmosphere conjured in the rooster's journey. The *Tortilla Flats* ethos. Cockfighting is a blood sport which can be traced back to Saint Augustine's time. And that old mystic, Augustine, was an aficionado of the game cocks.

Here's a key Gallo anecdote which turned around my life in music: In 1980 I moved to New York from San Francisco. I was going to be a novelist. Quit music awhile and drove taxi for a year. One night I picked up Robert Hunter, lyricist for the Grateful Dead, sang him "Gallo" *a cappella* in the cab. Robert loved the song. He came back to town and invited me up on stage to sing it at a show in the Village. He got me back into the music business. I hail him. I have a recording of Robert singing the song at the Glastonbury Festival in England. He states, "Here's a song I learned from a cab driver in Jamaica. Jamaica, Queens, New York."

The great Ian Tyson recorded "Gallo" on his first cowboy culture record, *Old Corrals and Sagebrush*, before I'd ever met him in person. He informed me the song was actually a *polka*. Tyson and I went on to write a dozen cowboy songs after he was on the road to reinventing western music. The definitive and most passionate version of "Gallo" must be Joe Ely's on the record *Letter to Laredo*. He also did it on one of his live records. Joe nails it. Rips it up. He even sang it for Bruce Springsteen, and Bruce wrote me a very nice letter, part of which is quoted above.

Most recently the song was mentioned in a very odd "tall tales" manner by the late Clarence Clemmons (Springsteen's sax player) in his book *Big Man*. There's a scene, also quoted above, in which Kinky Freidman, Clarence, and Bob Dylan are talking about Dylan seeing Joe Ely play in a roadhouse. Dylan mentions "Gallo."

I could go on and on with the anecdotes. The song evidently has a mythical, inherent magic all its own. The bird keeps flying. The legend lives on.

"Gallo" was on my first record, *Heart on a Sleeve*, and on the later records, *Poor Man's Dream*, *Cowboy Real* (a duet with Ian Tyson), *The Long Way Around*, *Songs of the West* (a duet with Tyson), and *Veteran's Day: The Tom Russell Anthology*.

CHORDS

I've usually played it in either F or E, but always in the "D" chord positions, capo up on either the second or third fret of the guitar.

Verse	*Chorus*
D-Em	G-A
A-D	Em-A
D-Em	G-A
A-G-A-D	Em-A-G-A-D

GALLO DEL CIELO

Carlos Zaragoza left his home in *Casas Grandes* when the moon was full
No money in his pocket, just a locket of his sister framed in gold
He headed for *El Sueco*, stole a rooster named *Gallo del Cielo*
Then he crossed the *Rio Grande*, with that rooster nestled deep beneath his arm

Now *Gallo del Cielo* was a rooster born in heaven, so the legends say
His wings they had been broken, he had one eye rollin' crazy in his head
He'd fought a hundred fights, and the legends say that one night near El Sueco
They'd fought *Cielo* seven times, and seven times he left brave roosters dead

   Hola, my Theresa, I am thinking of you now in San Antonio
   I have twenty-seven dollars and the locket of your picture framed in gold
   Tonight I'll bet it all, on the fighting spurs of *Gallo del Cielo*
   Then I'll return to buy the land Pancho Villa stole from father long ago

Outside of San Diego in the onion fields of *Paco Monteverde*
The pride of San Diego, he lay sleeping on a fancy bed of silk
And they laughed when Zaragoza pulled the one-eyed *del Cielo* from beneath his coat
But they cried when Zaragoza walked away with a thousand dollar bill

   Hola, my Theresa, I am thinking of you now in Santa Barbara
   I have fifteen hundred dollars and the good luck of your picture framed in gold
   Tonight I'll bet it all on the fighting spurs of *Gallo del Cielo*
   Then I'll return to buy the land that Villa stole from father long ago

Now the moon has gone to hiding and the lantern light spills shadows on the fighting sand
Where a wicked black named *Zorro* faces *Gallo del Cielo* in the night
But Carlos Zaragoza fears the tiny crack that runs across his rooster's beak
And he fears that he has lost the fifty thousand dollars riding on the fight

    Hola, my Theresa, I am thinking of you now in Santa Clara
    Yes, the money's on the table I am holding now your good luck framed in gold
    And everything we dreamed of is riding on the spurs of *del Cielo*
    I pray that I'll return to buy the land that Villa stole from father long ago

Then the signal it was given, and the roosters rose together far above the sand
Gallo del Cielo sunk a gaff into Zorro's shiny breast
They were separated quickly, but they rose and fought each other thirty-seven times
And the legends say that everyone agreed that *del Cielo* fought the best

Then the screams of Zaragoza filled the night outside the town of Santa Clara
As the beak of *del Cielo* lay broken like a shell within his hand
And they say that Zaragoza screamed a curse upon the bones of Pancho Villa
When Zorro rose up one last time, and drove *del Cielo* to the sand

    Hola, my Theresa, I am thinking of you now in San Francisco
    There's no money in my pocket, I no longer have your picture framed in gold
    I buried it last evening with the bones of my beloved *del Cielo*
    And I'll not return to buy the land that Villa stole from father long ago

Do the rivers still run muddy, outside of my beloved *Casas Grandes*?
Does the scar upon my brother's face turn red when he hears mention of my name?
Do the people of *El Sueco* still curse the death of *Gallo del Cielo*?
Tell my family not to worry, I will not return to cause them shame.

A ROSE FOR NADINE
Woodcut by Tom Russell
2012

CHAPTER FOUR

NEW YORK TO THE SAN JOAQUIN

HALEY'S COMET

"I was sitting at the kitchen table trying to write this tune. The first lyric was easy, 'Rock, rock, rock everybody!' Then I wrote 'Stomp, stomp, stomp everybody!' But it didn't fit. I then wrote in, 'Rock, roll, roll everybody!' It sounded better, I liked the two R's sound of rock and roll. The rest is history!"

Bill Haley, 1955

Bill Haley's "Rock Around the Clock," was the first rock and roll song I recall. Must have been 1955. The song was used in the opening of the movie *The Asphalt Jungle*. I have a strong memory of myself and a kid named Russ Williams opening up his parents' dining room window and blasting, at 45 rpm, this song out at the neighbors. Bad trouble ensued. The term *juvenile delinquents* was being batted about the neighborhood and the nation…then Elvis blew the roof off.

Fast forward to 1981. I'm working in a carnival in Puerto Rico as an *Urban Cowboy* singer. (See the song, "Road to Bayamon.") I recall sitting in the tent dressing room reading a copy of that rag, *The National Enquirer*, which someone left lying there. There was a back page article about Bill Haley dying drunk and alone in Harlingen, Texas, down in the Rio Grande Valley. The Rio Grande keeps cropping up in my life and songs, and now I irrigate my pecan trees off the brave river. But the Haley story shook me, and I'm always drawn to these sad tales about what really happens to certain American legends.

I made notes for a song and carried them around for eight or nine years, until I ran into Dave Alvin in New York. We finished the song in a hotel overlooking Central Park. Dave is a great writer and he kept checking the facts by calling our mutual friend, John Swenson, who wrote a biography on Bill Haley.

The song appears on Dave Alvin's *Blue Boulevard* record, and Doug Sahm and the Texas Tornados do a great version on *Wounded Heart of America: Tom Russell Songs*. Doug even throws a little *Rock Around the Clock* on there…My versions appear on *Hurricane Season*, *The Long Way Around* (with Dave Alvin and Katy Moffatt) and *Veteran's Day: The Tom Russell Anthology*.

CHORDS

I first recorded this in G, but now sing it in E. A bluesy, rock and roll treatment.

Verse	*Chorus*
E-A	E-A-B-E
E-B	A-B-E
E-A	E-A-B-E-C#m
E-B-E	A-B-E

HALEY'S COMET

"Do you know who I am?" said Bill Haley
In a pancake house, down near the Rio Grande
Well, the waitress said, "I don't know you from diddley,
To me you look like one more tired old man."

Well, he walked all alone, down on Main Street
Was a hot wind blowin' up from the south
There were two eyes starin' in a pawnshop window
A whiskey bottle lifted to his mouth

 There was no moon shinin' on the Rio Grande
 A truck of migrants pulled through town
 The jukebox was busted at the bus depot
 When Haley's Comet hit the ground

Well, he blacked out all the windows in his bedroom
He was talking to the ceiling and the walls
Then he closed his eyes and hit the stage in 1955
And the screams of the ladies filled the hall

 There was no moon shinin' on the Rio Grande…

Well, a cop walked in a pancake house in Texas
And he orders up two coffees to go
He tells the waitress, "Baby, we just found the body,
Of some old hillbilly who was famous long ago."

 There was no moon shinin' on the Rio Grande…

Co-written with Dave Alvin

LA GOULUE (THE GLUTTON)

La Goulue: *One day I'll go right down her throat, pull her heart out, and feed it to my cat!"*
Moulin Rouge
Directed by John Huston

Maybe I was drinking absinthe when I concocted this one. This has a French *bal musette* feel, and I could imagine Django Reinhardt ripping it to gypsy shreds. As I recall, most of the facts are true—*however strange*. La Goulue was the stage name of Louise Weber, a Moulin Rouge dancer whom Toulouse-Lautrec painted. She had a fondness for the drink, and emptied the glasses on patrons' tables as she danced around them, lifting her skirts up to reveal the heart stitched on her panties. Hence her title: "The Glutton." What a journey: chorus line star to lady wrestler to lion tamer to candy hawker to bordello maid. The *gamut*. She hit all the stops on her runaway carriage ride to the bottom rung of hell. I think I've also read that Lautrec's father drank the milk of Arabian mares, so of course I had to throw that in…Nashville hasn't been beating down my door for this song. Time will tell.

The only version I know of appears on my rarities album, *Museum of Memories*.

CHORDS

Key of A minor and also C on chorus. A *bal musette* gypsy waltz. With flare!

Verse
Am-E
E-Am
Am-Dm
E-Am

Chorus
F-C-G-C
F-C-E-Am

LA GOULUE (THE GLUTTON)

Toulouse-Lautrec trained his pen
In the *Cabaret de Assassins*
At *La Goulue*, the Alsatian girl,
Who drained the dregs from glasses
At sixteen, fierce with cobra's eyes
And an angel's magic feet
At twenty-five a worn-out dancer
And a jaded sideshow freak

Well, Count Alfonse was a lecher bold
And he spoke in drunken stutters
He drank the milk of Arabian mares
And he washed his shirts in gutters
And his only son, Toulouse-Lautrec
Was a toad four feet in height
A painter stuck on the thieves and whores
That stalked the Montmartre night

Now, a cutthroat moon was a-sinkin' low
The iguanas screamed in laughter
When *La Goulue* took the stage
They found what they were after
The cathedral bells of Notre Dame
Pealed in sacred warning
As the hunchback sot, Toulouse-Lautrec,
Staggered home by morning

    Father, I am La Goulue
    Will the Lord forgive me?
    Father, I am La Goulue
    Will my sins outlive me?

CONTINUED

Now *La Goulue*, the glutton
Long past her sideshow days
Became a lady wrestler
Bloody earlobes were her pay
And then a lion tamer
With tired beasts as friends
Until a cat tore off the arm
Of a child at La Rouen

She ended up a candy hawker
Outside the Moulin Rouge
Oh, once she danced upon that stage
She's now grotesque and boozed
Her last job—a bordello maid
At the age of thirty-nine
One night she screamed and called the priest
"Oh Father, it is time…"

    Father, I am La Goulue…

The posters of her traveling show
They cut 'em up in pieces
And hung 'em in the Louvre museum
To be viewed by nuns and nieces
And the hunchback sot Toulouse-Lautrec
Limps through the Montmartre dawn
Crying out for *La Goulue*
The Alsatian girl that's gone

    Father, I am La Goulue…

AMELIA'S RAILROAD FLAT

Some red French wine, when late awakening
In her warm hideaway...

Ian Tyson
"The French Girl"

There are certainly *international* flavors here. *Russia, Poland, Spain, Morocco, Denmark.* I can't recall writing this song, but I know Katy Moffatt has recorded it a few times, and she usually opens her show with it. This reminds me of a lot of nights in Oslo, Norway, back in the early 1980s, when I was working the clubs seven nights a week. We stayed in an old nunnery on the east side of town. Imagine four floors of musicians from around the world. Long nights of drinking and singing old folk songs and telling tales. And the ladies were quite beautiful. I recall meeting Randy Sparks, the founder of the New Christy Minstrels there, and two guys from the group King Harvest which had the hit "Dancing in the Moonlight." All of us working bar gigs for the Olav Thun organization. The lady who ran our musicians dormitory in Oslo (Red Karen) had a stock of cheap Polish vodka she'd deal to us. I loved it. If you survived it was magic. Most didn't.

This song appears on Katy Moffat's albums *The Evangeline Hotel* and *Up Close and Personal*. A demo of mine was also released on *Museum of Memories*. You can find performances on YouTube.

CHORDS

Played in E. Capo on second fret in D chord positions. Medium tempo country.

Verse	*Bridge*
D-G	Bm-G
A-D	Bm-G
D-Em	Bm-G
A-D	D
D-G	A
A-D	
D-Em	
A-D	

AMELIA'S RAILROAD FLAT

Amelia, she worked for the railroad
Doing what, I never knew
But I'd meet her down at the depot
Every day at half past two
And we'd climb the old wood stairway
Find the key below the mat
Watch the sun set on the freight yard
Up at Amelia's railroad flat

Russian vodka in the freezer
From the Polish liquor store
Spanish rice, Moroccan oranges
Persian rugs upon the floor
And Amelia came from Denmark
She brought a pair of Siamese cats
There was an international flavor
To Amelia's railroad flat

    And every night the Midnight Ghost
    Rolled out on time
    Rollin' down the line
    At 12.09
    And we'd sit, count the cars
    Out on the track
    As they shook the bedroom windows
    Of Amelia's railroad flat

But the freight yards, they are gone now
And the buildings block the sun
And Amelia sailed for Denmark
Way back in 1981
But every time I hear a freight train
Or watch the sun set on the tracks
I recall those summer evenings
Up at Amelia's railroad flat

And every time I hear a freight train
Blowin' lonely down the track
I hear those bedroom windows rattlin'
Up at Amelia's railroad flat...

HURRICANE SEASON

"Once a man I was leaving told me I could go if I would leave my skin behind. I was so young I didn't even know that I was wonderful…"

　　　　　　　　　　　　　　　　Ellen Gilchrist

I wrote this song (*I think*) on the same night I wrote "Chinatown in the Rain." There might have been vodka involved. And tonic water. This comes from reading Ellen Gilchrist short stories about the South, and also might have something to do with the relationship I was in at the time. It also smacks of Raymond Carver and Charles Bukowski. *Dangerous territory*. I used to imagine Roy Orbison singing this. *Scary*. This song somehow prefigures the great New Orleans flood. It's biblical in that way. It's the title song for the Tom Russell Band record *Hurricane Season*, which was recorded in Norway. Maybe Harry Dean Stanton will cover it?

CHORDS

Performed, tense and psycho, in D.

Verse	*Verse*	*Chorus*
First Form:	Second Form:	D-G
D-D	G-C-G	D-G
D-D	G-C-G	D-Em-A
G-G	D	G-F#m-Em-A
D-D	G-C-G	Bm-G
	G-C-G	Em-A
	D-D-A	

HURRICANE SEASON

Hurricane season on the home front
All the weak of heart are leavin' town
Well, baby and me ain't up to goin' just yet
Maybe we'll just drink until we drown
Me, I freshen up a pot of coffee
Baby puts the chain across the door
And pretty soon she's seein' things that I don't see
Like alligators on the bathroom floor

Hurricane season in the kitchen
Baby throws the eggs against the wall
She says, "Don't think I don't know what you've been up to, Jack
With that Puerto Rican slut lives down the hall
She told me all about it in the laundry room
She was foldin' her goddamn see-through underwear
She probably gave you some kind of rare tropical disease
Now I got it, you don't even care."

    Like a hurricane, hey, what's your name?
    Are you Donna or Marie? Are you Margaret or Elaine?
    Do you paint your toenails in the mornin'
    Yeah, fire engine red or baby blue?
    Then you roll downtown in a whirlwind
    Yeah, they ought to name a hurricane for you

We saw our bedroom set floating down Piedmont Street
Palm trees broken by the wind
So baby starts packing the essential things
Diet pills, potato chips, and gin
Next thing I know we're in a row boat
We're watching our apartment house go down
And baby's got a jar of gin and tonics
She says, "Christ, I hope the next door neighbors drown."

Last time I saw baby was in the Red Cross Store
She's trying to find a dress that she could wear
She said, "God protects the drunks and the adulterers
And He drowns everyone who says their prayers."
Now every time I drink a gin and tonic
I order up an extra slice of lime
Yeah, 'cause that's the way my baby used to drink 'em
Back when she was wild and in her prime

    Like a hurricane, heh, what's your name?...

WINNIPEG

"You go out on the road until your clothes don't fit."
Champion Jack Dupree

This one comes from those years of touring in an uninsulated Dodge van across Canada, dead of winter, with the Tom Russell Band. Late 1980s. I recall one afternoon driving into Thunder Bay for a gig at one of the worst dumps I'd ever seen. Our rooms were located above the topless disco where a gal danced with a snake, six shows a day, as the jukebox blasted out the beat through our bedroom floor. No chance of sleep. Wasn't my first encounter with a snake act. (See *Don't Look Down* for other snake-act footage.) Show business! The rest of the occupants of the hotel were old men on welfare. They sat on their beds, staring at the floor. We drove on across the desolate landscape and played another gig in Moose Jaw, and then on to Calgary. The one big reason for this song is to see if I could rhyme something with *Head-Smashed-in-Buffalo-Jump*, a colorful stop along our trail. I think I lost a few dollars at that horse track in Winnipeg, and rode in a taxi driven by a Sikh with a four-foot beard. These are the details that dreams are made of…and road songs.

CHORDS

Key of C. Capo on the fifth fret in G chord positions. Country style.

Verse
G-G
Am-Am-G
G-G
Am-Am-G
Am-Am-G

Chorus
C-D-G-C
C-D-G-C
C-D-G-C
Bm-Em
Am-D-G

WINNIPEG

How's the weather in Winnipeg? Broke-down nags with the bandaged legs
At Assiniboine Downs? The night we painted the town, a dark, dark blue
Stolen thunder in Thunder Bay, woke up knowin' that we came the wrong way
So we turned it all around, to the cold, hard sound, the turnin' of the gears
To the blood hard sound, the turnin' of the years

    I was thinkin' of you last night
    North of the border in the Northern Lights
    One horse town with the Indian name
    And all the gentle words I could never say
    Love shines in the night, in the morning it's gone away

Cup of coffee in old Moose Jaw, used to be the hideout of a bad outlaw
Name of Al Capone, his fedora on, walkin' through the snow
We headed west, then it all broke up, in *Head-Smashed-In-Buffalo-Jump*
A-rockin' and a-reelin', that old buffalo feelin', of fallin' through the air
And never really knowin' how the hell you ended up there

    I was thinking of you last night…

How's the weather in Winnipeg? When the ice melts on the first of May
On those desolate streets, one old Sikh in a powder blue cab
Is there an Indian name for all the love and the trouble we had?

    I was thinking of you last night…

THE EVANGELINE HOTEL

"I mean, it's hard to be an actor in the city—trying to make it as an actor—because you waitress all night, you get home really late and you're super tired and your feet hurt."
                              Piper Perabo

The Evangeline Hotel faces Gramercy Park in New York City. It's a residence for single women, run by the Salvation Army. I used to date an actress who resided there. The place was full of young ladies trying to make it, or at least survive, in the New York of the 1980s. A house filled with beautiful dreamers and out-of-work models and librarians. There are "No Men Allowed" at The Evangeline. I recall there was a curfew and each lady had a key to the gate at Gramercy Park. The rest is a beautiful blur. I believe the young lady in question went back to Oklahoma. This one is on the Tom Russell Band record, *Hurricane Season*, recorded in Norway. Katy Moffat also does a fine version on a Philo record, *The Evangeline Hotel*.

CHORDS

A Waltz in B flat. Capo on the third fret, played in G chord positions.

Verse	*Chorus*
G-C-G	G-D
C-G	C-G
C-G-D	G-D
G-C-G	G-C-G
G-C-G	C-G
G-D-G	G-D-G

THE EVANGELINE HOTEL

Well, she moves like Betty Grable
She's an actress waitin' table
And all her tips are kept inside a wishin' well
She's got an agent down the hall
He's got her photo on his wall
She's got a room at the Evangeline Hotel

And from the tenth floor fire escape
She can see the Great White Way
But not the street and not the eyes of those who fell
She dreams she sees her name in lights
She dreams that dream every night
Room 10-04 at the Evangeline Hotel

    It's "Rock of ages cleft for thee…"
    She's just a child of Tennessee
    Her daddy's girl, her golden curls locked in a spell
    Where you don't play your music loud
    And there ain't no men allowed
    On Friday nights at the Evangeline Hotel

You make it here, so they declare
And you can make it anywhere
Those old clichés ring through the halls just like a bell
But tell it to the ones who wait
Behind the 23rd Street gate
On Friday nights at the Evangeline Hotel

    It's "Rock of ages cleft for thee…"
    She's goin' back to Tennessee
    She's got a watch and winter coat that she can sell
    She learned the hard, unspoken rules
    And things you'll never learn in school
    All down the halls of the Evangeline Hotel

And you can knock on any door
Any room on every floor
It's all the same in the Evangeline Hotel
The House of Dreams called the Evangeline Hotel

MANZANAR

"Down in our hearts we cried and cursed this government every time when we showered with sand. We slept in the dust; we breathed the dust; we ate the dust."
            Joseph Kurihara
            Internee at Manzanar

"May the injustice and humiliation suffered here as a result of hysteria, racism and economic exploitation never emerge again."
            Historical Marker at Manzanar

In the wake of the bombing of Pearl Harbor, over 110,000 Japanese Americans were sent to internment camps in the U.S. Places like Heart Mountain and Manzanar. The spark for this song came from a book of Ansel Adams photos taken inside the Manzanar camp during World War Two. Manzanar was located up in the high desert of California, east of the Sierra Nevadas. Later, in Brooklyn, I lived next to a man named Mr. Moteki who had been in a camp during the war. A great cover version of this song was recorded by Laurie Lewis and appears on *Wounded Heart of America: Tom Russell Songs*. My versions appear on *Box of Visions*, *The Long Way Around* (which was a live version with Katy Moffatt), and on *Veteran's Day: The Tom Russell Anthology*.

CHORDS

Key of B flat. Capo on third fret, played in G Chord positions. *Fingerpicked.*

Verse
G-G-C-G
C-G-C-Am-D
G-G-C-G
C-Bm-F-D

Chorus
Em-G
Em-D
Em-B-C
G-C-G

MANZANAR

He said, "My name is, Nakishima, and I'm a proud American…
I came here in '27 from my homeland of Japan
And I picked your grapes and oranges, I saved some money, I bought a store
Until 1942, Pearl Harbor and the war.

"Came those relocation orders, they took our house, the store, the car
And they drove us through the desert, to a place called Manzanar
The Spanish word for 'Apple Orchard,' though we saw no apple trees
Just the rows of prison barracks with barbed wire boundaries."

    And we dream of apple blossoms
    Waving free beneath the stars
    'Til we wake up in the desert
    The prisoners of Manzanar

"Fifty years have all but vanished and now I am an old man
But I don't regret the day, that I came here from Japan
But on moonless winter nights I often wish upon a star
That I'd forget the shame and sorrow that I felt at Manzanar."

    And we dream of apple blossoms…

BOX OF VISIONS

"Yes: I am a dreamer. For a dreamer is one who can only find his way by moonlight, and his punishment is that he sees the dawn before the rest of the world."
   Oscar Wilde

"I used to think as I looked out on the Hollywood night—there must be thousands of girls sitting alone like me, dreaming of becoming a movie star. But I'm not going to worry about them. I'm dreaming the hardest."
   Marilyn Monroe

I wrote this for my youngest daughter Shannon (aka Quinn) who now has two lovely twin daughters of her own. Shannon sang the song at her high school graduation, and she's a very good songwriter and painter. The inspiration for the title came from a photo titled *Caja de Visiones,* by the Mexican photographer Manuel Alvarez Bravo. The photo showed a gypsy street vendor in Mexico and her *box of visions*. You paid a few centavos and looked into the windows in this ornate and mystical looking hurdy-gurdy thing—and I'm sure there were mirrors and images and candles and saints in there. A song is really just a box of visions.

I recorded this on the albums *Box of Visions* and *The Long Way Around*—this last one a live duet with Iris Dement.

CHORDS

Key of Bflat, played in G chord positions, capo on third fret.

Verse	*Chorus*
G-C-D	G-D-C-G
G-C-D	G-D-Am-D
G-C-D	G-D-C-G
C-D-G	G-Am-D
	C-Am-D-G

BOX OF VISIONS

I'll give to you a box of visions
I'll give to you a jar of hearts
I'll lend to you the gypsy's ear
To hear the Sacred Harp

I'll give to you a house of mirrors
A thousand eyes, they belong to you
A labyrinth of wild roses
I know you'll find your own way through

    Wait awhile and you'll grow older
    And never mind what the sad folks say
    Just keep an angel on your shoulder
    And never throw your dreams away
    For they might save your life one day

A song is just a box of visions
You can't unlock it with a key
A message rolled up inside a bottle
And dropped into the salty sea

A song is just a box of visions
A jar of hearts, a gypsy's ear
A labyrinth of wild roses
A journey through the house of mirrors

    Wait awhile and you'll grow stronger…

I'll give to you a box of visions…

BLOOD ORANGES

"The sky hides the night behind it and shelters the people beneath from the horror that lies above."
Paul Bowles

Here's a grotesque little parable fashioned loosely from the plot of a Paul Bowles story, "A Distant Episode." I spent a year in West Africa, during the Biafran war, teaching criminology. After that wild sojourn I travelled through Morocco, reading Bowles and Graham Greene and getting lost in the marketplaces of North Africa. At that point I had disdain for the academic lifestyle and had decided to try my hand at songwriting. This song is aiming a few arrows at academics I'd known who researched street crime, but really knew nothing about real life. This is the favorite song of a retired stomach doctor and patron of the arts in Fort Worth (and good friend) named John Jackson. John has odd tastes. He loves the dark stuff.

CHORDS

Key of Em, played in creepy medina-style.

Verse	*Chorus*
Em-D	C-Em
Em-B	C-Em
Em-D-C-B	C-Em
(repeat form)	B-Em

BLOOD ORANGES

It was an old hotel in Morocco
Caruso sang through the walls
Beat North African hipsters
Were muttering outside in the halls
An American waits for his interpreter-guide
Caffeine makes his hands itch and shake
She enters the room and calls with her eyes
Like a snake charmer summons the snake

      Blood Oranges, a copper buys you ten
      Come and see the dancing clown who lives with the Blue Men

He said, "I came here to study the language
Of a very rare nomadic tribe."
She chortled and clucked and hissed through her teeth
And motioned him to follow her outside
He wondered about the scars on her forehead
And the secrets behind her dark veil
As she led him out through the walls of the city
Through the moonlight on an old camel trail

      Blood oranges, a copper buys you ten…

They came upon a circle of nomads
Camped far from the lights of the town
Blue men with scars, malarial eyes
And teeth that were pointed, filed down
He said, "These are the people I've been searching for
This is more than I ever could have hoped!"
As they threw him down on a blanket
And tied him up with a hand-braided rope

They cut out his tongue and blinded his eyes
With coals from a *couscous* fire
Tied empty tin cans to his arms and his legs
That rattled on long copper wires
Now he's forgotten his name and why he came to the desert
As they lead him through oasis and town
And the people stare, throw coins, and laugh wildly
At the Blue Men and their white dancing clown

      Blood oranges, a copper buys you ten…

THE ANGEL OF LYON

*"I've been to Lyon. I've been to Tijuana too.
I've been everywhere, Tom, and the world is a zoo…"*
       Little Jack Horton
       Letter to Tom Russell

Steve Young, the songwriting legend, had mentioned he'd seen the "Angel of Lyon" at a concert in France. A beautiful woman who disappeared before he could meet her. I kept the remark in my subconscious and wrote the song one day. But Steve deserves half the song credit for his insight and title. Lyon is a French city known for its cuisine. The Rhone and Saone rivers divide the town, and there's a statue in the square of a Neptune-like figure, swimming in one direction, with a mermaid beneath him swimming in the other direction. Carved on the statue is, "The Rhône and the Saône." Our good friend Jacques Spiry used to hire us for concerts in that city. *Exit the Rainmaker,* as I recall, was a true crime book about a man who changes his name and disappears from his former life—which must be why that phrase is mentioned in the lyric.

Steve Young does a version of this on the album *Switchblades of Love,* my versions appear on *Box of Visions, The Long Way Around,* and *Veteran's Day*: *The Tom Russell Anthology.* Francesco De Gregori recorded a wonderful version in Italian, "L'Angelo Di Lyon." His brother Luigi Grecchi did the translation into Italian.

CHORDS

Key of C. The vibe and rhythm are like Dylan's *Series of Dreams.*

Verse
C-F-C
F-C-Dm-G
C-F-C
F-Dm-Bflat-G

Chorus
Am-Em-F-C
Am-Em-F-G
Am-Em-F-G-C
Am-Bflat-G

THE ANGEL OF LYON

He had a vision of Anne-Marie, with a rosary in her hand
So it's *Exit the Rainmaker*—the old grey flannel man
With a closet full of business suits, he left a letter near the phone
It said, "I'm on my way to Paradise to see the Angel of Lyon"

Then he caught the train to Brussels, he ordered cognac and croissants
He made a mental list, of things he owned but didn't want
Ah, the buildings and the real estate, the antique glass and stone
He'd trade a vow of poverty to see the Angel of Lyon

    And he sang *Ave Maria*, or at least the parts he knew
    And watched the shadow of the train on the towns that they rolled through
    And he closed his eyes and saw two rivers, the Rhône and the Saône
    The male and female spirit of the city of Lyon

Then he waited on the bridge, where they'd met the year before
But the days turned into weeks and then the seasons numbered four
And his clothes grew worn and ragged, as through that town he roamed
Searching every open window for the Angel of Lyon

    And he sang *Ave Maria*…

There's a thousand candles burning in the basilica tonight
Where Sister Eve Maria is the keeper of the lights
And down a dream of alleyways, walks a saint of rag and bone
The madman torn asunder by the Angel of Lyon

    And he sang *Ave Maria*…

Co-written with Steve Young

THE EYES OF ROBERTO DURAN

"Yes, it's true I once knocked out a horse. It was at a fiesta in my mother's home town of Guarare. Someone bet me a bottle of whiskey that I couldn't do it."
                                Roberto Duran

I paid five bucks once to watch the Panamanian boxer Roberto Duran workout at the 30th street gym in New York City. I believe he was preparing for the second Sugar Ray Leonard fight. The first was one was a bloodbath, won by Duran. Duran's nickname was *Manos de Piedra* (hands of stone). I paid my five and stood against the wall that afternoon. The gym was filled with Latino babes, and Duran was showing off. He did a skip rope routine where he got down in a squat and skipped rapid fire, hopping across the room. He hopped right up to me and snarled in my face. I looked down into those fierce eyes and recognized the look I'd seen in the eyes of a Mexican woman I was dating at the time. When those eyes turned angry the next thing coming at you was a shoe or a plate. She threw everything she owned. Later that afternoon the actor Joe Pesci showed up to spar with Duran—just fooling around for the cameras. Pesci made the mistake of slapping Duran a little too hard, and for a moment *that look* danced across Duran's eyes—the look of insane, *feral* anger. He was about to take off Pesci's head—then the moment passed and Duran smiled. I'll never forget it.

The late great Chris Gaffney did a cool version of this song on a Dave Alvin produced record, *Loser's Paradise*. You can see Chris, Dave, and I perform it on YouTube with Dave's band. My version is on the Hightone record *The Long Way Around*.

CHORDS

Key of D. Rock and Roll.

Verse
D-G-A
D-G-A
Em-G-A
Em-A-D

Bridge
Bm-F#m
G-A-Bm
G-D
C-A

THE EYES OF ROBERTO DURAN

Has anybody here seen Roberto Duran?
I met him once, yeah, I shook his hand
I looked in his eyes, and now I understand
The love and the anger, in the eyes of Roberto Duran

Has anybody here seen that Mexican girl?
She lives up on 3rd Street in her own little world
A saint in her window, and the rosary beads in her hand
Yeah, the smile of an angel, and the eyes of Roberto Duran

    Panama City, it's three in the morning
    They're talkin' 'bout the *Hands of Stone*
    New York City, Lord, the sun's coming up
    My baby's throwin' everything she owns

Has anybody here seen the woman I love?
She'll fight down and dirty when push comes to shove
She'll win every round, if the fight goes according to plan
With the smile of an angel, and the eyes of Roberto Duran

    Panama City, it's three in the morning…

THEY'RE CLOSIN' SUNNY'S DINER

Oh, somewhere in this favoured land the sun is shining bright,
The band is playing somewhere, and somewhere hearts are light;
And somewhere men are laughing, and somewhere children shout,
But there is no joy in Mudville—mighty Casey has struck out.
            "Casey at the Bat"
            Ernest Lawrence Thayer

I used to eat breakfast at Sunny's Diner on Ninth Street in Park Slope, Brooklyn. The real deal. Two eggs over easy, wheat toast, and home fries. Sunny had a big pile of home fries on the side of the grill and he'd keep scooping at the pile with his one good hand, while talking baseball. This place was about two miles from where the old Ebbetts Field used to be, home of the Brooklyn Dodgers. When the Dodgers moved to Los Angeles a lot of Brooklyn-ites never got over it. Including Sunny.

When the Dodgers arrived in Los Angeles (we're moving backwards in time now…1958?) my father became friends with a few of them, like Don Zimmer and Johnny Padres, and they'd come over to our house and play poker with the old man. This was before the family money dried up and the cards were put away for good. This was all back when baseball was *the great American pastime*, and fathers would recite "Casey at the Bat." I can name you the starting lineup for the 1959 World Champion Los Angeles Dodgers and have a signed baseball from the whole team. And Sunny's breakfast memories stay with me.

This one appears on *Museum of Memories*.

CHORDS

Key of C. Finger picked, talking blues.

Verse	*Chorus*
C (rundown to) Am-F-G-C	F-C
C-Am-D-G	F-C-G
C-Am-F-C	C-Am-F-C
C-Am-F-G-C	C-Am-F-C

THEY'RE CLOSIN' SUNNY'S DINER

Sunny lost his pitchin' hand in the Second World War
So he opened up a diner next to a hardware store
Roast turkey was a specialty, when the Dodgers played in town
Christ, did he turn bitter, when Ebbett's Field closed down

Sunny'd fall asleep each day with a tomcat on his lap
His wife says, "Since the Dodgers left, Sunny's always taking naps
He dreams he's still in Ebbett's Field, catching foul balls in the stands
You know, Sunny, he pitched semi-pro, before he lost his hand"

    They're closin' Sunny's Diner now, and 9th Street ain't the same
    The old men got no place to sit and analyze the game
    And talk of curves and spitballs, and work the triple play
    And curse the man who moved the Brooklyn Dodgers to L.A.

He ran the diner forty years, refills were always free
Breakfast went from twenty cents, to a dollar forty-three
He said, "It's three cents for the Governor, and a dime to pay the loan
And a penny goes into Sunny's fund to bring the Dodgers home"

    They're closin' Sunny's Diner now...

We buried Sunny Gilchrist in a Brooklyn baseball cap
His wife said, "He ain't dead, he's gone upstairs to take a nap."
And we cooked a twelve-pound turkey, and cleaned it to the bone
And we drank one toast to Sunny, and one to bring the Dodgers home

    They're closin' Sunny's Diner now...

SPARROW OF SWANSEA
(For Dylan Thomas)

"I hold a beast, an angel and a madman in me, and my inquiry is as to their working, and my problem is their subjugation and victory, downthrow and upheaval, and my effort is their self-expression."

Dylan Thomas

Dylan Thomas. The Welsh bard. There's something about Wales. North and South. The way the sea appears to wash up in slow waves and blend into the land. The coming and going of the tides. It wrenches poetry from the common man. This is the land of poets, actors, and orators. I like the list of pubs in the second verse—it all reminds me of the old song *The Bells of Rhymney*. Back then I was reading several books on Dylan Thomas: *Dylan Thomas in America*, and *A Portrait of Dylan Thomas*. I shared my thoughts on the matter with Katy Moffatt and we co-wrote this song. It was Kenneth Rexroth, the godfather of Beat poetry, who called Dylan Thomas the Sparrow of Cardiff. My copy of *The Selected Poems of Kenneth Rexroth* was sent to me by Lawrence Ferlinghetti; he put a note inside: "I can send you the original Fantasy recording of this poem from the album: Rexroth and Ferlinghetti and the Cellar Jazz Quartet 1959." That recording is well worth hearing. I recall walking through Greenwich Village one day with Dave Van Ronk; he took me into The White Horse Tavern where Dylan Thomas drank his last eighteen whiskey shots. Dylan is reputed to have stated, "I think that's the record." Fade to black. Caitlin Thomas, Dylan's wife, remarked, "Dylan and dying; Dylan and dying; they don't go together; or is it that they were bound to go together? He said it so often enough, but I did not heed him."

The song is on Katy Moffatt's *Midnight Radio* album.

CHORDS

Waltz time. Recorded by Katy in key of D. Capo on the 2nd fret, played in C position.

Verse
C-G-F-C
F-C-Dm-G
C-G-F-C
Am-C-Dm-G-G7

Chorus
C-G-Am-Em
F-C-Dm-G
C-G-Am-Em
F-C-Dm-G-C

SPARROW OF SWANSEA

(For Dylan Thomas)

From the back streets of Cardiff, to the halls of St. Vincent's
From a boathouse in Laugharne, to a bench in Times Square
They are tolling the bell for the Sparrow of Swansea
They are whispering his poems, they are sending him prayers

    Oh see how he flies, the Sparrow of Swansea
    The Sparrow of Swansea, see how he sails
    O'er the snail-horned churches, o'er the three legged horses
    Through the grey misty mornings, in the southwest of Wales

All the pubs they come open, at half-past eleven
You were likely to find him, down at Brown's Hotel
Or the Bells of Aberdovey, The Blue Bull, The Dragon
The Twill in the Wall, The Cat of Nine Tails

    Oh, see how he flies....

In the White Horse Tavern, on a bleak New York evening
The Sparrow of Swansea, was wounded in flight
He took eighteen straight shots from a barrel of whiskey
His Caitlin lies weeping; he is lost to the night

    Oh, see how he flies...

CO-WRITTEN WITH KATY MOFFATT

WINGS OF A BLACKBIRD

"I drank to drown my sorrows, but the damned things learned how to swim. "
                                            Frida Kahlo

"The art of Frida Kahlo is a ribbon around a bomb."
                                            André Breton

I was reading a biography about the Mexican painter Frida Kahlo when I wrote these lyrics. Someone described Frida's eyebrows as rising up "like the wings of a blackbird." Maybe it was Diego Riviera. I've visited Frida's house in Mexico City and her ghosts certainly dance around in there with the skulls and Mayan pottery.

   There are echoes of the Spanish poet Federico Garcia Lorca in this song – though I would never be foolish to overly invade Leonard Cohen's territory. He's the master of Lorca-esque lyrics. Still, this is a pretty melody. I co-wrote this with Katy Moffatt. Katy recorded the song on a record titled *Midnight Radio*.

CHORDS

Katy recorded this in B; capo on the 4th fret, played in G position.

Verse
G-Am7
Am7-D7-G-D
G-E7-Am7
Bdim-Am7-D7-G

Chorus
G-C-Bm
E7-Am7-Bdim-Am7
G-C-Bm-Bb add 2-E7-Am7
Bdim-Am7-D7-G

WINGS OF A BLACKBIRD

When she walks, men fall to their knees
Hearts hanging in trees, when she passes by
When she cries, rain on the clover
The oceans run over, she empties the sky

When she sings, the madmen they tremble
Children grow gentle, abandon their fears
When she dances, the music of silence
Soft passion and violence, only wild things can hear

    Her eyebrows rise up like the Wings of a Blackbird
    We search for the true words, escaping the lies
    Our hearts will rise up on the Wings of a Blackbird
    On the Wings of a Blackbird, she darkens the sky

When she loves, hear the clatter of locusts
Her eyes come unfocused, there's blood on the moon
When she sleeps, dreams speak from dark willows
The earth is her pillow, that old sorcerer's tune

    Her eyebrows rise up like the Wings of a Blackbird...

CO-WRITTEN WITH KATY MOFFATT

DENVER WIND

"I pictured myself in a Denver bar that night, with all the gang, and in their eyes I would be strange and ragged and like the Prophet who has walked across the land to bring the dark Word, and the only Word I had was 'Wow!'"
                                    Jack Kerouac,
                                    On the Road

I hitchhiked through Denver, back in the 1960s, probably with a dog-eared copy of Kerouac's *On the Road* in my sack, seeking out the ghost of Neal Cassady. This lyric echoes those early Ian and Sylvia and Leonard Cohen songs. The French Girl. Suzanne. You know…she feeds you tea and oranges that come all the way from China. That sort of thing. I include it in this collection because it's my Swiss friend Silvia's favorite song. There you have it. I believe it was an unreleased track from the early Tom Russell Band record: *Poor Man's Dream*, recorded in Oslo, Norway. It surfaced on a Rounder records compilation, *Raw Vision: The Tom Russell Band 1984-1994*, Vintage Americana.

CHORDS

Key of A, played in G chord positions, capo on 2nd fret.

Verse
G-D-G
G-C-D-G
G-C-D-Em-C
G-C-D
C-Em-Am-D-G

Chorus
Em-A-D
Em-A-D
C-Em-Am-D-G

DENVER WIND

Gonna lose myself in a dream of Denver
This borrowed time, Lord, it's too hard to spend
I'd crawl across the State of Texas
To sleep out in that Rocky Mountain wind
Yeah, and spend one night with the Denver girl again

Sweet Cora Lee, you're the red haired angel
With your spinning wheel and your ginseng tea
You wrote the book of love one night in Denver
Well, it's funny you ain't mentioned him to me
But I heard you got you a man down in Tennessee

    There's a lot of women there, will treat you as they please
    There's a lot of women there, will bring you to your knees
    Then blow you away like the wind through the Denver trees

And I remember Anne in her midnight window
She would sing that song about a dog named Blue
Drinking homemade wine, we were telling those stories
And writing songs we never could get through
Yeah, have another drink, girl, here's one more for you

    There's a lot of women there...

TEN CENT LEMONADE

"We are living in a world today where lemonade is made from artificial flavors and furniture polish is made from real lemons."
                                            Alfred E. Newman

I wrote this with Alan Rhody in Brooklyn back in the early 1990s. Alan is a successful Nashville writer. It's a sweet little song with a recipe for making lemonade thrown into the mix. A summer song. Memories of high school. I believe I drove a 1958 Ford Ranchero for awhile in high school, but I don't recall any Rebecca Martins. I do recall Mulholland Drive up in the Hollywood Hills as a great place to peer out on the City of Angels while trying to make out with too many virtuous Catholic princesses. And I don't recall any gin in the mix. I think the ice cream truck actually played "London Bridge is Falling Down." But hell, the past is quicksand. Quote Henri Matisse. Best not to go back there.

Alan Rhody recorded this on his record *Boxcar of Memories* (Ashwood Recordings) and my rough version appeared on *Museum of Memories*.

CHORDS

Played in the key of E, capo on the 2nd fret in D chord positions—medium tempo country style.

Verse
D-A-Em-Bm-G
D-G-D-Bm-G
D-G-D-A-D

Chorus
A-G-D
A-Em-A
D-G-D-D-G
D-G-D-A-D

TEN CENT LEMONADE

It was steamin' on the sidewalk, there was a plague of blue-tail flies
Dying days of August, the year was '55
When he met Rebecca Martin, in the weepin' willow shade
She was eight years old, selling ten cent lemonade

Young Rebecca Martin, she grew rawboned and lean
At twelve she hit the awkward stage, it passed by age sixteen
He had a '58 Ranchero, they parked up on the grade
Mixing love and cheap gin, with Becca's lemonade

    You take a gallon jug of water, and a jelly glass or two
    Slice a dozen lemons, add some sugar to the brew
    Just a chip off the old ice block, friend you've got it made
    Summer is for lovers, and ten cent lemonade

Well, the ice cream truck plays "Dixie," as it rolls on up the street
The years have cracked and splintered, like the porch beneath their feet
And sweet Rebecca Martin gave up her maiden name
And they sit out there on August nights, sippin' lemonade

Yes, God is in His heaven, and the Devil's down below
We're caught somewhere between 'em, 'neath the sun's hard, angry glow
Blessed with simple pleasures, that wash the thirst away
Like the love of a good woman, and ten cent lemonade

    You take a gallon jug of water...

CO-WRITTEN WITH ALAN RHODY

HOME BEFORE DARK

"Deep into that darkness peering, long I stood there, wondering, fearing, doubting, dreaming dreams no mortal ever dared to dream before."

Edgar Allan Poe

Darkness? Light? A simple song of hope. Brief and to the point. Written in Norway in the 1980s. And the wild, unholy boys line? I had my photo taken once, outside The Bottom Line club in New York, with George Jones and Andy Warhol. Somebody made a fake band poster out of it and named us The Wild Unholy Boys Trio—available for parties, etc. Can you imagine those three characters banging against each other on a New York street? I don't know what that has to do with this song. It's all fragments. One of John Cheever's daughters wrote a memoir of her father titled, *Home Before Dark*. There was also a Jean Simmons movie in the fifties with that title. In the last few years Neil Diamond's used the title. Maybe we're all trying to make it home before dark. Good luck.

Barrence Whitfield sang a version on the record we did together called *Cowboy Mambo*. Scott Joss covered it on his record *Souvenirs*, thanks to Dusty Wakeman, who always believed in the song. My versions appear on: *Road to Bayamon*, *Wounded Heart of America*, *Veteran's Day*, and *Raw Vision*.

CHORDS

Key of E#. Capo on 3rd fret played in the D chord positions. Rock.

Verse	*Bridge*
D	Bm-Em
D	Bm-G-A
D-Em	
A-G	

HOME BEFORE DARK

Listen to me little girl, it's a wild, unholy world, don't break my heart
You be home before dark
Long ago and far away, mama said, son, don't you stray, don't drift too far
You be home before dark.

    Last night I heard the devil, crawlin' 'cross the floor
    But I turned the light on, now he don't come round no more

Sometimes I close my eyes, I dream the sun won't ever rise, but don't lose heart
We'll make it home before dark

Listen to me little girl…

HALF MOON BOULEVARD

"One by one they were all becoming shades. Better pass boldly into that other world, in the full glory of some passion, than fade and wither dismally with age."
          James Joyce
          "The Dead"

Katy Moffatt tells me we were on tour in Europe, with a day off in Zurich, during a stretch of gorgeous autumn weather. Might have been 1989. I went for an afternoon walk and came back with this lyric. In Katy's words, "You said you had paused to sit a while on a park bench and wrote it down." I spent the rest of the evening with it and this song was the result. The realization that I wrote these lost love lyrics dispels my idea that I wasn't ever writing love songs back in the early seasons. Something in this reminds me of James Joyce's *The Dubliners*. Or Proust and *The Remberance of Thing's Past*, though I haven't read Proust in forty years. It's the yen of trying to get at the feeling of young love and linking it to wine and cafés and all the romance you may never have partaken in...but ah! Paris in the twenties! San Francisco in the fifties! The Beats, the Bohemian Girls, Rome! That sort of feeling. Was it France, Spain, Italy? Who knows? Beaujolais is a young wine, for a young song. Katy Moffat sings this one on the Philo record *The Evangeline Hotel*.

CHORDS

Katy recorded this in B—capo on the 2nd fret, played in A chord positions.

Verse	*Chorus*	*Tag*
Amaj7-E7sus4-D-F#m	Bm-E7-A-G#-G-F#	D-C#7-F#m-B7
D-A-Bm-E7	Bm-Bm7-E7-G#-E7-A-	BmeE7-Bm-E7-F#m-B7
Amaj7-E7sus4-Dmaj7-F#m	Amaj7-A7	Bm-E7-Bm-E7sus4-E7-A
D-A-Bm-E7-A	D-C#7-F#m-B7	
	Bm-E7-Bm-E7-A	

HALF MOON BOULEVARD

Old men playing dominoes, women hanging out their clothes
While children fell in love below, on Half Moon Boulevard
The moon came up, the sun went down, the wheel of time spun 'round and 'round
And love was the eternal sound on Half Moon Boulevard

    The courtyard, the Spanish Steps, our hearts beat loud as castanets
    And sadness hadn't caught us yet, and passion was the key
    Now broken dreams and better years, reflected in a shattered mirror
    As I walk this lonely path of tears called Half Moon Boulevard

Now it's a sad and empty part of town, they've closed that little café down
Where you and I danced 'round and 'round, on wings of Beaujolais
Where did all the old men go? That row of falling dominos
Like love that comes and love that goes, down Half Moon Boulevard

    The courtyard, the Spanish Steps…

        Were there really better times? Was it love that made us blind?
        Or was it maybe too much wine, on Half Moon Boulevard?
        I'll think of you, and better times, on Half Moon Boulevard

Co-written with Katy Moffatt

BILLY COLLINS

"A boxing match is like a cowboy movie. There's got to be good guys and there's got to be bad guys. And that's what people pay for—to see the bad guys get beat."
Sonny Liston

Billy Collins, Jr. was an Irish-American boxer following in the footsteps of his father, who'd also been a pro fighter. Billy, Jr. racked up fourteen straight pro victories, until the night he met Puerto Rican boxer Luis Resto in Madison Square Garden on June 16, 1983, on the undercard of the Roberto Duran / Davey Moore fight. Collins was the strong favorite, but took a savage beating from Resto and lost by decision. Billy Collins, Sr. noticed that Resto's gloves looked thinner and they were impounded for investigation. The boxing commission ruled that Resto's trainer, Panama Lewis, had removed an ounce of padding from each glove. The fight was changed to "no contest," and Lewis and Resto each were given prison terms.

Later, in the HBO film *Assault in the Ring*, Resto confessed that not only had padding been taken from the gloves, but his hands, beneath the gloves, had also been soaked in plaster of Paris, making them hard as rock. In effect Billy Collins Jr. had been bludgeoned almost to death. Resto also intimated that there was a lot of cocaine money gambled on him that night for a win. Dirty business. Billy never recovered, his eyesight was damaged, and he quit the ring and developed a drinking problem. He drove his car off the road one night in Tennessee in an alleged suicide.

Billy Collins, Sr. sent me a very moving note one night, about fifteen years ago, when I was performing in Nashville. We never got to meet. I wrote this with Katy Moffatt and a fine version appears on her record *The Evangeline Hotel*. Tine Valand also recorded it in Norway.

CHORDS

Katy Moffat Plays this is C.

Verse
C-Gm
C-Gm-C7
F-Dm7-Am
Bflat-F-Dm7-G

Chorus
C-F-G-C
C-Am-Dm7-G
C-F-G-E
Am-Dm7-G-C

BILLY COLLINS

They call me Billy Collins, boys, I'm as Irish as my name
And like my Pa before me, fightin' was my game
But to see the River Shannon has always been my dream
I've prayed I'd lay my dyin' soul, beside her lovely stream

    But I don't believe the River Shannon runs through Tennessee
    This muddy water filled with stone looks like Collins' Creek to me
    My father's kin have made their homes up and down this river bed
    And it's here beside this granite stone I'll lay my dying head

It was fourteen solid victories, fourteen bloody fights
That brought me north to New York, beneath the Garden lights
Where the Puerto Rican racketeers, played their money smart
They loaded up their fighter's gloves and destroyed my fightin' heart

So it was home I went in blind defeat, I never fought again
And the right and left which served me well, then served me pints of gin
And the roar of the thundering fight crowd, in one desperate scream is drowned
I was too damn drunk to see the things, that had thrown me to the ground

    But I don't believe the River Shannon...

So you can have your new world, boys, with all its fast machines
Your fancy cars and painted whores, and all your goddamn dreams
I'd trade it all to lay my head, on Lady Shannon's breast
But it's here beside this muddy stream they'll lay fightin' Bill to rest

Billy Collins lost his pride, but he never lost his nerve
He ran the straight and narrow, but couldn't make the curves
Ran off the road near Collins' Creek, blind drunk late one night
He lost the final round, but he may have won the fight

    But I don't believe....

Co-written with Katy Moffatt

THE ROSE OF THE SAN JOAQUIN

"When you get to readin` about where the music and John Steinbeck and all those people like that come from, the further you go the more interesting it becomes."
                                                        Merle Haggard

I wrote this with Ian Tyson one long afternoon in a motel out in the Mojave Desert, owned by the musician Dusty Wakeman. I'd wanted to show Ian the Joshua Tree National Monument and the big rock where Gram Parson's body was cremated. Mystical ground. The Rose of the San Joaquin phrase came from the Jim Ringer's great rewriting of the old ballad, "Tramps and Hawkers," which I also recorded on the album *The Rose of the San Joaquin*. That record was produced by Dave Alvin and Greg Leisz. Much of this album is centered in the San Joaquin valley, the great farming valley of California and home to the Bakersfield honkytonk scene. I grew up on those sounds.

The original version appears on *The Rose of the San Joaquin* and also *Veteran's Day: The Tom Russell Anthology*. The song was also used in a bar scene in Monte Hellman's film *The Road to Nowhere*.

CHORDS

Bakersfield country-style, in the Key of G.

Verse
G-Bm-C-G
G-Bm-C-G
G-Em-G-Em
C-Cm-G

Chorus
G-Em
C-Cm-G

THE ROSE OF THE SAN JOAQUIN

Farewell to the lights of Madera, I'm leavin' with the wind at my back
Tell all of my friends in Dos Palos, I'm gone but I'll be circling back
Now I'm crossing the Chowchilla River, by the light of a ragged moonbeam
And I miss the Rose of San Joaquin

I'll miss the sun on the Sierra Nevadas, adobe moon on the rise
Shining down on my love in Madera, shining into her dark Spanish eyes
Oh, she taught me those Mexican love songs, 'Volver, Volver' in my dreams
And I miss the Rose of San Joaquin

    Caught somewhere between
    The road and the Rose of San Joaquin

How her black hair fell on the blanket, in the tall grass wet with the dew
Making love through the night by the river, Magdalene, how my heart cries for you
Alone on this highway of darkness, you are the light of my dreams
And I miss the Rose of San Joaquin

    Caught somewhere between…

Co-written with Ian Tyson

HAND CARVED HEART

"Love many things, for therein lies the true strength, and whosoever loves much perfoms much, and can accomplish much, and what is done in love is done well."
              Vincent Van Gogh

This song seems like another reading, an alternative view, of *The Rose of the San Joaquin*. This has that Gypsy Davy, South Coast feel. The Spanish cowboy rides away—or Spanish is The Loving Tongue, and all that great early folklore wrapped around the enduring cliché of the dark-eyed, raven-haired Spanish beauty. It could be right out of Richard Henry Dana's *Two Years Before the Mast*, the early California novel of Spanish haciendas and vaqueros roping grizzly bears on the beach. There's a five-hundred-year-old oak tree on my sister-in-law's ranch in California. One day a cowboy looked up into the interior branches and saw the skeleton and head of a black bear which had crawled up in the tree and died. It balanced up there on a branch for many years, until it all fell down and was carried off by coyotes. I'd like to think this was the tree in the song. I think the track of this song turned out beautifully—it's on the record *The Rose of the San Joaquin*.

CHORDS

Key of G, Slow folk-rock ballad, rocks back and forth around G-C-D.

Verse
G-C-D
D-G-C-D
D-G-C
D-G

Chorus
G-C-D-G
G-C-F-D
D-C-D-G-C-D
D-G-C-D-G

HAND CARVED HEART

There's an old Spanish oak
Bent over a country road
If it could tell all that it knows
Of a hand carved heart

Once two lovers slept in the shade
His hands weaving through her dark braids
They shared the edge of his blade
Carved their names in the bark

> The heart it has darkened with the weather of years
> It may never fade away, washed clean with her tears
> The human heart breaks with a hurt that runs deep through the blood
> I wish it was made out of wood like a hand carved heart

Then he rode away
Down that old country road
Away from the old Spanish oak
With the hand carved heart

He said he'd be back one day
She wept and she waited, she prayed
She vowed she would never betray
The hand carved heart

> The heart it is darkened, with the weather of years…

WHAT DO YOU WANT?

"Life is a long and savage rowing towards happy hour."
Tom Russell
Notebooks

I wrote this with Peter Case. I think we were sitting around in Peter's front room in Santa Monica and he started playing a few lines of this chorus and a melody. We took it from there. It's a funny little song a guitar player would sing to his girlfriend. It's basic: What do you want from me, baby? I'm just a guitar player, I'm not a serial murderer. I know both Peter and I had both been through the twists and turns inside the romantic briar patch, and we chatted about that terrain. Other lines? I do have a Martin D-18 guitar that was made in 1946. It's sitting right behind me as I write this in Switzerland. It has a bullet hole in the back, but that's another story from a Puerto Rican carnival. (See, "The Road to Bayamon.") This guitar went to Africa with me back in 1969. As far as some of the other lines—I've never sold bibles door to door, but I've unloaded box cars. I was a butter-stripper at a creamery in Los Angeles. That's detailed in a later song, "What Work Is." The song appears on the record *The Rose of the San Joaquin*, and was also recorded by a UK country artist named Mike Shannon.

CHORDS

Played in C, capo on the fifth fret in G chord positions. Travis finger-picking.

Verse
G-C-(bass rundown to) Am
D-G
G-C-(bass rundown to) Am
D-G

Chorus
Basically the same chords as the verse.

WHAT DO YOU WANT?

This old Martin guitar was made in 1946
It's cracked, scratched and splintered by fingernails and picks
But it's been my close companion since 1962
Please don't ask me to decide 'tween this guitar and you

    What do you want from me? What do you want?
    Do I have to give you everything?
    What do you want from me? What do you want?
    Do I have to give you everything?

Well all my friends quit drinkin', you can't smoke nowhere no more
I think I'll take up smokin', though I've never smoked before
I'm gettin' tired of decaf coffee, I crave high-test in my cup
I'm too young to die of boredom and I'm too old to grow up

    What do you want from me? What do you want?...

Well, I've unloaded boxcars, I've sold bibles door to door
Hell, I'd be rich and famous if I weren't unknown and poor
Blessed are the poor in spirit for they'll possess the earth
But the day I hand the world to you, you'll ask me what it's worth

    What do you want from me? What do you want?...

CO-WRITTEN WITH PETER CASE

OUT IN CALIFORNIA

"A man that studieth revenge keeps his own wounds green."
Francis Bacon

The last bar on earth might be a desperate little joint in Naco, Mexico, across the border from Bisbee, Arizona. Dave Alvin and I had a few beers there one night and discussed the raw permuations of bad love. The place smelled like gun powder and piss. There were no bar stools, chairs, or tables. You stood at attention, ready to hit the floor when the bang bang started. The other customers were a handful of cat-eyed thugs too ugly to work as extras in a Sam Peckinpah movie. And that's ugly. I'd like to think we wrote the song that night, but it was probably in Dave's front room in Los Angeles. Dave is a fine California historian, poet, guitar picker, and songwriter of great reknown. He is The King of California. I noticed whenever I wrote with Dave that women were taking off their clothes, in the lyrics, or putting them on. That's rock and roll. The "If a man keeps runnin' he'll run right into himself" line I stole from Carl Perkins. Carl was talking about quitting the drink, I believe. This song appears on my records *The Rose of the San Joaquin* and *Veteran's Day: The Tom Russell Anthology*. Dave Alvin's versions appear on *Interstate City* and his live record, *Out in California*.

CHORDS

Key of A. Truck driving country-rock beat.

Verse
A-D-G-A
A-D-G-A
E-D-A

Chorus
A-G-D-A

OUT IN CALIFORNIA

I'm sittin' here drinkin' in the last bar on earth
I'm sittin' here drinkin' in the last bar on earth
Out in California she's takin' off her tight red skirt

The mountains out the window, they're a woman lyin' on a bed
The mountains here are shaped like a woman lyin' naked on a bed
She may be out in California, but I can't get her out of my head

    Out in California…

They killed off the Indians, they shot all the grizzly bears
Out in California they shot all the grizzly bears
She stands by the window, a-takin' down her long black hair

If a man keeps runnin', he'll run right into himself
If a man keeps movin', he'll run right into himself
Out in California she's lyin' down with somebody else

    Out in California…

Gonna buy me a Chevy as soon as my luck turns around
Gonna buy me a shotgun, soon as my luck turns around
I'm gonna drive on back to that California town

I'm sittin' here drinkin' in the last bar on earth…

Co-written with Dave Alvin

BETWEEN THE CRACKS

> *"I was astonished every time I met a young writer who could quote ecstatically line after line of dialogue from the down-and-out souls of* Fat City, *the men and women seeking love, a bit of comfort, even glory—but never forgiveness—in the heat and dust of central California. Admirers were everywhere."*
>
> Denis Johnson
> *Bronx Banter*

This one really gets down in the valley dirt. It reminds me of Leonard Gardner's great California boxing novel, *Fat City*. The book was made into a strong film by John Huston. This song also has echoes of Woody Guthrie's "Pastures of Plenty" and "Deportees." I co-wrote it with Dave Alvin. Dave is an inspiring person to write with because he really works hard getting inside the mind and body of who we we're writing about. What would this person really say or feel? There's also a film of this song (online) which makes passing reference to a boxer named Jesus Aguilar. I am also reminded of riding on a train through California when the train hit a car driven by a Mexican field worker...as I mentioned in the introduction to this collection. This song appears on my record, *The Rose of the San Joaquin* and Dave Alvin's release, *West of the West*.

CHORDS

Dave Alvin plays this song in B. I would put the capo on the 4th fret and play in G positions. Sort of a Tex-Mex rock ballad.

Verse
G-D
D-G
G-C
D-G

Chorus
C-G-C-D
C-G-Em-C-D-G

BETWEEN THE CRACKS

Sundown on the San Joaquin, an old woman walks home from work
Another day in the fields, another day in the dirt
She lights a sacred candle next to a faded photograph
She says a prayer for a young man who fell between the cracks

She stares at the photo of the young man who caused her so much pain
In countless twelve round bloodbaths when 'Kid Jesus' was his name
He was 'The Pride of the Valley' 'til the night he stayed down on his back
He took the dive and he disappeared down between the cracks

> She said, "Jesus was just a poor boy on the wrong side of the tracks
> He rose again but not before he fell between the cracks"

She re-reads all his letters that he wrote her from L.A.
He said, "Please don't worry about me, I'm coming home again someday."
Then she remembers the other stories that were whispered behind her back
About a shooting outside a grocery store, somewhere between the cracks

> She said, "Jesus was just a poor boy from the wrong side of the tracks…"

Sunrise on the San Joaquin, an old woman walks off to work
Another day in the fields, another day in the dirt
She stares at all the children dropping rich men's fruit into their sacks
And she says a prayer for all the souls trapped between the cracks

Co-written with Dave Alvin

TONIGHT WE RIDE
Woodcut by Tom Russell
2012

CHAPTER FIVE
COWBOY SONGS

NAVAJO RUG

"If Navajo rugs embody mythic time, they record historical time as well. Who the Navajos are today not only depends on the enduring voices that preserve the ancient stories, but on more recent ones born of living memory, voices that add to the poetics of weaving."
  Paul G. Zolbrod and Roseann Willink
  Weaving a World

Ian Tyson came to New York in 1986 for a show at The Bitter End. I invited him over to my "bunker" in Brooklyn for a few drinks. He'd recorded my song "Gallo del Cielo," and I was a big Ian and Sylvia fan, but prior to this we'd never met in person. Picture a small storefront, boarded over, on a side street in a Puerto Rican-Italian neighborhood. A loft bed and a desk and a small ice box. That was it. My bohemian home. My own Paris in the '20s. Ian took a taxi over from Manhattan and got lost on the wrong street, called from a phone booth, and I went out and rescued him. We drained a bottle or two of Cabernet or Merlot, and swapped songs. He sang an unexpurgated version of "The Castration of the Strawberry Roan." A fine evening. Before he left that night, I mentioned a song I was working on about a man and woman making love on a Navajo Rug, and I slipped the lyric fragments into his guitar case. He finished the song a few weeks later in a Super 8 Motel in Fort Worth, and then recorded it on the groundbreaking cowboy record, *Cowboyography*. His version of "Navajo Rug" was country-music single, and song, of the year in Canada in 1987, and topped the charts. It's also been recorded by Jerry Jeff Walker and Bill and Bonnie Hearne, and a few dozen other fine folks.

My versions appear on *Poor Man's Dream, Cowboy Real* (with Ian Tyson), *Veteran's Day: The Tom Russell Anthology*, and *Cowboy'd All to Hell*. Ian's version appears on *Cowboyography* and *All the Good'Uns*.

CHORDS

Key of A. I fingerpick it, with the capo on the second fret in the G chord positions.

Verse	*Chorus*
G-AM	G-EM
C-D	C-D
G-AM	G-Em
C-D	C-G

NAVAJO RUG

Well, it's three eggs up on whiskey toast, home fries on the side
You wash it down with that roadhouse coffee, it burns up your inside
Just a Canyon, Colorado diner, and a waitress I did love
We sat in the back 'neath the old stuffed bear, and a worn-out Navajo Rug

Well, old Jack, the boss, he'd close at six, then it's Katie bar the door
She'd pull down that Navajo rug, and spread it on the floor
Hey, I saw lightnin' cross the sacred mountains, saw the woven turtle doves
When I was lyin' next to Katie, on that old Navajo rug

> Ai-yi-yi, Katie
> Shades of red and blue
> Ai-yi-yi, Katie
> Whatever became of the Navajo rug and you?

Well, I saw old Jack about a year ago, he said the place burned to the ground
And all he'd saved was an old bear tooth, and Katie, she left town
Oh, but Katie she got a souvenir, too, Jack spat out a tobacco plug
He said, "You should have seen her a-runnin' through the smoke, haulin' that Navajo rug."

> Ai-yi-yi, Katie...

So every time I cross the sacred mountains, and lightnin' breaks above
It always takes me back in time, to my long lost Katie love
Ah, but everything keeps on a-movin', and everybody's on the go
They don't make things that last anymore, like a double-woven Navajo

> Ai-yi-yi, Katie...

Co-written with Ian Tyson

THE SKY ABOVE, THE MUD BELOW

LaBoeuf: *Fewer horses, fewer horse thieves.*
         True Grit
         1969

One time when I was writing songs with Ian Tyson, I took a break and drove into a town named Cochran, Alberta. There was a little western museum in back of a saddle and tack store, and inside one of the glass exhibit cases were two colorful bridle stocks—black, white, red, and yellow-tinted horsehair. The sign on the case said, "Braided by Mexican horse thieves, Montana State Prison, 1910." That triggered off the yen, in my mind, for a story about these bridles stocks. So I concocted one. I know now that Montana State Prison has had a horsehair hitchin' program for almost a century, and cowboys and horse thieves practiced the craft to mark time. A tedious craft it is. Harder than braiding rawhide *reatas*. Hard on the hands and eyes.

    My friend the poet Paul Zarzyski bought a wonderful bridle stock off a kid just out of Montana State Prison. It depicted Aces and 8s, the last poker hand drawn by Wild Bill Hickok. There was a documentary film once, in the *Mondo Cane* style of shock-docs, called *The Sky Above, The Mud Below*. Boquillas is a little Mexican town on the Rio Grande, in the Big Bend area of Texas.

    My versions of this song appear on *The Rose of the San Joaquin, Songs of the West*, and *Veteran's Day: The Tom Russell Anthology*. Ramblin' Jack Elliot and I did a duet of the song which is on my record *Wounded Heart of America,* and Ramblin' Jack's record, *The Last Ride*. Wylie and the Wild West recorded a cleaned-up version (without the phrase *sons of bitches*) on the record *Hooves and Horses*. The award winning fiction writer Annie Proulx used this song as an inspiration for her short story, "The Mud Below."

CHORDS

Finger picked, in the key of A minor.

Verse
Am-C-Am
G-Am
Am-C-Am
G-Am
C-G-D-F
Am-G-F-E
E-Am

Chorus
C-G
D-F
Am-G-F-E
E-Am

THE SKY ABOVE, THE MUD BELOW

Two men rode in from the South, one rainy autumn night
    The sky above, the mud below
They walked into the Deacon's bar, they was Mexican by sight
    The sky above, the mud below
They threw a horsehair bridle down
"We trade this for whiskey rounds."
The Deacon slammed a bottle down
The two men started drinkin'

Their hair was long and black, tied up behind their ears
Their faces were identical like one man beside a mirror
Someone whispered, "That beats all,
Their wanted poster's on the wall
Twin brothers name of Sandoval
Horse thieves from Boquillas."

Now the bridle and the belts they wore were braided grey and black
The color of a roan horse once belonged to Deacon Black
The fastest horse for miles around
He'd been stolen from the old fairgrounds
A month ago outside of town
We tracked but never found him

CONTINUED

Now the Deacon was a preacher who had fallen hard from grace
He owned the bar and a string of quarter horses that he'd race
Yeah, Deacon, he could drink and curse
Though he still quoted sacred verse
He was sheriff, judge, he owned the hearse
A man you did not anger

    The sky above, the mud below
    The wind and rain, the sleet and snow
    Two horse thieves from Mexico
    Drinkin' hard and singin'

One brother, he spoke English, Deak inquires as to their work
The man says, "Mister, we braid horsehair, bridles ropes and quirts
This fine bridle I did make
A roan horse killed by a leg-bone break
He's horsehair rope now, horsemeat steak
We cleaned him to the bone."

Now these brothers, they were ignorant or didn't know just where they were
The Deacon's face grew darker as he measured every word
He says, "You horsehair braidin' sons of bitches
Stole my claim to earthly riches
Someone go and dig a ditch
There may well be a hangin'."

One brother reached inside his shirt a-searching for his gun
Too late, for Deak had whipped around a sawed-off Remington
The twins they raised their hands and sneered
Deak was grinnin' ear to ear
He says, "Court's in session
Hear ye, hear! Yours truly is presidin'."

Well, the trial commenced and ended quick, they didn't have a hope
Deak says, "We'll cut your hair now, boys, and you can braid yourselves a rope
The Old Testament, it says somewhere
Eye for eye and hair for hair
Covet not thy neighbor's mare
I believe it's Revelations."

Now the fancy horsehair bridle, it hangs on Deacon's wall
Next to that wanted poster of the brothers Sandoval
And the twisted rope, so shiny black
The artifact that broke their necks
Their craftsmanship he did respect
They shoulda stuck to braidin'

    The sky above, the mud below
    The wind and rain, the sleet and snow
    The Deacon's hearse is rollin' slow
    In the first blue light of morning

THE BANKS OF THE MUSSELSHELL

"There were only two things the old-time cowpunchers were afraid of: a decent woman and being set afoot."
  We Pointed them North:
  Recollections of a Cowpuncher
  E.C. "Teddy Blue" Abbott

The Musselshell is a tributary of the Missouri River, named by Lewis and Clark during their expedition of 1805. The name refers to the freshwater mussels which lined the banks. The Musselshell rises up out of the Crazy, Little Belt, and Castle mountains in Central Montana. I co-wrote this ballad with Ian Tyson in Einer Brasso's cabin at the foot of the Canadian Rockies. Ian went home to the ranch one night and left me in the cabin with Teddy Blue Abbott's seminal book, *We Pointed 'Em North*, the true tale of a kid from Europe who hires on to a Texas trail herd. Larry McMurtry's *Lonesome Dove* owes a lot to Abbott's great account. So I read the book, drank a few jars of red wine, and, gathered notes. Next day we wrote the song. At that time Ian declared me the "king of whore and knife ballads." Somebody's gotta do it. I like the descriptions of the landscape in the first two verses. Ian and I both share a love of the West and it's one thing to write short stories filled with action and yet another to achieve a description of Hemingway's dictum, you have to describe how the country was. This song appears on my records *Song of the West* and *Cowboy'd All to Hell*, and Ian Tyson's *I Outgrew the Wagon*.

CHORDS

Key of B. Capo up on the 4th fret in G chord positions.

Verse	*Chorus*
G-C-F-G	F-C
G-C-F-G	F-D
F-G	F-C
G-C-F-G	D

THE BANKS OF THE MUSSELSHELL

I stare out every evening at the distant Northern Star
It leads us ever northward and it tells us that we are
Lost below the Yellowstone in a land unknown to me
Ten thousand miles from my loved ones and my home across the sea

We travel through an empty land, the benches are all strewn
With bison bones that shine ghost white 'neath the risin' of the moon
And the red wolf howls and answers as I try to sing on guard
Indentured to these Texans in a land so wild and hard

When I hired on to Bill Ducharm in the heat of the Texas sun
I was unaware of his darker side, his quickness with a gun
But I made a solemn promise, I'd ride with him through hell
And deliver the herd to the ends of the earth, or the mouth of the Musselshell

Well, I'd just turned about sixteen when we hit that first cowtown
I drank my first strong liquor, oh, and the women spun me round
But of all the barroom angels with their soft forbidden charms
I was stuck on blue-eyed Annie who belonged to Bill Ducharm

    And the boy became a man that night in Annie's arms
    Oh, Annie cried and begged me, "Beware of Bill Ducharm."

We left that Texas cow town, and we pointed the big herd north
But the first night when the moon was down, I rode back to old Fort Worth
They were closin' up the barroom, oh, they were rollin' up the floor
My heart was in my mouth as I knocked on Annie's door

    And the boy became a man that night in Annie's arms...

Oh, Bill Ducharm had one bad eye and his face was a devilish red
The result of a bygone prairie fire when he'd crawled back from the dead
And every night in dreams as I rolled in Annie's arms
I'd awake to face old Satan, in the guise of Bill Ducharm

CONTINUED

And each night 'cross the campfire I'd face that one bad eye
Did he know that I'd betrayed him? Had my hour come to die?
One promise he made true, we rode with him through hell
We delivered the herd to the ends of the earth at the mouth of the Musselshell

    And the boy became a man that night in Annie's arms…

And as we near the Yellowstone, the snow begins to fall
And soon this dreadful enterprise shall be ending for us all
It's then I'll need fast horses, to fly to Annie's arms
And stay one jump ahead of the guns of Bill Ducharm

    And the boy became a man that night in Annie's arms…

Co-written with Ian Tyson

HALLIE LONNIGAN

"A dame that knows the ropes isn't likely to get tied up."
Mae West

For about ten years now I've been working on a documentary film on the West which centers around my sister-in-law, Claudia, who's ranched alone for many years near the Central Valley of California. I believe she's the eighth generation of a family that has ranched or farmed in this historic valley of Spanish Land Grant ranches. One night Claudia had to shoot a bear which was climbing up the wall outside of her bedroom…It's all quite a story. Her great grandparents migrated to the Carissa Plains of California—in covered wagons from Texas. They almost starved to death. There's a lonely grave of Claudia's great grandmother out there on the plains. I hope we can get some of this in the film. Another touch point to this song was a remark made by the Canadian singer Cindy Church, who noticed that most of male cowboy poetry centered on the romance of horse work and the West, and the women's poetry centered on the plain old hard work. *Since the women were doing most of it*. I've noticed that around ranches. Men can sling the bullshit pretty damn good while the women cook, do the dishes, mend fences and wipe the snot off the noses of ten kids. For starters. There's a song there.

This one appears of my records *Song of the West* and *Cowboy'd All to Hell*. A group named *The Katy Creek Band* recorded it, as did Katy Moffatt.

CHORDS

Simple country-style, flat picked or finger picked: Key of C.

Verse
C-F
C-Am
F-C-G
Am-F-Bflat-F

Chorus
Am-F
C-G
E-Am
F-G-C

HALLIE LONNIGAN

My name is Hallie Lonnigan, I married Walter Jones
"For better or for worse," so said the Reverend Doctor Stone
But the better times are all used up and the worse times took control
Then drinkin' took my Walter, may the Lord protect his soul

Alone with two young kids to raise out on the western Plains
My children harmonized with wolves and sang just like the rain
But haulin' hay and water were the desperate daily facts
And the years have carved their memories in the muscles of my back

>   Hallie Lonnigan will tell these truths to you
>   Hard times, the only times I ever knew
>   Hard luck's the only horse I ever drew
>   Hard work's the only way I made it through

Then I married for convenience sake, a trader from in town
A blacksmith name of Charlie Hawk, who'd court me on his rounds
But he'd paw me like a wolverine and there was cheatin' in his blood
He fell upon my butcher knife and crawled off through the mud

Well no one was the wiser when old Charlie disappeared
And me and them poor children never shed one single tear
We can run this place on our own, don't need no drunks or cheats
And the men they step aside now when I walk down Market Street

>   Hallie Lonnigan will tell these truths to you…

This land was conquered by brave men, your history books will say
Proud men upon fast horses drove the Indian away
My name is Hallie Lonnigan, I'll have you all to know
That the secret of your history's in a working woman's soul

>   Hallie Lonnigan will tell these truths to you…

CLAUDE DALLAS

In 1981 Claude Dallas killed two game wardens, Bill Pogue and Conley Elms, in rural Owyhee country, Idaho. Dallas was poaching game, but his contention was, "A man's got a right to hang some meat when he's living so far from town." Dallas also contended that Pogue was threatening him and drew the gun first. Conley Elms was unarmed. Dallas dispatched both men and hid the bodies. A friend of Dallas's, Jim Stevens, was close by, but took no part in the incident. Dallas was eventually convicted of manslaughter and given a thirty-year sentence. He broke out in 1986, and was recaptured a year later and sent to a high security prison in Kansas and was paroled for good behavior in 2005. Around the time of the breakout, in 1986 or '87, Ian Tyson said to me, "We ought to write a modern outlaw ballad about Claude Dallas." There were two books out about the incident and I read them and did whatever research I could, and also talked to a bunch of cowboys in Nevada who knew Claude. The stories were wild and too numerous to mention here. Most were sympathetic to Claude. A few weren't. He was a controversial character. Like all "outlaws."

Years later a nephew of mine, working as a police officer in Los Angeles, was shot and killed in the line of duty, so I can surely sympathize with the families of the fallen officers. I think our attempt in the song was to show both sides of the story. It was clear the jury somewhat bought Claude's story that Pogue had been pushing Dallas. Elms, however, was unarmed.

Ian wanted to write this in the old ballad style which begins: "Come gather round me people…"

Ian's version appears on his seminal record *Cowboyography*. My versions appear on *Cowboy Real*, *Songs of the West*, and *Cowboy'd All to Hell*.

CHORDS

Finger picked in Am. In the opening bridge, the song begins with *Am* instead of *C*. Other bridges are normal.

Bridge (The song opens with the Bridge Form)
C-G
D-F
C-G
D-F
Am

Verse
Am-G
Em-Am
Am-G
Em-Am

CLAUDE DALLAS

In a land the Spanish once had called *The Northern Mystery*
Where rivers run and disappear and the Mustang still lives free
By the Devil's Wash and the Coyote Hole in the wild Owyhee Range
Somewhere in the sage tonight the wind calls out his name

    Aye Aye Aye

Come gather round me buckaroos a story I will tell
Of the fugitive Claude Dallas who just broke out of jail
You may think this tale is history from before the West was won
But the events that I'll describe took place in 1981

He was born out in Virginia left home when school was through
In the deserts of Nevada he became a buckaroo
And he learned the ways of cattle and he learned to sit a horse
And he always packed a pistol and he practiced deadly force

And then Claude became a trapper and he dreamt of the bygone days
And he studied bobcat logic in the wild and silent ways
In the bloody runs near Paradise and the Monitors down south
Trapping cats and coyotes and living hand to mouth

    Aye Aye Aye

And then Claude took to living all alone out many miles from town
A friend, Jim Stevens, brought supplies and he stayed to hang around
That day two wardens, Pogue and Elms, drove in to check Claude out
They were seeking violations and to see what Claude's about

Now Claude had hung some venison and had a bobcat pelt or two
Pogue claimed they were out of season, he says, "Dallas, you're all through."
But Dallas would not leave his camp, he refused to go to town
As the wind howled through the bull camp, they stared each other down

It's hard to say what happened next, perhaps we'll never know
They were going to take Claude into jail, and he vowed he'd never go
Jim Stevens heard the gunfire, and when he turned around
Bill Pogue was fallin' backwards, Conley Elms he fell face down

    Aye Aye Aye

Jim Stevens walked on over, there was a gun near Bill Pogue's hand
It's hard to say who'd drawn his first, but Claude had made his stand
Claude said, "I'm justified, Jim, they were going to cut me down
And a man's got a right to hang some meat, when he's livin' this far from town."

It took eighteen men and fifteen months to finally hunt Claude down
In the sage outside of Paradise, they drove him to the ground
Convicted up in Idaho, manslaughter by decree
Thirty years at maximum, but soon Claude would break free

There's two sides to the story, there may be no right or wrong
The lawman and the renegade, have graced a thousand songs
The story is an old one, a conclusion's hard to draw
But Claude's out in the sage tonight, he may be the last outlaw

    Aye Aye Aye

In a land the Spanish once had called The Northern Mystery....

CO-WRITTEN WITH IAN TYSON

ROANIE

A feller steps up and he said, "I suppose
You're a bronc fighter from looks of your clothes."
"You figures me right, I'm a good one," I claim
"Do you happen to have any bad ones to tame?"
                        "The Strawberry Roan"
                        Curley Fletcher

I used to work in my brother's western store in San Luis Obispo, California. There was a saddle maker there named Van, a southerner who'd moved out West. Van wore his hat on the side of his head, like a folded taco, and could really sling the bullshit in his southern drawl. "I used to ride them bulls but they started hurtin' me…hurt me real bad one time up in Dallas…so I married a sixteen-year-old gal…just a child she was…." Van could hold forth on bulls and women and whiskey and horses and he could twist anything into a romantic yarn, even though you knew it was mostly fiction. *A western character.* He had a sidekick named Ace who, in the grand tradition of cowboy sidekicks, backed up everything Van laid down. If Van wanted Ace to corroborate something, he'd say, "Ain't that true Ace?" Ace would answer, "Does a wild bear shit in the woods, Van?" Van would throw back, "The ones in the zoo don't, Ace." Then Van would wink and Ace would crack up. I used to drink beer with these characters on the weekends. They both lived in a cheap motel on the edge of town. I never saw them near a horse, cow, bull, or female for that matter. They lived inside their heads. I think a little bit of "Roanie" came from these guys. The folklorist Guy Logsdon (Baxter Black's father-in-law—Guy wrote the folk book *The Whorehouse Bells Are Ringing*) used to sing this song, and I recorded it on *Cowboy Real* and *Cowboy'd All to Hell*.

CHORDS

Fingerpicked in the Key of C.

Verse	*Chorus*	*Final Tag*
C-Em	F-Em	C-G-Am-G
Dm-G	Dm-G-C	Am-F-C-G
Dm-G-Dm-G	F-Em	C-G-C-F-C etc.
G-C	D-G	(Strawberry Roan
C-Em	Dm-G-C	melody)
F-Fm		
C-G		
G-C		

ROANIE

Mail Pouch Tobacco signs are crumblin' in waltz time
On the sides of forgotten old barns
And the rockin' chair's a-rollin', on the porch down at Dolan's
Where Roanie tells those wild western yarns
About a big roan caballo, that ruled the arroyos
Then he's hummin' "The Strawberry Roan"
Then the boys start to sighin', 'cause old Roanie's cryin'
He's forgotten the words to the song

    Roanie, you're nothin' but a drugstore Vaquero
    been tellin' your lies too damn long
    Hummin' the tune to "The Strawberry Roan"
    Forgettin' the words to the song
    Hey, Roanie, your Wild West is gone

Well, the Great Western Feed Lot's, turned into a truck stop
Where old Roanie drinks coffee all night
And he tells all the drivers he's an outlaw survivor
And he beat Jesse James in a fight
And the waitresses smile, Lord, they're lost for awhile
Makin' love in some gunfighter's bed
And the Wild West keeps dyin', and Ol' Roanie keeps lyin'
About the home on the range in his head

    He'd cough and he'd wink, he'd say, "Lord, I need a drink
    And I gotta get these dogies movin' on
    I'm pony ridin' mail down the wild Chisholm Trail
    Gotta make Laredo by dawn
    Hey, does anyone remember, the words to that ol' song?
        "As I rode out in the streets of Laredo
        As I rode out in Laredo one day..."

Well, the Mail Pouch Tobacco signs, are crumblin' in waltz time
On the sides of forgotten old barns
And the rockin' chair's been stolen, off the porch down at Dolan's
Where old Roanie told those wild western yarns
And that big roan caballo, has left the arroyos
He's swayback, plumb broken down
And ol' Roanie he's buried, in the new cemetery

Cause there ain't no more Boot Hills around

    Roanie weren't nothin' but a drugstore Vaquero...

        So it's beat the drum slowly, And play the fife lowly
        He had a pain in his chest, and he's bound to move on
        Singin,' *"Oh that Strawberry Roan...*
        He could turn on a nickel and give you some change...
        Who could ride that Strawberry Roan?"

TONIGHT WE RIDE

"Goodbye—if you hear of my being stood up against a stone wall and shot to rags please know that I think that a pretty good way to depart this life. It beats old age, disease, or falling down the cellar stairs."
Pancho Villa

"I have the duty to inform you that Pancho Villa is everywhere and nowhere at the same time."
An Officer with
Venustiano Carranza's Army

I wrote this in the Rancho Vistadores camp, in the mountains near Santa Barbara, California. Tequila might have played a part. It became a battle cry around the camp at happy hour. It reads like a Peckinpah movie, with a dash of Cormac McCarthy thrown in. This centers around the infamous Pancho Villa raid on Columbus, New Mexico. I live fifty miles from the town of Columbus and drive through there, on occasion, on my way to Arizona. Villa killed sixteen people during the raid (allegedly it was Villa and his army) and the U.S. sent General Black Jack Pershing after him (with a young George Patton in tow.) Using horses, mules, and bi-planes, they could never catch old Pancho. A great telling of this story can be found in the book *The General and The Jaguar,* by Eileen Welsome. I hadn't read it at the time I wrote the song, but it's a fine book for understanding the labyrinthine political history of Mexico…and you must understand Mexico (and Spain) to understand the West. "Siete Leguas" is a famous Mexican *corrido* about Pancho Villa's favorite horse. He was said to have been able to run *seven leagues* without tiring. A league is about three and one half miles. I used to request "Siete Leguas" from trios in the markets of Juarez, before the days of the drug war. I performed "Tonight We Ride" on *The David Letterman Show* and David introduced it by saying something like: "Here's a perfect song for getting on a horse and robbing a liquor store in Montana…" This song appears on my records *Indians Cowboys Horses Dogs, Veteran's Day: The Tom Russell Anthology,* and *Cowboy'd All to Hell.*

CHORDS

Key of C.

Verse	*Chorus*
C-F	Am-Em
C-G	F-C-C-G
Am-F	Am-F
C-G	C-G-C

TONIGHT WE RIDE

Pancho Villa crossed the border in the year of 'ought sixteen
The people of Columbus hear Pancho riding through their dreams
He killed seventeen civilians, you could hear the women scream
Black Jack Pershing on a dancing horse was waiting in the wings

    Tonight we ride, tonight we ride
    We'll skin old Pancho Villa and make chaps out of his hide
    Shoot his horse *Siete Leguas* and his twenty-seven brides
    Tonight we ride, boys, tonight we ride

We rode for three long years 'til Black Jack Pershing called it quits
When Jack he wasn't lookin' I stole his fine spade bit
It was tied upon his stallion so I rode away on it
To the wild Chihuahuan Desert so dry you couldn't spit

    Tonight we ride, you bastards dare
    We'll hunt the wild Apache for the bounty on their hair
    Then we ride into El Paso, climb up the whorehouse stairs
    Tonight we ride, boys, tonight we ride

When I'm too damn old to sit a horse I'll steal the warden's car
Break my ass out of this prison, leave my teeth there in a jar
You don't need no teeth for kissin' gals, or smokin' cheap cigars
And I'll sleep with one eye open, 'neath God's celestial stars

Tonight we rock, tonight we roll
We'll rob the Juarez liquor stores for the *Reposado Gold*
And if we drink ourselves to death, ain't that the cowboy way to go?
Tonight we ride, boys, tonight we ride

Tonight we fly, we're headin' west
To the deserts near El Paso, where the eagle makes his nest
If our bones rot on this frontier, we'll consider we are blessed
Tonight we ride, girls, tonight we ride

ALL THIS WAY FOR THE SHORT RIDE

> *It's impossible, when dust*
> *settling to the backs of large animals*
> *makes a racket you can't think in,*
> *impossible to conceive that pure fear,*
> *whether measured in degrees of cold*
> *or heat, can both freeze*
> *and incinerate so much*
> *in mere seconds...*
>   "All This Way for the Short Ride"
>   Paul Zarzyski

This one was written with the American master poet Paul Zarzyski, based on his original poem of the same title. The poem concerns the death, in a bull riding event, of Zarzyski's friend Joe Lear. I consider the poem one of the finest American poems of the past fifty years. The above quoted lines bear this out—and you ain't going to see this stuff in *The New Yorker*. The spooky thing is the child who was in his mother's womb, in the second and third verses of the song, now comes to my shows in Reno and thanks me for singing the song. It's quite moving to see this kid and sing the song in his presence. The song appears on my record *Indians Cowboys Horses Dogs*, and *Cowboy'd All to Hell*. Paul's poem is included in his book *All This Way For the Short Ride*, which won the Cowboy Hall of Fame Wrangler Award in 1996.

CHORDS

Key of E, capo on second fret (only covering the first five strings) in drop D positions. In waltz time, like *The Streets of Laredo*.

Verse
D-G-D
D-G-D
D-Bm-F#m
G-D

Chorus
D-Bm-E
E-C-G-D

ALL THIS WAY FOR THE SHORT RIDE

Well, the chute gate swings open, here we go again
The desperate dance, the kick and the spin
Dust risin' from a cross bred bull, fire meets with pride
A man come a long way, just for the short ride

His wife's in the grandstand, trying to swallow the fear
A little baby inside her whose time's drawin' near
The bull flyin' high now, then he falls to his side
Their love came a long way just for the short ride

>   Two hearts in the darkness, sing a blue lullaby
>   Beat the drum slowly for a cowboy's last ride

Well the dust is all settled, and the crowd's disappeared
The siren still echoes, in an unborn child's ear
Little boy's due in April, he'll have his daddy's blue eyes
He'll always remember his father's last ride

>   They preached at the service from John 25
>   How Christ came a long way, just for the short ride

CO-WRITTEN WITH PAUL ZARZYSKI

BUCKING HORSE MOON

"I didn't leave home for second place."
                              Casey Tibbs, Bronc Rider

I believe this is the first song I co-wrote with Paul Zarzyski, based around his poem of the same name. Along with the late great Buck Ramsey, Zarzyski has certainly injected much-needed fresh blood into the cowboy poetry scene. He's an outstanding performer as well. James Joyce once said, "There's the sound of words, the sound of words hitting against words, and the sound of the silence between words." Zarzyski seems to know this intuitively, and he's a man who savors each word as he recites them. He calls up a vision of his own poetical West. To understand and write about the West you have to have a profound appreciation of the landscape—that love of the terrain washes through this song. I recorded it on: *Indians Cowboys Horses Dogs*, and Wylie and the Wild West recorded a version on their record *Hooves of the Horses*. Wylie also performed this song with symphonies, and you can find films of this online.

CHORDS

Key of B flat—capo on third fret in G Chord positions. I fingerpick it.

Verse	*Chorus*	*Bridge*
G-D-Em	G-Am-G	G-Em-Bm
C-G-D-G	G-Am-C-D	C-G
G-D-Em	C-Bm	G-Em-Bm
C-D-Em	Am-C-G	Am-C-D

BUCKING HORSE MOON

Down a one lane road there's a dusty fairground
Where I learned the bronc trade and I fell in love
With a blue eyed twister and her smoky whisper
She said they call me *The Cimarron Dove*

We'd spool our bed rolls on down together
My callused hands combed through her hair
She'd stare at a star, through an old mesquite tree
See that moon shadow, there's a bucking horse there

> Sweet bird of youth, no easy keeper
> Flown with the seasons all too soon
> Beneath Montana's blue roan skies
> Nevada starlight, and the bucking horse moon

Our love reeled out like a western movie
Down heart-worn highways through the rodeo towns
Wrapped in her wings for the midnight flight
And that bucking horse moon kept shining down

> > Bucking horse moon, on the hood of her truck
> > She'd smile and say that means good luck
> > Bucking horse shadows through the purple sage
> > We'll ride forever, our love won't age

But heart and bone are made for breaking
The Cimarron Dove's gone with the wind
Then a bronc in Prescott rolled on my back
I'll never ride rough stock again

> Sweet bird of youth, no easy keeper...

I lost my youth on the dusty fairgrounds
I'm an old bronc fighter long past high noon
But on the haunted night wind I can hear her whisperin'
As I search the heavens for the bucking horse moon
    The Cimarron Dove and the bucking horse moon

> Sweet bird of youth, no easy keeper...

Co-written with Paul Zarzyski

BACON RIND AND CHIEF SEATTLE

"When the green hills are covered with talking wires and the wolves no longer sing, what good will the money you paid for our land be then?"
            Chief Seattle

These poetic fragments are not so much songs as introductions to Peter La Farge's powerful song, "The Ballad of Ira Hayes," which I recorded on a record called *Indians Cowboys Horses Dogs*. The cowboy poetry movement needs more songs and poetry concerning Native Americans. Peter La Farge was the son of Oliver La Farge who won the Pulitzer Prize for his novel *Laughing Boy*. Johnny Cash recorded an album largely composed of Peter's songs, *Bitter Tears*. "Ira Hayes" is the standout, a true story of one of the Marines who raised the flag at Iwo Jima. Ira came home a hero and dissolved into white man culture. One of the lines reads, "…then Ira started drinking hard, jail was often his home, they let him raise the flag and lower it, like you'd throw a dog a bone…" Strong stuff. Bitter irony.

 Bacon Rind is depicted on one of the gas station glasses I have in my cabinet at home. A western souvenir. I read Chief Seattle's speech on the side of an art museum one day in Seattle and it chilled me. His words speak to the spiritual differences between white Christians and Indians.

CHORDS

This is basically a folk-rap, finger picked in C. Like a talking blues. Play whatever chords move you.

LYRIC 1

Bacon Rind was an Osage Chief
He wore a regal hat
I found him in a gas station on
One of those give away glasses that
Said, "The Indians of Oklahoma—
You can collect the entire set."
Hunting Horse, Sequoia, Dull Knife,
I don't have 'em all yet
As I drive across this wild ground
For what wisdom I can find
I thought of those gas station drinking glasses
And a chief called Bacon Rind

LYRIC 2

Chief Seattle stared into the yellow eyes
Of the mission padre
And then spit on the ground and said:
"Your religion was written on tablets of stone
By the iron finger of an angry God
Our religion is the tradition of our ancestors
And the dreams of our old men
Given to them in the solemn hours of the night
By the Great Spirit
Our religion is in the vision of our leaders
And it is written in the hearts of our people."
The mission father rode off
And preached the Ten Commandments
To those who had stopped listening with their hearts.

THE BALLAD OF EDWARD ABBEY

> "The sneakiest form of literary subtlety, in a corrupt society, is to speak the plain truth. The critics will not understand you; the public will not believe you; your fellow writers will shake their heads. Laughter, praise, honors, money, and the love of beautiful girls will be your only reward."
> Edward Abbey
> *A Voice Crying in the Wilderness*

I guess Edward Abbey was a cowboy. *Of sorts*. An enigma. A great writer on the West and environmental concerns, though he could swing his bat to any field. A character who stood before an audience of cattlemen, pistol clanked down on the podium, and told them *to get their goddamn cattle off of public land*. Then he could turn back around and make anti-government statements whilst throwing beer cans out the window, as he rock and rolled his old convertible through the desert. Ed's theory was that the road shouldn't be there in the first place. He wrote the novel *The Brave Cowboy*, which became the Kirk Douglas movie *Lonely Are the Brave*. Basically I used Ed, in this song, to take a pot shot at developers who've destroyed the West around my hacienda. After George Custer, your average developer rates high on the list of the great assholes of Western history. The melody to this one is borrowed from the old cowboy song *The Buffalo Skinners*, which I've heard Ramblin' Jack Elliott sing on many occasions. This appears on my record *Indians Cowboys Horses Dogs*.

CHORDS

Finger picked in Am.

Verse
Am-F-Am
Am-F-Am
Am-F-Am
Am-F-G-Am

Chorus
Am-G
G-Am
(Occasional added lines:
Am-C-E-Am)

THE BALLAD OF EDWARD ABBEY

'Twas in the town of Tucson in 1983
A man named Edward Abbey came a-walkin' up to me
He pulled his cigar from his mouth, said, "I smell lawyers here"
The politicians' running dogs, they crawled away in fear

    Sing a Doo Ri Doo, Sing a Doo Ri Day

Ed walked across the desert, at least a thousand times
He spoke with javelina, and slept 'neath piñon pine
And if he saw a billboard there, Ed chopped that bastard down
Ed said, "If a man can't piss in his own front yard, he's livin' too close to town."

    Sing a Doo Ri Doo, Sing a Doo Ri Day
    Lord, I wish Edward Abbey, were walking round today

Ed had a taste for women, in fact he married quite a few
He said, "I fall in love, boys, but I'm only passing through
You know I like 'em all, boys, and some more than the rest
I've tried my hand at monogamy, now I'm off to save the West."

    Sing a Doo Ri Doo, Sing a Doo Ri Day

Ed died one day at sundown, in his Tucson writing shack
They wrapped him in a sleeping bag, and drove him way out back
Beneath the wild Saguaro, the coyotes chewed Ed's bones
And on a hidden marker, was "No comment" carved in stone

    Sing a Doo Ri Doo, Sing a Doo Ri Day

Now I'm living in the desert, but the towns are closing in
Those cracker box developments, Ed would call a sin
We stole this land from a Mexican, and now we'll sell it back
And they'll live like mortgaged prisoners, in those goddamn housing tracts

Tell me who votes for the mountain lion? Tell me who votes for the fox?
Who votes for the spotted owl, who hides there in the rocks?
I wish that Ed would come again, with a chainsaw in his hand
And carve on up them housing tracts, and take on back the land

    Sing a Doo Ri Doo, Sing a Doo Ri Day

LITTLE BLUE HORSE

The time has come, the Walrus said,
To talk of many things:
Of shoes, and ships, and sealing-wax
Of cabbages, and kings
And why the sea is boiling hot
And whether pigs have wings.

Lewis Carroll
Through the Looking Glass

Pony Boy, Pony Boy
Won't you be my Pony Boy
Don't say no
Here we go
Off across the plains

Heath and O'Donnell
"My Pony Boy"

This one's a lullaby which references the medieval verse, "Ride a Cock Horse to Banbury Cross," a nursery rhyme I remember as a kid. That rhyme is also in *Tom Thumb's Pretty Song Book,* published in 1744. I was looking for something to finish one of my cowboy records and wrote this. I'll dedicate it to Izzy, Lulu, Patrick, Molly, Quinn and Jessica. Let's all be kids forever. This is on *Indians Cowboys Horses Dogs*.

CHORDS

A slow waltz in C.

Verse
C-G-C-C7-F-Fm-C-C7
F-Fm-C-Em-Am
C-G-C

Bridge
F-Em-F-G-C
C7-F-Em-D-G
F-G-C

LITTLE BLUE HORSE

Go and saddle your little blue horse,
We're riding for better or worse
'Cross the blue midnight sky, where the stars never die
On the wings of your little blue horse

He's got a Navajo brand on his hip,
He's got "Made in Japan" 'neath his lip
He's got burrs in his mane, he won't ever be tame
Baby, saddle your little blue horse

    Down all of my days, I never figured his ways
    He rides on that sandman moonbeam
    He's a nursery rhyme horse, from Banbury Cross
    Where morning's never as far as it seems
    And lullabies are the mysteries of dreams

He's got rocking chair legs made of wood,
He'd be a real horse if only he could
Through all kinds of weather, on a bed of goose feathers
We'll ride on your little blue horse

So baby lay down on your bed,
Chase the troubles and trials from your head
Close your sweet little eyes, we'll mount up and ride
Through the hills on your little blue horse
      Over blankets on a little blue horse

THE BASQUE

The red, red grass a thousand miles—
And Spanish Johnny, you!
                    "Spanish Johnny"
                    Willa Cather

I wrote this in Ian Tyson's writing cabin one night. It seems highly influenced by Willa Cather's poem "Spanish Johnny," which Tyson recorded on the record *Ole 'Eon,* and versions were also sung by Emmy Lou Harris and Paul Seibel. I changed the main character into a Basque, since I'm interested in that Northern Spanish culture. I've performed in Bilbao and Guernica. Love the food (squids in their own ink, etc.) and was always interested in *pelota*—the Basque ball game, which came to be known as Jai Alai as it arrived in America and prospered awhile on the Mexican border. I wrote a song called "Jai Alai" on the album *Mesabi*. Jai Alai is still played down in Florida. The Basques also brought their sheep herding culture to the Western states, and I've enjoyed fine evenings in Basque restaurants in Northern Nevada. I'm fond of Spanish wine, as is the cowboy in this song. This one appears on the record *Cowboy Real*.

CHORDS

A Tex-Mex waltz in C.

Verse
G-C-G-C
G-C-D-G
F-C-F-G
C-C7-F-G-C

Chorus
C7-F-C-F-G
C-C7-F-G-C

THE BASQUE

At night his spirit is singing, through the cactus trees and scrub
An old song of fever and passion, of a cowhand crippled by love
A song alive with the sorcerer's touch, handed down from the past
And there's only one man who could sing it, the cowboy that we call The Basque

    He'd sing, "Lay me down by the river, boys, facing the hot desert sun
    And the wind will scatter my spirit, after the coyotes are done."

He'd a gap 'tween his teeth that would whistle, when he sang or he snored or he chewed
And he was skilled at braiding *reatas*, or cooking his wild shepherd stew
With a goatskin full of his burgundy wine, he was armed for the trail or the task
And if matters called for endurance, we knew we could count on the Basque

    He'd say, "Lay me down by the river, boys…"

But the wine began to take over, and bitterness poisoned his tongue
And he'd curse in his sleep at a woman, and all of the damage she'd done
With pity we watched his derangement, as he conjured a ghost from his past
But none of our words could console him, we feared we were losing The Basque

One night he walked out in the desert, and he sang and he moaned all night long
We found his remains three days later, after the coyotes were done
In the sand he'd written in Spanish, a poem to a Tonopah whore
Who'd taken his love and his money, and crippled him deep to the core

    So we laid him down by the river, facing the hot desert sun
    Where the wind would scatter his spirit, after the coyotes were done

THE HEART OF A BUCKING HORSE

Tipperary, Steamboat, Gray Bob, Flying Devil, Coyote, Prison Bars, Flaxie, Midnight, Five Minutes To Midnight, Hell's Angel, Descent, Miss Klamath, Come Apart, High Tide, Three Bars....

Legendary Bucking Horses

This is another Russell-Zarzyski composition. Paul Zarzyski used to ride bareback broncs, and I grew up watching my brother Pat go from bulls to bareback broncs to bull dogging, to rodeo stock contractor to senior citizen snowboard champion. The names of the classic bucking horses were always lyrical and elegiac. *War Paint. Trail's End. Five Minutes to Midnight. Steamboat. Hell's Angel.* My brother owned one called *Vertical Drop.* You can imagine how he bucked. Straight up. Straight down. The stories surrounding these horses are as legendary as their names. That image of a cowboy on a bronc is probably the central image of the West, and in the rodeo business the great buckers are honored, in life and death, as much as the champion cowboys. I spent a little time one day with Jim Hanum, a childhood buddy of the great Casey Tibbs, and Jim could rattle off the names of dozens of great broncs and why they were legendary and how they moved. Jim had ridden a few of them himself, including Painted Smile. There's nothing like listening to one of these old boys talking about the classic bucking horses. It's always pure poetry. In the last verse we mention, "a cowboy's eyes intent on the try…" and I recall seeing a saddle bronc rider, in the chute, with the word *try* carved into the leather seat of his saddle. I never forgot that. Seems like a good mantra for all of us.

I wrote this for a western documentary and did a demo of this song which appears on *Cowboy'd All to Hell.*

CHORDS

Key of G. Medium tempo, flat-picked country.
Instrumental Interlude: Cm-Bm/Cm-Bm.

Verse
G-Am
D-C-G
G-Am-
D-C-G

Chorus
D-Em
A-Am-D
C-Em
D-C-G

THE HEART OF A BUCKING HORSE

Old Roman nose, long tangled mane, not built for town parade
But ugly lies in the eye of man, God makes broncs a different way
The buckskins, roans, and dappled grays, let's cut down to the source
I come here to tell you boys, 'bout the heart of a bucking horse

    Of names that ring like carnival games, in the dusty old fairground night
    Whiplash, Cyclone, Kewpie Doll, Hootchie-Kootchie, Dynamite
    And when they throw their weight 'gainst the hand of a man
    With the whirl and the suck and the force,
            there's nothing that defines the West, like the heart of a bucking horse

From the hurricane deck of a rank old wreck, roars the wild volcanic blood
The resin squawk is the anthem talk to the gelding, the mare, and the stud
The shouldered spur, the snort, the whirr, the screaming in a red dust rain
It echoes up from Mexico—to the Blackfoot rider out on the Plain
    (*Or/alternate*: it echoes up from Patagonia back to the Moors in Southern Spain)

    War Paint, General Custer, Empty Saddles, and Trail's End
    Grey Wolf, Midnight, Indian Sign, Snake Eyes and Descent
    And when they throw their weight…

This old rodeo life just a big ole painting, Maynard Dixon skies that roll away
Some come to ride, and some come to hide, 'near the chutes in the Cottonwood shade
But forever out in the forefront, the great western image, the soul, the source
A cowboy's eyes intent on the *try*, and the heart of a great bucking horse

    Yellow Fever, Dream Boat Annie, Painted Smile and Jesse James
    Red Wing, Banjo, Widow Maker…how I love them old bronc names!
    And when they throw their weight…

Co-written with Paul Zarzyski

HOPI MAN FROM NOWHERE
Woodcut by Tom Russell
2012

CHAPTER SIX

THE MAN FROM GOD KNOWS WHERE

THE MAN FROM GOD KNOWS WHERE

Into our townland on a night of snow
rode a man from God knows where;
None of us bade him stay or go,
nor deemed him friend, nor damned him foe,
but we stabled his big roan mare;
for in our townland we're decent folk,
and if he didn't speak, why none of us spoke,
and we sat till the fire burned low.
                    Florence Wilson
                    "The Man from God Knows Where"

The Man from God Knows Where is my "Folk Opera," as it's been called, centered on twenty-six pieces of original song, old folk songs, poetry, traditional melodies, and instrumental music which form together and *sing up* the story of my ancestors coming from Ireland and Norway a hundred and fifty, or so, years ago. I began a song-cycle on family history with the working title, "American Primitive." Then one night in a bar in Downpatrick, Ireland, an old man came up and asked me if I was Thomas Russell. He said, "They hung your namesake, Thomas Russell, right across the road in 1798, during the United Irish Rebellion. There's a poem about him called 'The Man From God Knows Where.'" The old man recited most of the poem that night, and a powerful piece it is. I took the title for this opera. This first song winds in and out of the whole opera—the voice of the omniscient narrator, citing folks songs and distorted American history. He's going to set the record straight and deliver us from the myths. He is Thomas Russell, rising up with the moon, out of his grave.

CHORDS

Finger picked in Am.

Verse   *Chorus*
Am-G-Am   C-Am-C-G
Am-G-Am   C-Am-C-E
C-Am-C-E   Am-Am-G-Am
Am-G-Am   Am-Am-G-Am

THE MAN FROM GOD KNOWS WHERE

Come gather round me, children, a story I will tell
I've been around since Jesus met the woman at the well
I've walked these roads ten thousand years, I'm a ragtime millionaire
I am the rake and the ramblin' saint, I am the man from God knows where

Oh, they hung me in Downpatrick, up near Saint Patrick's tomb
My ghost rose up in the peat fire smoke toward the rising of the moon
Now as I drift through your villages, all the maidens stop and stare
"There goes old Tom, the vagabond, he's the man from God knows where."

   So rise up all you ancestors and dance upon your graves
   I've come to hear your voices now so maybe I'll be saved
   Cursed are we who forget the past, but pray and don't despair
   My song might haunt your dreams tonight, I'm the man from God knows where

I've slept beneath your bridges, near your oil refineries
I've gambled on your river boats, *Shenandoah, Kankakee*
I'm the homeless lad, I'm an orphan child, leaves of grass sewn through my hair
Yeah, me and old Walt Whitman, we're the men from God knows where

I rode the rods on steam trains with a banjo on my knee
While the voice of Stephen Foster, he whispered songs to me
Of a storefront church and a chain gang choir—black sorrow filled the air
Then Stephen died on the *doss house* floor, like a man from God knows where

I heard the sound of Indian drums, I heard the bugles blow
Before they rewrote history into a Wild West Show
My kin sailed toward America to steal their Indian ground
They passed Bill Cody's circus ships, European bound

   So lock up all your daughters, your whiskey and your gold
   I've come to claim my bounty for the lies that I've been told
   As I look out on this crowd tonight, I see most of you don't care
   Come lift your glass, reveal your past, to the man from God knows where

PATRICK RUSSELL

"There was another America out there that remained unsung; a rawer, more primitive America, where the spirit had not been tamed by the restless machine of modern materialism."
                    Jack Kerouac

This was taken *almost verbatim* from Patrick Russell, my father's grandfather, as he dictated it to one of his daughters at the end of his life in Iowa. He was eighty-five. The story, in plain talk, gives you the idea of what kind of people these were. Strong characters who crossed over the ocean with very little but their tremendous heart and a potato spade "for cultivation." They were dirt famers and horse traders. The Malloys were the Irish on my mother's side, and the Larsens came from Norway. They all met up in Northeast Iowa and built up their quarter acres. I don't know if there were wolves in Iowa back then, as he mentions, maybe so. Or perhaps they were coyotes. It was wild country and they were stalwart people. I still have an Aunt Mary living in Templemore, and she comes to my concerts. When I play Roscrae, she sits in the front row and says, "Ah, the Russells are shining tonight!"

CHORDS

Key of A. Sort of medium blues rock.

Verse	*Chorus*	*Bridge*
A-D-E-A	A-D-E	E-A-E-A
A-D-E	A-D-E	E-A-E-A
D-A-D-E	A-Cm-D-A	B-E-B-E
A-D-E-A	A-E-A	B-E-B-E

PATRICK RUSSELL

My name is Patrick Russell, I have led a Christian life
I speak of family history as it's transcribed by my wife
I sit here in New Hampton, the year is 1910
Looking back from Iowa toward Mother Ireland

I was born in Templemore, in 1825
Recall a happy boyhood until my mother died
Starvation crept across the land, America's our dream
Six cruel weeks on stormy seas aboard the ship Tyrene

    American Primitive man
    In an American Primitive land
    I wash my face in a fryin' pan
    American Primitive man

At last we docked in old Quebec, the English offered farming ground
But we'd lived too long under English rule, to United States we're bound
By train and then by cattle boat, ah, the filth down in that hold
We landed in Milwaukee, trekked two hundred miles or more

        A sack of new potatoes was carried by each man
        Four spades for cultivation that we'd brought from Ireland
        We worked at splittin' railroad ties, bought one old milking cow
        A quarter section uncleared land, two oxen and a plow

At nights we heard the wolves howl on our newly purchased farm
And starving lads from the Civil War took shelter in our barn
The Larsens and the Cooneys, the Russells, the Malloys
We tilled the soil of Iowa, grew a spate of girls and boys

    American Primitive man
    In an American Primitive land
    A whiskey still in an oatmeal can
    American Primitive man

THE OUTCAST

A sideshow carousel plays the old carny tune, "Over the Waves," as the painted ponies go up and down and a carnival barker steps out and delivers his spiel. In this case it's Dave Van Ronk taking the holy piss out of American history in one of the favorite things I've yet written. Barnum and Bailey time. To have Van Ronk sing "The Outcast" was a dream. Drunkenness, political corruption, racism, hatred, inbred sex, dirty family history... an amusing little rap about the drunk/insane relative we've all tried to hide in a dark closet. In this case the relative is Uncle Sam himself. *Tongue in cheek*. My vision was that the tribes of incoming immigrants are being released from the ships and they run smack dab into a welcome delivered by the carnival huckster "outcast" who tries to sell them the Brooklyn Bridge or forty acres on a flood plain. It's the American way. I have this slight theory that our relatives went a bit *off* when they left their homeland, their tribes, music, and local taverns behind forever. Lost in the cornfields of America. So they reinvented themselves. This one is from *The Man from God Knows Where*. There are two versions on the record.

CHORDS

Key of D. Carny Jazz.

Verse form #1
(Two verses in a row)
D
G
D-Bm-F#m
Em-A-D

Verse for #2
(Or bridge/ two in a row)
G-D
G-D
D-Bm-F#m
Em-A-D

THE OUTCAST

Oh, gather round me people, lend an ear now if you please
Your promised land was settled by bastards, drunks, and thieves
Excuse me if it offends you, but I'm the worst of all of these
I destroyed the family tree, I am the outcast

I'm yer inbred second cousin that was kept inside a shed
I'm the cross-eyed little stutterer who always wet the bed
I'm yer queer Uncle Harry, yer retarded Uncle Fred
I'm the one they left for dead, I'm the outcast

I've embarrassed folks at weddings, birthdays and at wakes
I'm the cur who passed out face down in your anniversary cake
I'm the black sheep, the philanderer, the louse, the souse, the rake
The remittance man, the snake, the bloody outcast

Forbear with yer pity, my function's very plain
We've all come here from the Olde World, and we've gone a touch insane
On yer social scale ya need a foil to bear the family stain
I am the joker in yer game, I am the outcast

Oh, the black man and the Indian, the Chinaman, the Jew
They built yer friggin' railroad, they picked yer cotton, too
They washed yer dirty laundry, they tied yer children's shoes
They got a right to sing the blues, 'cause they were outcasts

Now we worship politicians as if they all were saints
Put their faces on our money, pillowslips, and plates
We should love this land for what it is, and not for what it ain't
Oh, their game is fueled by hate, the hate of outcasts

The Norwegians hate the Swedish and the Swedes they hate the Finns
The Finns they hate the Russians and the Russians hate the Yids
Spicks and Wops and Greasers, Kikes and Spades and Ginny Hens
Hatred's blowin' in the wind—ten million outcasts

Oh, beautiful for spacious skies and amber waves of grain
Grain distilled to make the rye that pickled ol' Thom Paine
Old Georgie built the White House with slaves that died in pain
But George's quarries made the gain, from blood of outcasts

Move in a little closer now, the sideshow must begin
History will repeat itself, again, again, again!
On the immigration totem pole the low man never wins
Competition ain't a sin. God help the outcast!

So step right up ye pilgrims, the trains a-leavin' soon
We got acreage out in Iowa for the likes of folks like you
A quarter section on a flood plain, forty acres and a mule
Sign right here ye bloody fools, welcome, ye outcasts!

AMBROSE LARSEN

As a person grows older, memories of childhood and early youth are often recalled…when I listen to old melodies and especially when I sit alone in my room at twilight, I see mountains and meadows, hills, and valleys which I knew so well and loved so much; I hear the clang of cowbells, the murmur of the brooks, and the song of the lark in the sunlit sky. I live over again many episodes. Sometimes I laugh, and sometimes I don't.

Nils Nilsen Rønning
The Boy from Telemark

Ambrose Larsen was a great-great-grandfather of mine who emigrated from Bergen, Norway in the late 1800s. Norwegian television did a special on my quest to find his childhood home and birth information, but I'm not convinced we found the right Larsen. Larsen is like "Smith" in Norway. Common name. This track on *The Man from God Knows Where* begins with the Norwegian traditional singer Sondre Bratland singing in Norwegian, then a Hardanger fiddle enters and we're transported by that lonely, drone sound to the fjords of west Norway. The fiddle is played by Annbjorg Lien. (The record was actually recorded near the Hardanger Fjord in Norway.) Then Sondre Bratland sings up Ambrose Larsen, with Iris Dement harmonizing. Ambrose married Bridget O'Malley, and Bridget's heritage traces back to the Irish pirate Queen Grace O'Malley. My sisters are quite proud of this. Grace was a legend. The rest is Ambrose's story of Iowa farm life in the 1800s. Hard ground. Tough people. Good whiskey.

CHORDS

Key of Bm, played with capo on second fret in Am position.

Verse
Am-Am-E-Am
Am-Dm-Am-E
Am-E
Am-Dm-E-Am

Chorus
Am-G-Am
Am-G-E
Am-G-C
E-Am

AMBROSE LARSEN

My name is Ambrose Larsen, from the Bergen shore I've come
I've been cheated for my wages, couldn't speak the native tongue
My wife and child are terrified of these Midwestern storms
But we settled down in Lime Creek, next to Jim Cooney's farm

The blackbirds and the locusts destroyed our corn and wheat
The hawks, they ate the chickens, the wolves our mutton meat
With traps and plows and shotguns loud, we fought this old wild ground
Our children caught the fever, but no doctors were around

    American Primitive man
    American Primitive man
    Norway Bible in my hand
    American Primitive man

I married Bridge O'Malley, she is Grace O'Malley's kin
That Pirate Queen from the Isle of Clare who led two hundred men
"Invincible on land and sea," was the O'Malley cry
Her spirit's in my children's blood, they'll prosper here or die

I learned to plow a decent row, make candles, knives and gloves
And how to balance misery with God's eternal love
Cooney taught me whiskey craft and when hardships are extreme
Jim and I, we take a sip and disappear in dreams

    American Primitive man
    American Primitive man
    Bought my share of the promised land
    American Primitive man

THE DREAMIN'

For I'm drunk today and I'm rarely sober
A handsome rover, from town to town....
    Carrickfergus (Traditional)

On Raglan Road, of an autumn day
I saw her first and knew...
That her dark hair would weave a snare
That I would one day rue...
    Raglan Road
    Patrick Kavanagh

Ah the old songs! Ah, the Irish! Ah, the dreamin'...My God, I wished Liam Clancy had sung my part on this song. Or Finbar Furey! Or Tommy Makem! Or Luke Kelly! I wish I would have spent more time on my singing of this—or maybe I shoulda drank a few Guinness. *If wishes were horses then beggars would ride.* This one is for all those Irish dreamers bent over a Guinness, a glass of Jameson, or even a cup of coffee...in the bars of Dublin. I can picture the bard Zozimus, his cane tap-tapping down a cobblestone alley. Or Brendan Behan at the end of the bar. Even Shane McGowen, for God's sake. Deep singers all. God save the Irish! I wrote the words and Katy Moffatt the melody. I sang it on the record with the great Irish singer Dolores Keane. *An honor.*

CHORDS

Key of C played with capo on 5th fret in G positions.

Verse
Em-C-G-D
Em-C-G-D
C-G-C-G
C-Bm-Am-D

Chorus
C-Bm
Am-C-D
C-Bm
Am-D-G

THE DREAMIN'

Oh, whiskey is the life of man, but whiskey's mostly water
And it's whiskey fuels the worker and corrupts his sons and daughters
The mountain water in the still, the copper pipes are steamin'
There'll soon be whiskey in the glass and dreamers gone to dreaming

    Oh, it's the dreaming, it's the dreaming
    A young girl's prayer, an old man's thoughts a-reelin'
    Two lovers stealin', the moonlight beamin'
    The search for meanin', leads through the dreamin'

Oh, I met her down in Dublin town, like a bottle fly I fell
To the spider in the Blackbush of the old Railway Hotel
She spun her web from Liffey's walls to the back rooms down at Whelans
But oh, how sweet her poison, now I'm drowning in the dreaming

    Oh, it's the dreamin', it's the dreamin'...

Oh, whiskey's made of water, lads, barley, corn, or malt
And man and woman's water, mixed with poetry and salt
Bring on the pullin' of the tides, the flash of eyes a-gleamin'
When passion blends the elements the yeast is but the dreaming

    Oh, it's the dreamin', it's the dreamin'...

CO-WRITTEN WITH KATY MOFFATT

ACRES OF CORN

"The first mile that leads away from the old home is a long mile."

C.A. Clausen
A Chronicler of Immigrant Life

On *The Man From God Knows Where,* Iris Dement brings this one alive with her singing. She's perfect for it. You can picture her in a print dress lying out in a corn field. Half drunk and lost in battered dreams. It reminds me of a Wyeth painting, *Christina's World,* which portrays a woman lying in a barren wheat field, staring up at an old Victorian farm house on a far hill. Or maybe something out of a painting by Grant Wood, or a short story by Flannery O'Conner. *Desolation in Iowa.* It carries a feeling I have—that my ancestors immigrated here and went a little crazy—missing their homeland. *Their roots.* Their blood memories. The wedding dress. The old songs. The first boyfriend. The dream of Paris.

CHORDS

Iris sings this one in F#. So to follow her, I would put the capo on the 4th fret and play in D positions. I think it's a 6/8 time. Double waltz.

Verse	Bridge
D-G	D-A-Bm
G-D-A	Bm-E-A
D-G	A-G-Bm
G-D-A-D	Bm-E-A-D

ACRES OF CORN

When I was a child, I spoke as a child
Now I'm a grown woman, but my thoughts are still wild
I thought I'd see London, or maybe *Paree*
But I'm starin' at cornfields, and they're starin' at me

    Dreams are just things that you keep in a jar
    You bury your dreams, or you wish on a star
    For an ocean line ticket, back to where you were born
    Away from these hard times, and the acres of corn

Every now and again I take a small drink
From the blackberry brandy hidden under the sink
And I pull out that steam trunk, I put on my gown
And I waltz through these cornfields, 'til I fall to the ground

    But dreams are just things that you keep in a trunk
    'Til the men are out workin' or you've gone a bit drunk
    Then you unlock your dreams but they're tattered and torn
    So you stare out the window, at the acres of corn

    Dreams are just things that you keep in a jar…

SITTING BULL IN VENICE

"If the Great Spirit had desired me to be a white man he would have made me so in the first place. He put in your heart certain wishes and plans, and in my heart he put other and different desires. It is not necessary for eagles to be crows."

Sitting Bull

There's a great photo of Buffalo Bill Cody and four Sioux chiefs sitting in a gondola in Venice, Italy, in April of 1890. Cody's Wild West Show was touring Europe. I found out later that Sitting Bull was actually *not* one of the chiefs in that gondola, as I'd imagined in this song. Two of the Lakota were American Horse and Long Bear. Sitting Bull was the last major Native American chief on the northern Plains to surrender to the U.S. Army. Some people claim he was the one who killed Custer, but that's never been substantiated. He joined Cody's Wild West Show in June of 1885 in Buffalo, New York. Buffalo Bill knew the great chief would sell tickets, and indeed he did. People came to *boo him* because of the Battle of the Little Big Horn. *Tough shit*, thought Sitting Bull, as he made a good bundle of money signing photos. Sitting Bull quit after a long tour through the United States and Canada. I don't think he made the Europe gig. Cody gave him a grey circus horse and a white sombrero. You can't make this stuff up. The American West! I wanted a Native American twist in this folk opera, so I placed Sitting Bull in that gondola in Venice.

CHORDS

Key of Am.

Verse
Am-F-E
Am-F-C-E
Am-F-C-E
Am-F-E-Am

Chorus
Am-F
Am-F

SITTING BULL IN VENICE

Look at me, brave Sitting Bull, in this gondola canoe
Bill Cody brings us smoke and meat, so what are we to do?
I came across the water, in a boat no man could row
To play a war in front of strangers, in Cody's Wild West Show

 Whoop a-ti, whoop a-ti-yi-yo

I've seen their Eiffel Tower, and the wonders of your world
Saloons where drunken white men stare at naked dancing girls
And I close my eyes and see the Bighorn Valley, harvest moons ago
The bloody hair of Custer hanging from our victory pole

 Whoop a-ti, whoop-a-ti-yi-yo

See me staring calmly from your magic photograph
In this gondola canoe—am I about to cry or laugh?
My spirit rides with Red Cloud, Black Bear and Buffalo
My dreams fly with the heron, the grey crane and the crow

 Whoop a-ti, whoop a-ti-yi-yo…

WHEN IRISH GIRLS GROW UP

"Whatever else is unsure in this stinking dunghill of a world, a mother's love is not."
       James Joyce
       A Portrait of the Artist as a Young Man

"I'm an Irish Catholic and I have a long iceberg of guilt."
       Edna O'Brien

This song is one of my favorites off *The Man from God Knows Where*. It's sung by two great singers, Dolores Keane and Iris Dement. It gave me the chills to watch them sing it together in an ancient farmhouse on the West coast of Norway—where we recorded the record. It's an Irish mother—warning her daughter of the evils of the big city. As someone educated for twelve years in Catholic schools, there's a bit of satisfaction in being able to poke fun at this devout old Catholic lady. But these are certainly my people. I wrote it with my daughters in mind, Jessica and Shannon (Quinn). I met Dolores Keane, the great Irish singer, when we were both touring with Nanci Griffith. Dolores set the tone for this song—she told me how Irish women get away with being gossips—before they lay down the gossip on somebody they ask for God's forgiveness. God forbid me gossipin', but she's a slut…etc. I put that in the second bridge.

CHORDS

Dolores and Iris sing this in the key of A. For ease, then, I would play it with capo on second fret in G positions. Fingerpicked.

Verse
G-C-G-C-D-G
G-C-G-A-D
G-C-G-C-D-G
G-C-G-C-D-G

Bridge
G-C-G
G-A-D
G-C-G-C-D-G
G-C-G-C-D-G

WHEN IRISH GIRLS GROW UP

Darlin' don't go to the city, you'll get lost there in the crowd
All the boys there in the city drink and smoke and talk too loud
And the women in the city sneak their whiskey from a cup
Oh, isn't it a pity when Irish girls grow up?

      Have you heard of Mary Gilligan? She's gone about three weeks
      She's painted up her lips, when all the color left her cheeks
      She never goes to mass no more, she gave her virtue up
      Oh, isn't it a pity when Irish girls grow up?

Have you heard about the Cooneys, the Russells, and Malloys?
Their girls all left the farm and went to chasin' city boys
Their mothers pray to Mary that their girls won't turn corrupt
Oh, isn't it a pity when Irish girls grow up?

      Oh, God forbid me sayin' it but I swear that it's all true
      The Lord should strike me dead should this beset the likes of you
      Your lips will not touch alcohol, it's tea that you shall sup
      Oh, isn't it a pity when Irish girls grow up?

Darlin' don't go to the city, you'll get lost there in the crowd…

THROWIN' HORSESHOES AT THE MOON

"Success is the ability to go from failure to failure without losing your enthusiasm..."
                                                Winston Churchill

Probably the most personal song on *The Man from God Knows Where*. It took me a long time to come to terms with my father's ghost. He was a gambler, and he pushed it all to the table limit, tried to raise the stakes, and paid the price. So did my mother. There's a more detailed account of his rise and fall in the song "Chickasaw County Jail," which tells it all from a jail cell. My father came out of Chickasaw County, Iowa, and migrated west to make his fortune. Son of a sheriff and horse trader. My old man owned gas stations, furniture stores, race horses, and Cadillacs. He played poker with Hopalong Cassidy. He kept pushing the limit higher until he found himself in jail for some sort of misappropriation of a lot of money. He was going to win it back but he never made it. I have a memory of us kids in the big Cadillac, rolling through his hometown in Iowa when he was at the top end of his high roll. I have another memory of the Cadillac being towed away when the empire crumbled. It's an American story. I have sympathy for his journey now that I have a clearer perspective gained from time.

Iris Dement sings harmony on the original version. This is also on *Veteran's day: The Tom Russell Anthology* and *Cowboy'd All to Hell*.

CHORDS

Key of Bflat. Finger picked with capo on third fret in G chord positions.

Verse
G-D-F-Em
C-G-D-C
C-G-C
Bm-Em-F-D

Chorus
D-Em-C-G
C-G-D-Em
C-G-C
Bm-Em-F-D
D-Em

THROWIN' HORSESHOES AT THE MOON

My father was a gambler, he threw horseshoes at the moon
He won a million dollars, he lost a million too
They repossessed the house, they towed the Cadillac
My daddy he just smiled and said, "One day I'll win it back."

My daddy bought that Cadillac off a Detroit motor line
Then he drove it through his hometown to prove he'd hit his prime
With hundred dollar bills in a Saint Chris money clip
And four kids staring proudly from that big ol' sinking ship

> Throwin' horseshoes at the moon, boys, it's mighty risky odds
> Sometimes you hook the Milky Way or the outstretched hands of God
> But mostly they just fall to earth in a dark and a dusty hole
> And the sound of falling horseshoes, it pulls upon the soul
>   Throwin' horseshoes at the moon

My daddy was a gambler but he had an honest heart
He never did complain when the whole thing fell apart
He just swam a sea of alcohol 'til he hit the other side
How can you be a loser if you never lose your pride?

> Throwin' horseshoes at the moon…

THE OUTCAST (REVISITED)

"Alive! Alive! Alive! Terrors of the Amazon! Deadly piranhas, able to strip the flesh from a cow in seconds and leave just the bones! The two-headed pig—a two-faced calf! Freaks of nature!"

Bally, Sounds of the Sideshow

Our carnival side show pitchman, Dave Van Ronk, who sang both versions of "The Outcast" on *The Man from God Knows Where*, here launches into a revisited gander at those people he welcomed off the boats one hundred years back in the song, "Outcast #1." Some are cooking hamburgers in the suburbs, others dying in ghettos, a few jumping off of high buildings…I always return to the idea that we as a people have lost our *blood memory*. Our connection to our tribal roots. Tradition. Songs. Where are those potato spades my great-great-grandfather brought over from Ireland? Where's that old Bible with the family history written in the front? Some of our ancestors went insane in the desolate wilds of America. Others kept going until they were like my father—standing on the western edge of the continent, trying to figure out how to turn one dollar into ten—as the carousal went round and round on the Santa Monica Pier.

CHORDS

Key of D. Carny Jazz.

Verses 1 and 4
D
G
D-Bm-F#m
Em-A-D

Verses 2, 3, 5, 6
G-D
G-D
D-Bm-F#m
Em-A-D

THE OUTCAST (REVISITED)

Gather round me people, lend an ear now if you please
This land was settled by bastards, drunks and thieves
They came to see the elephant but were driven to their knees
But greed is no disease when you're an outcast

The ones we lost in foreign wars are buried on the hill
Survivors in the suburbs, cooking meat upon a grill
Out here a man is measured up in hundred dollar bills
Cheap apartments must be filled by kins of outcasts

Some will live like monarchs, and some will ride the dole
The dead will sleep 'neath monuments or rot in unmarked holes
Give me your poor, your tired, your restless! The olde Americana soul
We dug your gold and stripped your coal and died like outcasts

The Indian, the buffalo, were slaughtered for their hides
We've created a new species from the melting pot, a tribe
Boastful, lustful, arrogant, with unsatiated pride
We rule the world, can't be denied, and we're all outcasts

But where are those potato spades you brought from Ireland?
The ghost of Patrick Russell? Ambrose Larsen, Bridget's man?
The orphans and the dreamers, those who died by their own hands?
Strike up McNamara's Band! Salute the outcasts

Have you forgotten who you are? Forgotten why you came?
The graveyards back in Templemore. Bergen town in flames
The recipe for whiskey, the family tree, the family name
Loss of memory's such a shame, you bloody outcasts
    Stand up and clap your hands, salute the outcasts

LOVE ABIDES

"Love was invented in the eleventh century by the troubadours."

Graham Greene
The Heart of the Matter

"Love Abides" ends *The Man from God Knows Where*. I sang it with Iris Dement as a duet. I wanted to end the record on a note of hope. There is so much minor key tension in this *folk opera* that I felt it had to be resolved. *Let loose*. In 1997 I moved from New York to El Paso, crossing many barren deserts—figuratively and realistically. El Paso is the final frontier, and the end of the line, right across the river from the most dangerous city in the world—*Juarez, Mexico*. I was walking down the road near my house one day and saw three crosses at an intersection. Three teenagers were killed there in a car wreck. It's an eerie place overlooking corn and cotton fields. They're angels now.

I also recorded *Love Abides* on my current record (as I write this) *Mesabi*. I was singing it solo in a studio in Tucson one afternoon and my wife remarked I should record it again, because she loved it. So I put that solo demo on the record.

CHORDS

Key of D. Capo on second fret in C chord positions. Ballad.

Verse	*Bridge*
C-F	C-F-Am
G-C	Am-F-G
C-F	G-F-G-Am
G-C	Am-F-G-C

LOVE ABIDES

Hey, look how far we've come, do we know who we are?
Stranded on a mountain top, trying to catch a falling star
Here's to what we've left behind us, here's to what we've kept inside
May the road that lies before us lead to a place where love abides

I went walkin' with my baby through the early morning frost
Saw three crosses by the roadside where three young souls were lost
She said, "They're flyin' with the angels, Jesus took 'em for a ride
High above the Rio Grande, they'll find a place where love abides"

    You may cross the barren desert, you might walk your path alone
    But a sudden storm may blind you, shake your spirit to the bone
    Seeking shelter for a weary heart, somewhere to rest, somewhere to hide
    Then somewhere down that troubled road, you find that place where love abides

Our people came across the water with their fearful, untamed hearts
Standing on a foreign shoreline, they prayed for a brand new start
Then hand in hand across the mountains, and the ragin' rivers wide
They reached the distant ocean, or found that place where love abides

    You may cross the barren desert, you might walk your path alone…

THE SAGUARO MOON
Woodcut by Tom Russell
2012

CHAPTER SEVEN
THE BORDER YEARS

TOUCH OF EVIL

> Quinlan: *There was an old lady on Main Street last night picked up a shoe…and the shoe had a foot in it. We're gonna make you pay for that…*
> Orson Welles
> *Touch of Evil*

The film *Touch of Evil* opens with a three minute pan-shot of a car crossing into the United States from Mexico. The car blows up. Drug chaos ensues. A while later Orson Welles walks into a Mexican whorehouse. The cathouse madam is played by Marlene Dietrich—her blonde hair dyed black to affect a Mexican look. Orson, a fat corrupt American cop, is jamming a chocolate bar into his mouth. Dietrich says, "Hank, you look like hell." Fade out. Fade into *my life* around the time I moved to El Paso. I stumbled right into *Touch of Evil*. My relationship went sour and I'm stuck in a cheap apartment overlooking an El Paso mall, right above a Chinese, all-you-can-eat buffet joint. Above the mall I can see the shantytowns of Juarez. Raymond Chandler meets William Burroughs. To quote Raymond Chandler, "…nobody cared whether I died or went to El Paso." The end of the line. That's the feel of this song *Touch of Evil* and the entire record *Borderland*—produced by Gurf Morlix. I think I wrote this in the Kentucky Club bar in Juarez. Back when you could cross over the bridge without stepping through a pile of bodies.

CHORDS

Key of A. Tense galloping beat. Like a team of mules dragging your head away.

Verse
A-D-A
A-D-A
A-D-A
A-D-A
D-C#m
Bm-D-E-A

Chorus
A-D-D-A
A-E-A
A-D-D-A
A-E-D-A

TOUCH OF EVIL

Last night I crossed the river, they were tearin' up Juarez Avenue
Like the movie, *Touch of Evil* I got the Orson Welles/Marlene Dietrich blues
Where Orson walks into the whorehouse, and Marlene says, "Hank, you look like hell."
And Orson's chewin' on a chocolate bar, as the lights go on in the old Blue Star Hotel
    "Read my future," says old Orson, "down inside the tea leaves of your cup."
    She says, "You ain't got no future, Hank—I believe your future's all used up."

    Why don't you touch me anymore? Why don't you touch me anymore?
    Why do you run away and hide? You know it hurts me deep inside
    Why do you close the bedroom door? This is a brutal little war
    What good is all this fightin' for? If you don't touch me, anymore...

They shot *A Touch of Evil* in a Venice, California, colonnade
And I grew up near those dead canals where they filmed the longest pan shot ever made
Now I'm thinkin' about the movie, this bar I'm in, the bridge, the Rio Grande
Now I'm dreamin' about my baby, and the borderline 'tween a woman and a man
    I was drunk as Orson Welles, that night I crawled backwards out the door
    And I was screaming, "Baby, baby, how come you don't touch me anymore?"

    Why don't you touch me anymore? Why don't you touch me anymore?...

Won't someone roll the credits now, on twenty years of love turned dark and raw?
It's not a Technicolor love film (it's a brutal document—its *film noir*!)
It's all played out on a borderline where the actors were tragically miscast
Like a Mexican burlesque show where the characters are wearing comic masks
    "It's just love and love alone," I cry to the barman in this Juarez waterhole
    As we raise a glass to Orson, and the touch of evil livin' in our souls

    Why don't you touch me anymore? Why don't you touch me anymore?

DOWN THE RIO GRANDE

"Men like to pursue an elusive woman, like a cake of wet soap in a bathtub—even men who hate baths."
Gelett Burgess
1866 to 1951

The Rio Grande river runs from the headwaters up in Colorado on down through New Mexico. It hits Texas and El Paso then turns left and becomes the border of Texas-Mexico—all the way down to the Gulf. The Mexicans call it the *Rio Bravo*—the brave river. We irrigate our pecan trees off the river and I've always enjoyed that facet of small farm life. Don Juan Oñate crossed over this river in the 1500s and celebrated the first Thanksgiving on the El Paso side. He evidently had a Spanish priest travelling with him who owned a guitar and wrote songs. The first songwriter to enter the West. I've seen herons and egrets in the water ditches and I've travelled down many times into the Big Bend, which is one of the most spectacular parts of this country. *Wild*. I wrote this song with Dave Alvin, and Dave is great at going after detail, and coloring songs with romantic passion—like the silk stocking dangling from the bedside light. Dave is also a fine poet. This song is on my record *Borderland*, and also *Veteran's Day: The Tom Russell Anthology*. Dave Alvin's version (words slightly different) appears on his record, *Ash Grove*.

CHORDS

Key of B. Capo on second fret in A chord positions. Finger picked. Wistfully.

Verse
A-G-D
A-G-D
D-A
G-A
D-A

Bridge
D-G-A
D-G-A
A-G-A

DOWN THE RIO GRANDE

Baby pulled her blue dress on and walked out in the night
Left one silk stocking danglin' from the bedside light
I sobered up and called her name just before the dawn
I followed footprints through the sand, I knew where she had gone
    Down the Rio Grande, down the Rio Grande

I pulled out of Albuquerque, must have been past eight
Four cups of coffee and I hit the interstate
Rollin' through Las Cruces, I thought I saw her car
She always said she'd go someday, she never said how far
    Down the Rio Grande, down the Rio Grande

    Maybe she's in Brownsville, she got some family there
    She always talked about the salty Gulf Coast air
    Where the river ends, down the Rio Grande

Saw an old grey heron flying south against the wind
Storm clouds over Juarez rollin' down to the Big Bend
I called her name in Esperanza's dusty desert rain
But who knows what the hell I'd say if I found her again
    On the Rio Grande, down the Rio Grande

Turned south on Highway 90, sky begin to clear
Black mountains out ahead, red sundown—rear view mirror
Haunted by her dark, wet skin movin' next to mine
I swore that things would change if I could hold her one more time
    On the Rio Grande, down the Rio Grande

    Maybe she's in Brownsville, she got some family there…

I bought a bottle in Del Rio, I pulled out off the road
Spent the night a-starin' at the lights of Mexico
I walked down to the border bridge around the break of day
I threw that empty bottle off, watched it float away
    Down the Rio Grande, down the Rio Grande

CONTINUED

Now I'm on my way to Brownsville and the Gulf of Mexico
Just like that empty bottle, I may sink or else I'll flow
To the river's end, down the Rio Grande

Baby pulled her blue dress on and walked out in the night…

Co-written with Dave Alvin

AGAVE
Woodcut by Tom Russell
2012

WHEN SINATRA PLAYED JUAREZ

"I feel sorry for people who don't drink. When they wake up in the morning, that's as good as they're going to feel all day."

Frank Sinatra

My good friend Tommy Gabriel used to tell me great stories of the 1940s and '50s in Juarez, when such luminaries as Frank Sinatra, Nat King Cole, and the Kingston Trio worked the nightclubs. Those were the golden years of the quickie divorce, when everyone from Marilyn Monroe to Zsa Zsa Gabor dissolved their marriages there in style. All it took was one overnight stay, so a Las Vegas scene grew up around it—until the Mexican government changed the laws and many American states would not recognize the divorces. Oh what a time! Bullfights, dog races, horse races—and the invention of the margarita. Tommy used to play piano over there in joints like *The Office* and the *Fiesta Club*. You can see some of these places pictured in old postcards. Most of those clubs have been torn down now during the drug wars. This one's for Uncle Tommy. This song is on the record *Borderland*.

CHORDS

Key of D. Sort of Tex-Mex feel.

Verse
D-G-D-A
D-G-A-D
D-G-D-A
D-G-A-D

Bridge
Bm-F#m-G-D-A
D-A-Bm-G-A-D

WHEN SINATRA PLAYED JUAREZ

Uncle Tommy Gabriel, he played the blue piano
While Frank and Ava Gardner danced the wild *Juarense Tango*
"Those were truly golden years," my Uncle Tommy says
"But everything's gone straight to hell since Sinatra played Juarez."

    "I wish life was still like that," Uncle Tommy says
    "But everything's gone straight to hell since Sinatra played Juarez.

"You could get a cheap divorce, get your Pontiac tuck-n-rolled
And take your Dolly to the dog track in her fake Chinchilla stole
The Fiesta Club, the Chinese Palace, the Old Kentucky Bar
The matadors and the baseball heroes and grade-B movie stars.

    "Those were truly golden years," Uncle Tommy says,
    "But everything's gone straight to hell since Sinatra played Juarez."

Now Uncle Tommy Gabriel, he still plays Fats Domino
He speaks that border *Spanglish* well, he owns a carpet store
He lives out on his pecan farm, "I don't cross the bridge," he says
"'Cause everything's gone straight to hell since Sinatra played Juarez.

    "I wish life was still like that," Uncle Tommy says
    "But everything's gone straight to hell since Sinatra played Juarez.
    Everything's gone straight to hell since Sinatra played Juarez."

WHERE THE DREAM BEGINS

> Martha: *Make me another drink…lover.*
> George: *My God, you can swill it down, can't you?*
> Edward Albee
> *Who's Afraid of Virginia Woolf?*

I was hesitant to put this song in the book. It seems to evidence a potential breakdown, while knocking at the fragile, useless door of self-pity. People like and request it, though I never plan to sing it again. One verse was written for my two daughters, in a bout of guilt about being on the road all the time when they were young. It's hard to look at now. The whole record *Borderland* bears witness to a former, doomed relationship gone to hell at the end of the road: *El Paso*. Lock up the guns. Then the lyric slips into my old favorite platitude from the Gnostic Gospel of Saint Thomas: *Everything you bring forth will save you. Everything you do not bring forth will destroy you.* True enough. The good news is (if there is any here!) the man in the song reaches a point where he's going to try to write himself out of the hole. Which is exactly what happened…the records *Borderland* and *Love and Fear* were my cathartic ventures in writing about the dark side of love and relationships. No holds barred. *Blood on the Tracks*. Raymond Carver territory. This song is on *Borderland*.

CHORDS

Key of D, capo up on 7th fret played in G chord positions. Finger picked.

Verse:
G-C-G
G-D-G
G-C-G
G-D-G

Bridge:
C-F-C
G-D-G
C-F-C
G-D-G
G-D-G

WHERE THE DREAM BEGINS

What happened to the kid in the baseball cap?
Well, he's tryin' to get home but I think he lost the map
What happened to the kid with braces on his teeth?
He had an autographed picture of Muhammad Ali

    He's just a wise-assed, buck-toothed, near-sighted fool
    Always starin' at the girls in the swimmin' pool
    Thirty years later he's starin' again
    He's searchin' for the place where the dream begins
    Searchin' for the place where the dream begins

Then he bought a bunch of records and he heard a man sing
He said, "If I could write a song, I believe I'd be a king."
But it took him twenty years until he got the nerve
He's got boxes full of papers and papers full of words

    And the words fly away like swallows on the wind
    But they never flew back to the nest again
    Never took him to the place where the dream begins

Then he finally got married and he had two little girls
But he didn't see them much 'cause he had to see the world
And the lie that he told 'em is, "I'm like most men
It's always down the road that the dream begins."

    And the girls grew up to be pretty and wise
    They said, "You could've seen the dream by lookin' in our eyes
    You were always livin' in a world of pretend
    You kept runnin' away from where the dream begins
    Runnin' away from where the dream begins."

Now he's livin' with a woman out on Borderline Road
But her love's turned bitter and her eyes turned cold
She said, "We came to the desert to let the sickness mend
But hell ain't the place where the dream begins."

CONTINUED

        Look out boy, something's gainin' on you
        He's Old Blind Joe Death in his alligator shoes
        He's got a pocketful of pills and a pint of sloe gin
        He's gonna show you to the place where the dream begins
        Follow him down where the dream begins

At the end of the road there ain't nothin' but fear
Just a big ol' room and a big ol' mirror
And the man in the mirror, his hair's turnin' grey
And his hands begin to shake in a funny kind of way

        He knows everything you bring forth will save your soul
        Everything denied will condemn you to the hole
        With his hand on his heart, he picks up his pen
        He goes searchin' for the place where the dream begins
        Lookin' for the place where the dream begins

What happened to the kid in the baseball cap?
Well, he's tryin' to get home but I think he lost the map…

CALIFORNIA SNOW

"The border means more than a customs house, a passport officer, a man with a gun. Over there everything is going to be different; life is never going to be quite the same again..."
                        Graham Greene
                        The Lawless Roads

I wish Merle Haggard would sing this. It's probably my favorite among the songs I've co-written with Dave Alvin. I imagine we wrote it in his house in California. I don't recall. There had been reports in *The Los Angeles Times* about migrants crossing over the border in Southern California, climbing into the high mountains and freezing to death up there. They had not expected the change in the weather. This has that Woody Guthrie/Merle Haggard feel, songs like "Deportees" and "Mama's Hungry Eyes." It's written through the eyes of a Border Patrol officer who's been on the job too long. This is on my record *Borderland*, and also *Veteran's Day: The Tom Russell Anthology*. Dave Alvin's version appears on his album *Black Jack David*.

CHORDS

Key of B-flat. Capo on third fret, played in G chord positions. Slow ballad.

Verse
G-C-G-C
G-C-D
G-C-G-C
G-C-D-G

Chorus
C-D-G-C
G-C-D-G

CALIFORNIA SNOW

I'm just tryin' to earn a livin'—I'm an old man at thirty-nine
My two kids and my ex-wife moved up to Riverside
I'm an agent on the border, I drive the backroads late at night
The mountains east of El Cajon, north of the Tecate line
    Where the California summer sun will burn right through your soul
    But in the winter you can freeze to death in the California snow

                                                        CONTINUED

I catch the ones I'm able to, I watch the others slip away
And some I know their faces, I might even know their names
I guess they think—that we're all movie stars and millionaires
I guess they think their dreams and hopes will all come through up here
      And I bet the weather's warmer way down in Mexico
      And no one ever warned them of the California snow

Last winter I found a man and wife, it was just about daybreak
Lyin' in a frozen ditch north of the Interstate
I wrapped them in a blanket, Lord, but she'd already died
We shipped the man on back alone, south of the borderline
      And I don't know where they came from or where they'd hope to go
      But he had carried her body all night long through the California snow

Man, the things I've seen up here make me think about my life
I might go back to Riverside and try to fix things with my wife
Or maybe I'll just get in the truck and drive as far as I can go
Away from all these ghosts that haunt the California snow
      And the California summer sun will burn right through your soul
      But in the winter you can freeze to death in the California snow

CO-WRITTEN WITH DAVE ALVIN

WHAT WORK IS

In his poem, "What Work Is," Philip Levine said something to the effect that if you're old enough to read, you know what work is. But "you may not do it."

I borrowed Phillip Levine's poem title to write a song based around three blue collar jobs I had back in the 1960s. A talking blues poem. In the summer of '63 I worked as a butter stripper at a large creamery in Los Angeles. I joined the union. It was a tough job. Butter stripping involved pulling seventy-pound boxes of one-foot-square butter cubes off of refrigerated freight train cars—you grabbed the box, ripped the top flaps open, then lifted the box by the flaps and yanked upwards so the large cube of seventy-pound butter slipped out of the box, onto a wooden pallet. You stacked the butter onto the pallets until the box car was empty. It was hell on your forearms and shoulders, and my wrists still hurt fifty years later. A violent little Mexican man working next to me used to stab wooden sticks into the butter—imagining they were a person's chest. Frankie, you see, had slight anger management problems. Those splinters weren't so good for the butter consumers either.

Then I got a job running a wood chipper in Inglewood. You throw in tree limbs and pray your sleeve doesn't catch on a branch and pull you into the sausage machine. Those chippers can chop up human bodies (murderers have employed this method—*I know*—I'm a *criminologist*.) I was working my chipper near Watts when the riots broke out. Scary times. Finally I worked as a truck driver, driving roses to the market, from Santa Barbara down to skid row in Los Angeles. I drove all night. The good news is I got to eat at *The Pantry* in Los Angeles three times a week at five in the morning. Two eggs over easy on a T-bone steak. This song is on the record, *Borderland*.

CHORDS

Key of C. Finger picked, talking blues.

Verse
C-F-C-F
C-F-C-F
Am-F-C-G
Am-F-C-G

Chorus
Am-F-Am-G
F-G-Am-C-G-(Am)

WHAT WORK IS

I used to work with a guy named Frankie Acosta
We were butter strippers down at the Challenge Creamery
Strippin' the cardboard off seventy-pound cubes of butter
Yeah, it was hot back then, summer of 1963
And Frankie, man, he'd get so angry
He'd say, "See what the women make me do."
Then he'd break off a splinter from a dirty wooden pallet
And stick it like a knife in one of them big ol' butter cubes

    That's what work is, that's what love is
    A little pleasure and a little misery
    Now every time it gets hard out here
    I think of L.A. back in 1963

Then I got a job workin' for the City of Inglewood
Running the chipper, chippin' limbs off of trees
I worked with a guy named Crazy Dave Macklin
One day he almost ran a tractor over me
We were out choppin' weeds near South Central
When the riots broke out, and the sky turned fiery red and brown
I called up my girlfriend on a payphone and said:
"Baby, I love you, but I think God's gonna finally burn Gomorrah down," and she said:

    "That's what work is, that's what love is
    You build a house of straw and the flames lick the sky."
    Now every time I fall in love out here
    I think of L.A. back in 1965

I finally got a job drivin' a rose truck
Santa Barbara midnight to L.A. Fifth and Main
All jacked up on coffee, cheap speed, and donuts
Walkin' 'round the L.A. flower market in the rain
Every morning I'd eat breakfast at *The Pantry* down on Figueroa
The waiters were always old-time ex-cons
Then we'd load the truck back up with empty rose boxes
And drive on up the coast through the California dawn

    That's what work is, that's what love is
    Two eggs over easy on a T-Bone steak
    Every time I see the sun rise on the ocean
    I think of L.A. back in 1968

That's what work is, that's what love is...

THE KID FROM SPAVINAW

"If I knew I was going to live this long, I'd have taken better care of myself."

Mickey Mantle

Here's a true American story. Mickey Mantle, New York Yankee, and the greatest switch hitter of all time. I used to treasure his baseball card when I was growing up, and I played centerfield on our little league team, just like Mickey. Hollywood could not have dreamed up Mantle's journey. He was the son of a zinc and lead miner named "Mutt" Mantle who pitched baseballs at young Mickey as soon as the child could hold a bat. The town was Spavinaw, Oklahoma. Mick was later discovered by a Yankee baseball scout in an old wooden stadium out on Route 66—*the Mother Road of America*. Mantle went up to the big leagues and replaced the retiring Joe DiMaggio in the Yankee centerfield spot. (Remember: Joe was once married to Marilyn Monroe...American dreams!) Yankee Stadium! The house that Babe Ruth built! Mantle drank and wenched his way through his career... ending up in the Betty Ford clinic later in life. I think of Mickey whenever I pass his bar on 59th street, near Central Park in New York City. I wonder if I still have that baseball card. This song is on the records *Modern Art* and *Veteran's Day: The Tom Russell Anthology*.

CHORDS

Key of C. I play it with the capo on the 5th fret in G chord positions. Finger picked.

Verse
G-C-C-G
G-C-C-G
C-D-G-C
Bm-Em-F-D

THE KID FROM SPAVINAW

I was born in Oklahoma, 1931
Outside the town of Spavinaw, where the red dust clouds the sun
And I ran beneath your diamond skies, and I drank your waves of grain
My name is Mickey Mantle, boys, and baseball is my game

My father's name was Mutt, boys, and he worked down in the mine
He pitched to me in the evening, at least a thousand times
A thousand times again, in my nightmares and my dreams
You're gonna live in the house that Ruth built, kid, gonna make that Yankee team

Sure enough, the Yankee scout came drivin', right down Route 66
He had never come to Spavinaw, Class D Ball in the sticks
But I happened to be playing in an old wood ball park, way out on the Mother Road
The Yankee scout, he signed me, and I went up to *The Show*

Strike one, that was the drinking, *Strike two*, there go the knees
Then my old man died in Denver, some type of lung disease
When God starts throwing change-ups, you can't swing with fame or wealth
If I'd known I was going to live this long, I'd taken better care of myself

I don't miss the lights of Times Square, I don't miss Toots Shor's Bar
I miss my old man pitchin' baseball, near the shed in our backyard
I wish that he were still around, to see the trophies on my shelf
If I'd have known I was going to live this long, I'd taken better care of myself

I was born in Oklahoma, 1931
Outside the town of Spavinaw, where the red dust clouds the sun…

THE BOY WHO CRIED WOLF

When the villagers saw no wolf they sternly said, "Save your frightened song for when there is really something wrong! Don't cry 'wolf' when there is no wolf!"
                                            Aesop's Fairy Tales

"Little pig, little pig, let me come in."
"No, no, not by the hair on my chinny chin chin."
"Then I'll huff, and I'll puff, and I'll blow your house down."
                                            The Three Little Pigs

The Boy Who Cried Wolf meets the *Three Little Pigs*, in this cheery little jazz song which I must have written after surviving the heartbreaks outlined in the songs on the previous record *Borderland*. We keep thinking we learn the lessons of life and love, only to find ourselves stuck in the same briar patch, because we never fully absorb the basic truths contained in old songs and nursery rhymes. Both the ancient tales referenced in this song have to do with *wolves. The Big Bad Wolf* of reality, vengeance, hatred, regret, depression...what have you? I like this song, for some odd reason, and enjoyed singing it. I would have loved to hear Sinatra do it on one of those records like *Wee Small Hours*. Or maybe Chet Baker! Andrew Hardin plays a brilliant jazz influenced guitar solo on the original, which appears on the record *Modern Art*.

CHORDS

Key of G. Finger picked ballad with a jazz attitude.

Verse
G-Am-D-G
G-Am-D-G
G7-C-D-Em
Em-Am-D-Cm-G

Chorus
G-C-D-G
G-Am-D-Cm-G

THE BOY WHO CRIED WOLF

The boy who cried wolf, he don't cry wolf any more
For one day he opened his eyes, and the wolf was at the door
And all his faithful hound dogs, couldn't chase the wolf away
The boy had cried wolf one too many times, now the real wolf came today

    Sing la la la one more time, then the fairy tale is through
    Fairy tales are funny little things, unless they're happening to you

The boy who cried love, he don't cry love anymore
The wolf of love opened up his heart, left it bleeding on the floor
And a thousand healing love songs, couldn't take the pain away
The boy did not know true love, 'till love had gone away

    Sing la la la one more time, then the fairy tale is through...

Some live in houses made of straw, some live in houses made of glass
Surrounding walls of brick and stone, they say, "I'm safe at home at last."
Then the wolf comes prowling late one night, and he blows their safe house down
Nursery rhymes go running through their mind, as they lay curled up on the ground

    Sing la la la one more time, then the fairy tale is through...

The boy who cried wolf, he don't cry wolf anymore

MUHAMMAD ALI

> *"Impossible is just a big word thrown around by small men who find it easier to live in the world they've been given than to explore the power they have to change it. Impossible is not a fact. It's an opinion."*
>
> Muhammad Ali

My grandmother was a painter. I talk about her quite a bit in my art book, *Blue Horse/Red Desert*. When I was in high school she painted pictures for me of all my sports heroes…foremost of which was Muhammad Ali. I have her painting of Muhammad (then Cassius Clay) standing over the fallen Sonny Liston. What a moment in history! I'm sure Ali was shouting, "Get up you big ugly bear." It was the beginning of his incredible career. I remember sports writers writing such hateful things about him and he turned out, in the end, to be one of the most courageous athletes who ever lived. And a kind man. I would recommend the film *When We Were Kings*, as a manifestation of Ali's character—the defeat of George Foreman (via the rope a dope) and the very moving images of Ali dancing and playing with African children that next morning. He's a big man. The most famous man in the world, they say, and a minister of peace. I have a photo of Ali and Bob Dylan in a dressing room during the Rolling Thunder tour. A pair of Americans who changed my life for the better. Far more than politicians or priests. This song is on the record *Modern Art*.

CHORDS

Key of G. I play it capo on 5th fret in D chord positions. Reggae style. Chunky.

Chorus
(Float like a butterfly…etc.)
D-Em
A-D

Verse
D-G-A-D
D-Em-A-D

MUHAMMAD ALI

    Float like a butterfly, sting like a bee,
    my name is Muhammad Ali

Down there in Louisville back in the day, a skinny little black kid name
    of Cassius Clay
I won the gold medal for the Land of the Free, refused Vietnam,
    they took my license from me

    Float like a butterfly, sting like a bee…

No Vietcong ever called me a nigger, no Sonny Liston ever called
    me a quitter
I threw the gold medal in the Mississippi River, changed my name
    to Muhammad Ali

    Float like a butterfly, sting like a bee…

I came back and fought where the fighting was fair, in the tropics of Manila,
    in the jungles of Zaire
Up against George Foreman they said I had no hope, I fooled the world
    with my *rope a dope*

No Vietcong ever called me a nigger, no George Foreman ever called
    me a quitter

    Float like a butterfly, sting like a bee, my name
    is Muhammad Ali

Now my hands may tremble and slowly I walk, I was *the Louisville lip*,
    now it's painful to talk
But all the little children know my heart is free, don't cry
    for Muhammad Ali

    Float like a butterfly, sting like a bee, my name is Muhammad Ali
    His heart is tender, his soul is free, don't cry for Muhammad Ali

RACEHORSE HAYNES

"Say you sue me because you say my dog bit you. Well, now this is my defense: My dog doesn't bite. And second, in the alternative, my dog was tied up that night. And third, I don't believe you really got bit. And fourth, I don't have a dog."
                    Richard "Racehorse" Haynes

Racehorse Haynes is a famous Texas criminal attorney known for his wild and imaginative (and successful) attempts to defend wealthy murderers. One of his most notable cases was his defense of T. Cullen Davis, a Fort Worth millionaire accused of shooting his ex-wife and killing her daughter and boyfriend. Mr. Davis was acquitted of that crime and a subsequent charge of trying to murder the judge in that case. Racehorse Haynes stories are legion around Texas courtrooms. I used to read a lot of good true crime books, like the classic *Blood and Money*, and Racehorse appears in quite a few of them. One night, at a gig called the Mucky Duck in Houston, Racehorse walked in (he's about ninety now) and said he "came to hear his song." I was a little reticent of getting sued, but after I sang it he stood up and waved his hands over his head like a boxing champion. Later I introduced him to my young wife and he looked at her, and then at me, and declared, "Son, you're in way over your head." I have his card in my wallet. If you have any legal grudge with me please see my attorney…Racehorse Haynes.

I wrote the words and Andrew Hardin wrote the music.

CHORDS

Key of Am. A John Lee Hooker type boogie.

Chorus
Am-G (F-G-Am)
Am-G (F-G-Am)

Verse
Comping on Am,
whole verse

Bridge:
(Down here in
Texas…)
F-C-E-Am
F-C-E

RACEHORSE HAYNES

    Somebody better call Racehorse Haynes
    Somebody better call Racehorse Haynes

I didn't kill nobody, never seen her before,
A man of my means and a Chinese whore?
I got a lawyer in Houston with the juice and the brains,
Let the big horse run, get me Racehorse Haynes

    Somebody better call Racehorse Haynes…

He's a thoroughbred lawyer, he ain't no hack
He's Man o' War runnin' tearin' up your fairground track
He could run on the grass or the mud when it rains
Yeah, put all of your money on Racehorse Haynes

    Somebody better call Racehorse Haynes…

        Down here in Texas, you see, money still talks
        You murder your wife, you're still gonna walk
        You blacks and Chicanos, whoa, ain't it a shame?
        You're going to Huntsville if you can't afford Haynes

    Somebody better call Racehorse Haynes…

Show me the phone, lend me a dime
I ain't rollin' over, I ain't doin' no time
Ain't coppin' no plea, I'm hip to your game
I ain't talking to no one, 'cept Racehorse Haynes

    Somebody better call Racehorse Haynes…

Co-written with Andrew Hardin

ISAAC LEWIS

> *"It was one of those hot, silent nights, when people sit at windows listening for the thunder which they know will shortly break; when they recall dismal tales of hurricanes and earthquakes...and lonely ships at sea, struck by lightning."*
>
> Charles Dickens,
> *Martin Chuzzlewit*

It was a bar in Northern Wales, *of course*, where I heard the core of this story. The bartender lady was pretty and poured a good pint of Guinness, and I liked to hang out there and listen to the old men. Well this gent comes up and says he knows my songs, then starts telling me sailing ship stories about all the famous shipwrecks which happened right outside the window where we were drinking. The story that caught my ear was one about the wreck of the sailing ship, *The Royal Charter*, and a local kid named Isaac Lewis, who drowned and washed up on shore, right near his father's door. It was a damn good story and I followed up on it and found that it was true. I even found his grave. The rest of the color and human elements I added, but I think the moral of the song is a strong one. *Tell your loved ones what they mean to you.*

This is on the records *Modern Art* and *Veteran's Day: The Tom Russell Anthology*. It's also been recorded by several Welsh groups, in the Welsh language—one of these is the artist Tich Frier.

CHORDS

Key of B flat, capo on third fret played in G Chord positions. Finger picked.

Verse	Chorus	Bridge:
G-C-G	(Sail on...)	(For every night
G-Am-D	G-C-D-G	I dreamed...)
D-G-G-C	C-Bm-Am-G	D-G-G-C
Bm-Am-D		Bm-Am-D
		D-G-C
		Bm-Am-D

ISAAC LEWIS

My name is Isaac Lewis, I'm an able-bodied man
On the ship The Royal Charter, bound for Von Damien's land
Oh, the sea that took six months to cross, we could do in two
So it's up that Mersey River, out of Liverpool we flew

And some of us were sailors, all hearties young and old
And some of us were pioneers, bound off for the gold
There were merchants and musicians, Christian soldiers of the cross
We stared into that foamy sea, saw our dreams there in the broth

    Sail on, sail on, and on, and on
    My name is Isaac Lewis, and this shall be my song

So we landed there in Botany Bay, and the boys went on the town
And I met a girl named Emma Gray, and I loved her up and down
And I swore that I'd return for her, after one more tour of sea
But I had to tell my father, what he meant to me

    For every night I dreamed a dream, as the wind swept through the sails
    That I was in my father's house, back in Northern Wales
    And I reached out for my father, and said, "I love you very much."
    But the ship rolled o'er and the dream was drowned, before we got to touch

    Sail on, sail on, and on, and on…

So I kissed the lips of Emma Gray, and set sail for Liverpool
And the parrots perched in the rigging, boys, and the dolphins swam in schools
Our trip it was a pleasant one, 'til we reached the coast of Wales
And one day out of Liverpool, God unleashed a gale

Lord, I've seen some squalls, me boys, and hurricanes at sea
And many nights I'd rediscovered Faith on bended knee
But I'd never seen it blow so hard, we anchored her at last
But the waves rolled o'er the top of us, and we had to cut the mast

                                                                                             CONTINUED

And all the mining magnates clutched their gold, believing they'd be saved
But their bloody greed destroyed them first, beneath God's angry waves
All the women and the children, lost to eternity
Ah, man has tamed and shaped the land, but he'll never tame the sea

    For every night I dreamed a dream…

    Sail on, sail on and on and on…

We were caught upon the rocks, just ten yards from the shore
And we saw men standing on those rocks, maybe three or more
And I swear I saw my father, waving at me through the squall
And I screamed that I was coming home, but that's all that I recall

For the waves they swept me overboard, with the broken mast and sails
And I drowned where as a child I'd fished, on the rocks of Northern Wales
And in three days' time I washed upon the white and sandy shore
One hundred yards from *Moelfre* and my father's white oak door

    Sail on, sail on and on and on…

And some will shout coincidence, or say this can't be true
I only say just tell your loved ones, what they mean to you
For you shall sail the seas of life, pursuing golden schemes
Yet drown so closely to your home, the cradle of your dreams

    Sail on, sail on and on and on…

        My name is Isaac Lewis and this has been my song.

GRAPEVINE

"It sounds like something from a Woody Guthrie song, but it's true; I was raised in a freight car."
                                                        Merle Haggard

The Grapevine Hill is on Highway 5 in California. It runs from a high grade on down into the great San Joaquin Valley—the breadbasket of our nation. There's a runaway truck ramp at the bottom of the grade for trucks with burnt out brakes—then you're headed for Bakersfield and the echo of that high twang from all that great music that came out of there when I was a kid. We're talking Merle Haggard, Buck Owens, Tommy Collins, Wynn Stewart, Rose Maddox, and the rest. It was music made by the sons and daughters of folks who migrated to the San Joaquin from Texas and Oklahoma—looking to escape the dust and poverty in the 1930s and '40s. This song is really, *almost*, Merle Haggard's story. John Steinbeck territory.

Dave Alvin and I produced a tribute to Merle called *Tulare Dust,* which is now out of print, but we got to work with Merle on that occasion. A *high honor.* One of Merle's ex-guitar pickers, the great Red Volkert, plays some killer guitar on this track, and Joel Guzman rips up the Tex-Mex accordion. It's one of the hottest music tracks I've had the pleasure of singing on.

This one is on my record *Hotwalker*, a largely spoken-word, concept album about the stuff I heard and read when I grew up in L.A. Kerouac, Bukowski, Lenny Bruce, Dave Van Ronk, Ramblin' Jack Elliott, Harry Partch, Edward Abbey and a few others make short cameo appearances. Also—a methamphetamine-crazed circus dwarf named Little Jack Horton narrates it all. *Tickets please.*

CHORDS

Key of C. Bakersfield country.

Verse
C-Dm-G-C
C-Dm-G-C
C7-F-G-C
C-Dm-G-C

Chorus
C7-F-G-C
C-Dm-G-C (Guitar riff: B-flat-F-C)

GRAPEVINE

Well, the dust it started blowin', 'neath the windows and the door
Blew us out of Oklahoma, in a 1940 Ford
Living rough beside the highway, on Mexicali rice and beans
The dust blew us to California, the valley of the San Joaquin

We were living in a boxcar, sleeping in our old work clothes
Friday nights down at the dance hall, we heard the Maddox Boys and Rose
My Papa picked the grapes and kept some, my Mama made that sweet blue wine
We vowed someday that we'd see Hollywood, drive back on up that old Grapevine

    We come runnin' down those canyons, that old engine how it whined
    Seems like you could see forever, from that hill they call Grapevine

Some found Jesus in the prayer tents, some drank themselves to hell
Me, I finally made old Hollywood, desk clerk in a big hotel
Where I write movies in my head all night, just like Steinbeck in my mind
I'll tell of all my Okie brothers, whose dreams fell down the old Grapevine

    Now the hands that picked the cotton, are lost to tractors and combines
    Left our souls out in the orchards, down below the old Grapevine

WOODROW

"Woody was just a weird guy. Most people couldn't get along with him...except for fans of his songs."
Ramblin' Jack Elliott

"Left wing, chicken wing, it don't make no difference to me."
Woody Guthrie

Ramblin' Jack Elliott told me that Woody Guthrie was probably responsible for three of Jack's marriages breaking up. Woody, it seems, had some bad habits and taught them to Jack. Jack says all his ex-wives mentioned Woody in their divorce briefs. I used to buy Woody's books from The Ash Grove in Los Angeles when I was a kid. The Woody I remember from his books seemed to be a wild-assed artist given to great bursts of raw poetry, and gritty biographical sketches, and pencil drawings of naked women. I heard he was busted once for sending obscene letters through the mail. Woody never grew up, and at the shake of a stick he was out the door and down the road. *Human*, for sure. This doesn't fit with the saintly folk-radical image now painted of him. I think in this song I was trying to get at that fractured view of a man—the accepted image folkies paint—verses the reality of an unrepentant outsider artist. This song is on the record, *Hotwalker*.

CHORDS

Key of C. Capo on 5th fret played in G positions. Fingerpicked.

Verse
G-C
G-Em
C-G-C-D
Em-Bm-C-D-G

Chorus
G-Em-Bm
C-G-C-D-G

WOODROW

When people twist your words, Woodrow, ah, they'll twist at every whim
It's thugs that run the unions now and use your songs like hymns
Once your music danced on women's thighs and the arch of a hobo's brow
Aw, Mrs. Guthrie, look what they done to your brown-eyed baby now

Oh, the trains leave every morning, some go east and some go west
And the clacking of the iron is the sound you love the best
It's the great escape from railroad bulls and the Coney Island girls
Aw, Mrs. Guthrie, look what we done to your brown-eyed boy with curls

    Sing the truth, sing it loud
    Aw, Mrs. Guthrie, look what they done to your brown-eyed baby now

All those boxcars full of Chinese junk, the caboose has been junk piled
And we're all buying groceries now from men with crooked smiles
You were a drunken, wild misogyny-eer and your politics were crude
As you sat home writing nursery rhymes and drawing women nude

And all those politicians' breaths stink bad, be they left or be they right
And the ones who play with rhetoric are not the ones who fight
Don't go coming 'round here, Woodrow, they'll stretch you from a rope
And your corpse won't ever find a bar where a man can drink and smoke

    Sing the truth, sing it loud...

Did you hear the screen door slam, Ma? Woodrow's gone again
He's writin' obscene letters now, the Feds might bring him in
But every song he ever wrote is hangin' on the breeze
With the laundry in the Guthrie yard full of Huntington's disease

So, Woodrow, rest in peace, old pal, there ain't nothin' for you here
We're in the scrub oak country, the land of dread and fear
And whitey's in the wood pile and the writing's on the wall
But your ring of truth still echoes down the Greystone Clinic halls

    Sing the truth, scream it loud

So here's to all outsiders, all the ones who don't fit in
The troubadour, the prisoners, the drunken Indian
Ah, the circus freaks, the wounded lovers, we'll make it through somehow
Ah, Mrs. Guthrie, we are ridin' blind with your brown-eyed baby now

    Sing the truth, scream it loud…

THE PUGILIST AT FIFTY-NINE

He went into AA. Went to a gym and started boxing.
He left his girlfriend and got a room.
Slept on the floor and quit talking,
His sister asked why he quit talking.
He said when he was sober he didn't know nothing.
Nothing at all.

Willy Vlautin
"The Pull"

After the love trials and tribulations played out in records like *Borderland,* I think I decided to stand my ground, like an old pugilist, and take a harder look at love and relationships. I remember one freezing night in El Paso when I was staring out at the lights of town, five miles away. I was cold and sober and in between relationships. I called my oldest daughter and said, "I can't survive another winter like this. I need to do one of three things: start drinking, get a girlfriend, or buy a good wood stove." She said, "Dad—buy a wood stove." Archie Moore, the wise *old Mongoose* boxer, is referenced in here as well as *The Sweet Science*, the great boxing stories by A. J. Liebling. I don't know why I kept returning to the boxing metaphor—but it works when you're trying to learn to dance like Muhammad Ali for all fifteen rounds. I dedicate this song, now, to the great boxing writer and friend—the late George Kimball. This one is on the records *Love and Fear* and *Veteran's Day: The Tom Russell Anthology*.

CHORDS

Key of G. Rock and roll.

Verse	*Chorus*
G	Am
G	G
G-C-G	Am-C
F-C-G	D

THE PUGILIST AT FIFTY-NINE

Rolled out of bed, threw some water on my face
Twenty-five sit ups, then I run in place
I put the coffee on, but the pot ain't clean
Oh you little devils of alcohol and caffeine

A handful of vitamins, dropped 'em on the floor
My ex-girlfriends are laughin' from the icebox door
I put their photos up there, yeah, we talk all the time
But they ain't talkin' back now the pugilist is fifty-nine

Cold chicken salad, a glass of iced tea
Phone bills, gas bills, electricity
And the mortgage and the junk mail, one old Father's Day card
Yeah, go sweat it out kid, it's 108 in the yard

Water the lawn, trim them old trees
Pray that your gut don't fall down to your knees
Then Archie Moore whispers in your ear, "Get up, kid, you're still in your prime."
No, no, the champ's on the ropes, Arch, the pugilist is fifty-nine

    And the rock and the roll, and the fight for your soul,
    Goes on and on,
    You put on the gloves, you're always ready for love,
    Pray your passion ain't used up, burnt out and gone

The harder we love the harder we fall,
Its cauliflower hearts and old medicine balls
And backstreet affairs in all the water tank towns
Where there's a mighty thin line between a heavyweight champ and a used up old clown

But this is Hollywood, kid, fear strikes out
Miracles turn around one-sided bouts
Get off the floor, kid, the sweet science of them old romantic lines
Hey, the champ's coming back, boys, the pugilist is fifty-nine

    And the rock and the roll...

Rolled out of bed, water on your face...

BEAUTIFUL TROUBLE

> *"I feel as if I've come to a place...where a little harmless dreaming and then some sleepy, early-morning talk has led me into considerations of death and annihilation."*
> Raymond Carver
> "Where I'm Calling From"

This song was written during a savage little interlude when I broke up with somebody—then met my wife in a honky-tonk in Switzerland. She saved my life, but I was still at that stage where everything up to that point had blown up in my face, so I was looking over my shoulder...but, hell, that's why God invented novels and soap operas and Raymond Carver stories. To wallow in the drama of Shakespearean love angst. I was at the point of wondering whether the car was going to fly off the road again. But I was *game*. It all worked out.

This song appears on *Love and Fear*.

CHORDS

Key of G—sort of Leonard Cohen-esque—spoken.

Verse
G-Em
G-Em
G-Em
G-Em

Chorus
D-Em
D-Em
F-C-G (Em)

BEAUTIFUL TROUBLE

You go out on the road 'til your clothes don't fit,
Champion Jack Dupree used to speak about it
Old dressing rooms lined with the smoke and the blood and the spit
     Of trouble, beautiful trouble

You stand up on your head on the vaudeville stage,
You fall in love with ladies half your age
Other women point their finger, sour with the rage
     You're gonna find trouble

Then you're spinnin' and you're tumblin' you've taken it too deep
The soft hair on the back of her neck, the fire in her cheek
Her breasts, her eyes, her thighs, the quirky way she speaks
     You found trouble, beautiful trouble

  You scratch the surface at your own peril,
  Now you're starin' down a double barrel
  Trouble finds its very own level,
  Of trouble, beautiful trouble

The lights go out, the steering wheel won't steer
Ninety miles an hour down the alleyways of love and fear
The brakes are gone and you've stripped the gears
With trouble, beautiful trouble

You wake up face down in the bottom of a ditch
She screams, "What are your intentions toward me you rotten son of a bitch?"
You wonder who and how and why and whether and which
Forms of trouble, you are in trouble

    Just when you thought you had a take on her
    The mask fell off, real people emerge
    Welcome to the night of the living, loving world
    Of trouble, beautiful trouble

CONTINUED

So if you see me out on your street tonight
Better close up your curtains, better shut out the lights
I'm a runaway kid with a savage appetite
For trouble, beautiful trouble

I'm just looking for that gin joint right up your road
Where if you look at somebody cross-eyed, the place might explode
You flirt with the wrong set of dark eyes, you've taken on a load
Of trouble, beautiful trouble

I'm just looking for that little yellow haired girl
Like Sterling Hayden in a beat up film noir world
I'm staggering toward the end of the world
Of trouble, beautiful trouble

    I scratch the surface at my own peril…

FOUR CHAMBERED HEART

"I'm for decency—period. I'm for anything and everything that bodes love and consideration for my fellow man. But when lip service to some mysterious deity permits bestiality on Wednesday and absolution on Sunday—cash me out."
  Frank Sinatra
  Playboy
  February, 1962

Tom takes heavy rap-boogie aim at everything—family dysfunction (yawn), anger management, forgiveness, *The Gnostic Gospel*, *The Four Agreements*, the Catholic Church etc. Hail to Lenny Bruce!

It's all wrapped up in my discovery that crocodiles and alligators have four chambered hearts. Hence the metaphor. Go figure. Christ said, "My kingdom is not of this world," but hell, here comes religion and all the insane tribal-religious wars that religion engenders. I had twelve years of Catholic education (*untouched* was I, folks) and a great Jesuit formal education to boot—but the current Catholic Church handling of child abuse is beyond shameful. Jesus Christ is rolling his eyes so much now he'll need eyeglasses and heavy doses of valium to look down on the scene…and Saint Peter can't wait to pass judgment on fifty thousand pedophile priests….But I digress. This song is on *Love and Fear,* and there's been a few interesting films put up about it on YouTube. And you can dance to it. Gurf Morlix plays the boogie guitar.

CHORDS

Boogie in the key of A. Think John Lee Hooker.

Verse	*Chorus*
Mostly hammering on A chords, with the guitar riff: A-G-D	D
	A
	D
	E
	D-A
	G-A. G-A

FOUR CHAMBERED HEART

We break and train our children just like animals
We fill 'em up with parasites and poison dreams of fear
We hand them false Gods on a golden platter
Then remind them to wash behind their ears
We gave up our own dreams so the kid could go to college
Then they grow up and resent us, accuse us with impossible psychological crimes
The normal relationship in hell is about getting even
But you won't find that in your Sunday *New York Times*

Anger, sadness, hatred, envy, these are just fear wearing the same old cheap mask
You're doomed if you don't live forgiveness, sister
We're all driving around lost, we don't know who to ask
We're all stopping at abandoned gas stations to ask directions
There's no more road maps to tell us who the hell we are
Raised on TV commercials and organized religion
Following corrupt wise men who've been navigating by the wrong star

> When a man and a woman couple up
> There's really four people talking
> Hidden people, outer images
> Where you gonna start?
> So two people in love are like one big old crocodile
> And crocodiles have four chambered hearts...

Now they tell me there's some guy down in Dallas named Oly
He's running some type of early Christian community down there, I'm told
Well, the Gnostic says *everything you bring forth will save you*
Everything you don't bring forth will shatter your mortal soul
Christ said, "My kingdom is not of this world."
But hell, they went and built their earthly kingdoms anyway
Then they paid out millions of dollars to defend pedophile priests
Meanwhile, people are living in the gutter holding signs, "Have you hugged your kid today?"

We reach the end of the road and find out no one else can make us happy
We've waged all the wars of drama and control
We've sacrificed it all for wives, husbands, money, children, false religion
That old line about gaining the world but losing your soul
So it's always back to living with yourself or whoever it is living in your body
Grandpa said, "Don't put the horse before the cart."
Me, I'm just an old alligator swimming through dark, uncharted waters
And alligators have four chambered hearts

    When a man and woman couple up...

STEALING ELECTRICITY

"You don't want to love—your eternal and abnormal craving is to be loved. You aren't positive, you're negative. You absorb, absorb, as if you must fill yourself up with love, because you've got a shortage somewhere."
  D. H. Lawrence
  Sons and Lovers

It seems like every few months along this border, there's a gruesome photo in the Juarez newspaper of a charred corpse hanging from a power line. A poor person was trying to tap into the electric lines and got zapped. Naturally I'd employ that image as a metaphor for love gone bad. You don't mess with high voltage situations. You have to pay the tab. I must have still been shivering from several bad love deals when I wrote this. I sang it on Letterman a few years back. I think some people are a bit shocked when they realize the twist to this one—but, hell, when you're living on the frontier, next to the most dangerous city in the world, you take what metaphors you're given. This is on the records *Love and Fear* and *Veteran's Day: The Tom Russell Anthology*. The great American poet Lawrence Ferlinghetti also recorded this, as a spoken word piece—it appears on *Wounded Heart of America*.

CHORDS

Key of E. Capo on 2nd fret, across first five strings—played in D chord positions.

Verse
D-Bm
G-D
D-A
Em-D

Chorus
G-D
A-D
G-F#m
Em-D
G-D (back and forth)

STEALING ELECTRICITY

There's a Mexican dead on a power line
He's deader than yesterday's communion wine
He was trying to get something he couldn't afford for free
Just a poor man stealing electricity
His heart went da da da…da da

    Ten thousand volts and now he's gone
    Hangin' on a cross high above Babylon
    Hey baby, ain't that just like you and me?
    Love is like stealing electricity
    Two hearts go da da da…

When the poverty of your spirit and the weakness of your flesh
Go dancing every night through other people's trash
You don't love yourself, woman, what the hell you doin' with me?
You're gonna burn baby, burn, from stealing electricity
Two hearts go da da da…

    We climb so high in search of a kindred soul
    'Till we grab hold of a live wire up on a high line pole
    The laws of nature say you get nothing for free
    And love is like stealing electricity
    Two hearts go da da da…

There's a Mexican dead on a power line…

THE SOUND OF ONE HEART BREAKING

"I could hear my heart beating. I could hear everyone's heart. I could hear the human noise we sat there making, not one of us moving, not even when the room went dark."
    Raymond Carver
    What We Talk About When
    We Talk About Love

I wrote this song with Sylvia Tyson, the great Canadian songwriter. I believe she spoke about seeing a fat man in an overcoat singing a brokenhearted song to himself—as he walked alone down an empty street. Maybe he was singing opera? The song title, of course, plays off the old Zen koan: *What is the sound of one hand clapping? Hell if I know. If a tree falls in the forest does anybody hear it?* That sort of thing. But now I hear the song again, after so many years, it's become one of my favorites. Simple yet complex in its tone and message. The *wounded heart like a broken bell.* The voice changing. I learned a lot writing with Sylvia. She has the ability to bring her deep knowledge of literature and folklore to the table and then wrap it all up in a simple, beautiful melody. It's very hard to broach new territory when creating love songs. This one is on my record *Love and Fear*, and on Sylvia Tyson's album *Gypsy Cadillac*.

CHORDS

Key of C. Capo on 5th fret in G positions. Finger picked.

Verse
G-Am
D-Em-D
G-Am
D-G

Chorus
C-Em7-Am-G
C-Em7-Am-G
Am-C
C-Em7-Am-G
C-Em7-Am-G
Am-D
Am-D-G

THE SOUND OF ONE HEART BREAKING

There's a fat man in an overcoat,
Singin' as if his heart is broke
He sings like an angel in an overcoat,
On a street where nobody hears

    He said, "A wounded heart's like a broken bell,
    Keeps on beatin', anyone can tell
    It's not the same, the voice has changed
    Like the wind through the leaves on an empty street,
    That's the sigh of a heart when it skips a beat
    You can almost hear it aching,
    That's the sound of one heart breaking."

They say true love's hard to find,
Bad love's hard to leave behind
No love at all is the hardest kind,
When you feel so weary of life

    For a wounded heart's like a broken bell…

There's a fat man in an overcoat
Singin' as if his heart is broke
He sings like an angel in an overcoat
On a street where nobody hears

    He says a wounded heart's like a broken bell…

Co-written with Sylvia Tyson

ASH WEDNESDAY

"When one burns one's bridges, what a very nice fire it makes."

Dylan Thomas

Once again I plumb the depths of twelve years of Catholic education to fish up a metaphor for heartbreak and spirit destruction. I recall getting those ashes on our foreheads on Ash Wednesday, the day lent begins. A moveable feast. Then we had to give up something until Easter came: Candy, desserts, or foul language. If you were older, you gave up drinking for lent and your teeth began to grind when happy hour approached. Those ashes represent mortality (*ashes to ashes, dust to dust*), repentance, and humility. In El Paso, near our hacienda, there's a mountain called Cristo Rey, with a statue of Jesus on top. Jesus looks down on Rosa's Cantina. The drunkards look up. The penitents crawl on their knees, five miles up that hill—ah, the things we do for love and forgiveness! Gretchen Peters sings this as a duet with me on the records *Love and Fear,* and *Veteran's Day: The Tom Russell Anthology.*

CHORDS

Key of D. Capo on 2nd fret played in C chord positions. Rock ballad.

Verse	*Chorus*	*Bridge*
C-F	C-G	Am-Em
C-G	C-F	Dm
C-F	C-G	F-G
C-G	C-F	
F-G-C	C-G	
	C-F	
	Am-G	
	F	

ASH WEDNESDAY

There once was a man who thought love was war
Hey, stop me if you've heard the story before
He's got a purple heart, but who's keeping score?
There's a lot of purple hearts in the purple heart store
He was a commandant, now he's a penitent, on Ash Wednesday

There once was a woman, a pretty young thing
She sold her soul for a diamond ring
She read about love in a magazine,
Saw it every Friday night on the movie screen
She was a debutante, now she's a penitent, on Ash Wednesday

    They're both love sick, they're love tired
    They strayed a little close to the edge of the fire
    Their hands got burned and their eyebrows singed
    They're walking down the streets of oblivion
    They got holes in their pockets, holes in their minds
    They're holy people in an unholy time
    Headin' for the church at the end of the line
    Ash Wednesday

        See them hangin' out in every lonely place
        They tell you love can't hurt them now
        But they've got ashes on their face

We're all love sick, we're love tired…

IT GOES AWAY

"Oh, you weak, beautiful people who give up with such grace. What you need is someone to take hold of you—gently, with love, and hand your life back to you."
                                                        Tennessee Williams

When I was a kid in Catholic first grade we had to deal with the terror of the nuns and their constant threats that the communists were going to arrive, torture us, and try to make us give up our religion. Yikes. And then there was that bomb that was gonna drop on us. When I said my prayers at night, I rattled off: *God bless, mommy and daddy, and I hope the bomb won't drop.* We did bomb drills where we had to hide under our desks. I guess we should have been hiding under there from the priests, too. But I made it out alive. Only to be confronted by love and sex and our unpreparedness for it all. The nuns never told us anything about that. So we were hit—*head on*. Years later—about forty years later to be exact—an Irish lady who ran a B & B in Kilkenny sat in the kitchen with me one morning, over a pot of strong tea, and laid out all the facts of love life that I'd missed. I'd just gone through a rough break up. "Now Tom," she said, "a woman's got an on-and-off switch. When it's off, it's off. For *good*, usually. And it's not about *you* anyway. Don't take it personal. It's about *her*. Get on with your life…it goes away." Welcome to first grade. Better late than never.

CHORDS

Key of B flat. Capo on 3rd fret. G chord positions. Sort of reggae feel.

Verse	*Chorus*
G-C-Em	G-Bm
C-G-D	C-Em
G-C-Em	C
C-G	C-G-D

IT GOES AWAY

A young boy scrapes his knee, or he falls out of a tree
And his momma hears his screams from far away
She runs to dry his eyes, she says, "It's okay to cry
'Cause everything that hurts will go away

    It goes away, it might take years
    Or a hundred thousand tears
    But one day the sky will clear
    It goes away

The boy just turned sixteen, ah, he's bashful, lives in dreams
And his heart breaks when the girls go by his way
He's chokin' deep inside, from swallowin' false pride
'Til he remembers that old prayer, *it goes away*

    It goes away, it might take years…

The older that we grow, the less we seem to know
But we still recite the old prayers every day
How we hope the bomb won't drop, yeah, and all the wars will stop
And when our heart breaks, that the pain will go away

    It goes away, it might take years…

OLD HEART

"I'm for whatever gets you through the night."
Frank Sinatra

"Old Heart" was written during a particular loveless season when I'd quit drinking for a year and spent a lot of time reading Don Miguel Ruiz's, *The Mastery of Love*. The song strikes me now as a cross between Sinatra's version of "A Very Good Year," and a fine old Ralph McTell song, "The Grand Affair." The jazz chordal changes add to the nostalgic vibe. I have this dream of one day doing a cabaret sit-down gig in a grand old New York hotel. A pianist and a jazz guitar player behind me. Maybe a saxophone. Singing songs like this and "The Dutchman," by Michael Smith, and Piaf songs and Leonard Cohen and old Broadway gems. And, of course, Sondheim's masterpiece, "Send in the Clowns." I really dig a singer named Karen Akers who does a great version of that. This one's dedicated to Carey of the Acoustic Music series in San Diego. He loves the song. It appears on the record *Love and Fear*. Barry Walsh plays some cool jazz piano.

CHORDS

Key of A. Capo on 2nd fret in G chord positions. Jazz/cabaret mood.

Verse
G- F6
Am/maj 7- Cm
G-E
Am/maj 7- D

Chorus
C-Bm
Am/maj 7-C-D
Cmaj7-Bm
Am/maj7-F-Em7

OLD HEART

Old heart get out of bed, time to face another day
Don't lie there feelin' sorry for old debts you'll never pay
Shake the poison from your clothes, put some polish on those shoes
Old heart you've survived worse than this, all those yellows, greens, and blues

Your body drank its fill, the well has been used up
But love's an endless banquet, in love go fill your cup
Yeah, go out and fill your cup, boy, and drink until you're blind
Or drink until you see the light, it's eternity this time

> Let the big heart rage 'n' run, love is wasted on the young
> We'll dance with those with whom we come, or else we'll walk away
> Yeah, we'll turn and walk away from them, and a new dream will begin and then
> We'll master love, we'll not pretend, old heart get out of bed

All the cities of this world, all those nights in strange hotels
All the walks along the shoreline, moonlight on oyster shells
The sadness, the parting, the aching in the eyes
Go and throw those wounded memories, off a healing bridge of sighs

> Let the big heart rage 'n' run, love is wasted on the young…

THE DEATH OF JIMMY MARTIN

"People wonders why country music is a-dropping and the reason is it's not coming from the heart...I sing with feeling and give it all I've got...If I don't got that, I don't got nothing."
Jimmy Martin
Interviewed by Silvie Simmons

I read Tom Piazza's great article, "A Night with Jimmy Martin," that later became the book, *True Adventures with the King of Bluegrass*. Jimmy was a throwback to the days when people sang the living piss out of every verse of every country and bluegrass song—and *meant* it. It seems now that much of bluegrass music is pristine and flawless guitar and banjo picking, and stacked, perfect harmonies and wonderful melodies—but where in hell is the soul of the music? Listen to Jimmy rip it up. He also, in this book, walks backstage at The Opry, drunk and looking for trouble. And he finds it. The Opry never allowed Jimmy to be a member. Well, they kicked Hank Williams off too. The boys were blunt, honest, real. Occasionally prone to lift the bottle. But, hell, that's country, ain't it? Like his beloved hound dogs, Jimmy seem to be able to sniff out all that is phony in modern country music. And he never shut up about it. (*Pete*, referenced in this song, was one of Jimmy's hounds. *20/20 Vision* was one of his hit songs.)

I sang on the Opry once—with Kinky Freidman and his Texas Jewboys...I snuck on stage and joined them on "Amazing Grace" during the gospel hour. But that, friends, is another story. This Jimmy Martin song appears on the records *Wounded Heart of America* and *Veteran's Day: The Tom Russell Anthology*.

CHORDS

Key of D. Capo on 2nd fret played in C chord positions. Raging bluegrass.

Verse
C-F-C
C-G-C
C-F-C
C-G-C
Am-F
C-G
C-F-C
F-C
C-G-C

Chorus
G-F
C-G
Am-F
C-F-C
C-G-C

THE DEATH OF JIMMY MARTIN

There's a hound dog runnin' all alone through the piney woods
Lord, his howlin' tears the soul out of me
There's a jay bird calling out a funeral dirge
In ancient harmony
Barbary Allen rolled over in her grave all morning
With roses growing out of her head
Hey, God's gonna burn down Nashville, boys
'cause Jimmy Martin's dead
Ah, the great Jimmy Martin's gone dead

You got 20/20 vision but you're walkin' round blind
You Grand Ole Opry fools
With your hypocritic judgments and your self-righteous snobbery
And your goddamned false hearted rules
You scorned Hank Williams, you shunned Jimmy Martin
Boys who sang with tongues of fire
So God's gonna burn down your Grand Ole Opry
Hear the screams of the hypocrites and liars
They feel safer now that Jimmy Martin has expired

> Yeah, run Pete, run, your master's callin' you
> He's waiting on up ahead
> Don't look back, Pete, Nashville's burnin' down
> 'Cause Jimmy Martin's dead
> Ah, the great Jimmy Martin's gone dead

Yeah, don't call me no country singer
These are poisoned words to me
'Cause I ain't heard a good country song, since 1973
Ah, the King of Bluegrass has died for your sins
The Whore of Babylon is sleepin' in your bed
So God's gonna burn down Nashville, boys
'Cause Jimmy Martin's dead
Yeah, the great Jimmy Martin's gone dead

> Yeah, run Pete, run, your master's callin' you…

GUADALUPE
Woodcut by Tom Russell
2012

CHAPTER EIGHT

BLOOD AND CANDLE SMOKE / MESABI

EAST OF WOODSTOCK, WEST OF VIET NAM

"So one always starts a journey in a strange land—taking too many precautions, until one tires of the exertion and abandons care in the worst spot of all."
                                Graham Greene
                                The Lawless Roads

A few days after the United States landed a man on the moon, 1969, I was in a cinema in West Africa, during the Biafran War, watching a newsreel of the landing. The audience was jumping up and down on their seats, laughing at the funny little spaceship. Drunken, hysterical Nigerians. Screaming and swilling beer. They thought the landing was all a hoax. I agreed with them. It looked like a cartoon. I was probably drunk too. I was over there to teach criminology for a year. That season I didn't go to the Woodstock Festival. I didn't go to Viet Nam. I went to Nigeria during the Biafran War—I grew up. I met a woman named Suzanne Wenger who was a white priestess of the Yoruba cult—I'm still transfixed by her visions of art. I drank beer laced with Sprite (the English call this a *shandy*), a fine drink when you're roasting to death in the tropics. I discovered Graham Greene—from moldy old Penguin paperbacks found in a bookstore basement. I learned to carve wood from a Yoruba artist in the market place. I got dysentery. I played my guitar. I decided to leave academia behind.

This song was recorded with the band Calexico in Tucson. I sang it on the Letterman show the night David announced he was being blackmailed. Strange. This appears on *Blood and Candle Smoke*.

CHORDS

Key of E. Capo on 2nd fret over first five strings. Played in D chord positions.

Verse	*Chorus*
D-G	D-G-D
D-D-A	D-D-D-A
D-G	D-G
D-A-D	D-A-D

EAST OF WOODSTOCK, WEST OF VIET NAM

I slept through the 1960s, I heard Dory Previn say
Me I caught me the great white bird, to the shores of Africay
Where I lost my adolescent heart, to the sound of a talking drum
East of Woodstock, West of Viet Nam

On the roads outside Oshogbo, I fell down on my knees
There were female spirits in old mud huts, iron bells ringing up in the trees
And an eighty-year-old white priestess, who made juju all night long
East of Woodstock, West of Viet Nam

> Raise high the roof beams, carpenter boy, we're comin' through the rye
> In the cinema I watched the man on the moon, I laughed so hard I cried
> And it was somewhere in those rainy seasons, that I learned to carve my song
> East of Woodstock, West of Viet Nam

Africa, Mother Africa, you lay so heavy on my breath
You old cradle of civilization, *Heart of Darkness*, blood and death
But we had to flee you runnin' scared, when the crocodile ate the sun
East of Woodstock, West of Viet Nam

I think it's gonna rain tonight, I can smell it comin' off the sage
As I sit here readin' ole Graham Greene, I taste Africa on every page
And then I close my eyes and see those red clay roads at sundown and boys I'm gone
East of Woodstock, West of Viet Nam

> Raise high the roof beams, carpenter boy…

SANTA ANA WIND

"... a harsher California...devastated by the hot dry Santa Ana wind that comes down through the passes at 100 miles an hour and whines through the Eucalyptus windbreaks and works on the nerves..."

                Joan Didion
                "Some Dreamers of the
                Golden Dream"

It was Joan Didion's fine essay, noted above, which inspired this song. This is a story from her collection *Slouching Towards Bethlehem*. The essay tells of a murder in California—a classic piece of true crime writing from a master. The Santa Ana wind blows from the Mojave to the ocean—an ill, dry wind that leaves forest fires and madness in its wake. I was born in Los Angeles, so I'm entitled to lay out this dark rhyme on Armageddon in The Promised Land. This is on *Blood and Candle Smoke,* and I'm backed up by Calexico.

CHORDS

Key of G# (or A flat)—Capo on first fret played in G positions. Galloping.

Verse
G-C-G
G-D
G-C-D-G
G-D-G

Chorus
D-Em
A-D
C
G-C
Em-C
G-D-G

SANTA ANA WIND

When these old adobe walls turn to dust and then they fall
And the creatures of the night call out your name
Mother Nature, she'll grab hold of everything that we've let go
Here comes an ill-intentioned wind that knows your name

Out in the desert night it builds, behind those Gila Monster hills
A wisp of dust, then a whisper, then a curse
Soon it's ninety miles an hour, past El Centro water towers
Look out, El Cajon, you'll be the first

    When those Santa Ana winds begin to blow
    From Death Valley to the wide Pacific shore
    Won't be no saints come marchin' in
    No movie stars or clergy men
    Where will you run when that wind knocks at your door?
    When that Santa Ana wind begins to roar

California, my home state, cars of people sit and wait
They know what's coming, they can feel it in their bones
All that real estate and pride, all those Indians that died,
While those Spanish priests danced the drunk fandango

The troubadours invented love, a thousand years before the flood
They rode from town to town singing up the mystery
Well, the wind sings its own song, moving patiently along
Burning down the lies of western history

NINA SIMONE—THE RAVEN
Woodcut by Tom Russell
2012

NINA SIMONE

"Jazz is a white term to define black people. My music is black classical music."
                                                    Nina Simone

I was in a bookstore in San Cristobal de las Casas, in the Yucatan of Mexico. The American who owned the little store was playing an LP of Nina Simone singing Dylan's "Just Like a Woman." Or it might have been her version of "Just Like Tom Thumb's Blues."

I was transfixed. I realized she could sing *anything*. Great art defies categories. Great songs. Great singers. The bottom line. I notice no critic ever dropped the foppish, ridiculous term *Americana* on Nina's music—or Dylan's or Leonard Cohen's. It's above and beyond that. Categories are trashbins for rack jobbers. I wrote this in two different dressing rooms: Kansas City and London. It's on the record *Blood and Candle Smoke,* and I'm backed up by Calexico, Nick Luka, Gretchen Peters, and Barry Walsh.

CHORDS

Key of B. Capo on fourth fret in G chord positions. Mexican waltz.

Verse
G-D-G
G-D-G
G-C-Bm
Bm-Am-D

Chorus
D-C
C-Bm
Bm-Am-D-G

NINA SIMONE

The trains used to run, all across Mexico
Way down through the Yucatan, wherever in hell, ya know?
It was down in San Cristobal, that I first heard the sound
Nina's voice on the jukebox, spinning darkly around

    And I was so lost down there,
    Out of love and walking alone
    But walking beside me, was Nina Simone

Tonight in my dressing room, the tea kettle rattles
Water pipes are dripping down, on a plate of Spanish apples
Outside in the freight yards, trains they rattle and moan
It's just Hank Williams talking to Nina Simone

    Yeah we've been to hell and back,
    Where love cut us right down to the bone
    But walking beside us, was Nina Simone

I've driven your highways and back roads—I rode your Grey Dog
Through the snow and sleet and hail, through the sunlight and fog,
I've heard the ravens call morning up, with their little raw saxophones
But the darkest of ravens was Nina Simone

FINDING YOU

"Finding You" is a simple love song. One of my favorites. I met my wife in that Swiss honky-tonk. About eight years ago, as I write this. We were engaged in Venice, Italy a few years later. My wife is a psychologist who's certainly helped me keep mind, body, and spirit fit. She saved my life at a time when I'd all but given up on love. This one's for her. I also got *the blessing of the shoeshine boys* into the song, somehow, and a nod toward the troubadours, like Ian Tyson, who've taught me so much about the minstrel trade.

CHORDS

Key of open D. (The low E string is tuned down to D.)

Verse
D
D-D7
G
D

Chorus
G-D
D-A
D-G
Bm-A
G-D

FINDING YOU

They are blessing the animals, in the old Cathedral square
Tonight they'll bless the shoeshine boys, and baby I'll be there
For I need all the blessings to keep this heart at home
To remember all the troubled nights when I slept alone

    'Til I found you—and now I'm blessed and I am pleased
    When no one else is looking I will fall down on my knees
    And I will pray to any God who keeps the light on late at night
    For the miracle of miracles, the one that changed my life
        Finding You, Finding You…

So blessed are the shoeshine boys, for they'll inherit the earth
Blessed are those who sleep alone, may then find what love is worth
And blessed are the troubadours who handed me the feather
Who taught me how to write the songs that brought us both together

    I found you….

CRIMINOLOGY

"If I know a song of Africa, of the giraffe and the African new moon lying on her back, of the plows in the fields and the sweaty faces of the coffee pickers, does Africa know a song of me?"
                        Isak Dinesen [Karen Blixen]
                        Out of Africa

"I have loved no part of the world like this and I have loved no women as I love you. You're my human Africa."
                        Graham Greene
                        The End of the Affair

I have a master's degree in Criminology—never much mentioned it until I wrote about it in songs on *Blood and Candle Smoke*. Tongue in cheek. A year teaching criminology in West Africa led me to dropping the academic routine, and I started over, at the bottom of the song trade—playing the bars of British Columbia. I remember the night Picasso died, and news came on the TV in our motel room in Prince George. The Indians in the next room began to moan and chant. *The death chant*. Picasso was a heavy cat. *An Indian*. This is a cubist song about guns. But back to Africa—one time I bribed my way through an armed road block by offering a grapefruit to a drunken soldier who had a gun in my face. Excuse me, if I'm boring you…This is on *Blood and Candle Smoke,* and Winston Watson, who used to play with Dylan, is on the drums. Nick Luka plays the West African palm wine guitar.

CHORDS

Key of G. Finger picked—sort of West African *Juju* music. Palm wine guitar.

Verse	*Chorus*
G	Em
G	G
C-G	Am
D-G	D-G

CRIMINOLOGY

I've had a gun pointed at my head on several occasions, yeah Nadine, I was scared
Something 'bout a black man with machine gun, made you wished you'd said your prayers
It was Nigeria—the year was 1969
I was teaching Criminology and played a little guitar on the side

In Apache Pass, Prince Rupert, Indian Jack put a gun to my head
He said, "How you like it now, Mr. White Boy? How's your blue-eyed boy, Mister Death?"
It was Canada—the year was 1971,
I was performing at the Smiling Buddha, in the neon world of knives and guns

> Excuse me if I am boring you, dear listener
> Please except my humble apology
> You may think that I'm just a folksinger
> No! I'm a Master in the Art of Criminology

When Picasso died the Indians cried, in a Prince George hotel room
We were drunker than a thousand white men, playing lumber camp saloons
It was Canada again, the year was 1973
There were grizzly bears walkin' down Main Street, what an amazing sight to see

Well, the Devil rides a cubist horse, the devil he's got angles
But God is an expressionist, he's got the Devil strangled
Down in Purgatory and Limbo and Hell, and all them southern rib joints just like that
God's waiting room is full of painters and poets, and old black jazz saints in pork pie hats

> Excuse me if I'm boring you...

So I got off that plane in Ibadan, Nigeria, 1969
Arrested by *Ton Ton Macoutes*, taking photos was a war zone crime
They were gonna hack me up with machetes, and a U.S. ambassador come pay my bribe
So I played guitar with *Sir Victor Uwaifo*, and taught a little Criminology on the side

> That's my story and I'm stickin' to it, No regrets, no surrender, no apologies
> I know a little bit about a lot of things and I'm a Master in the Art of Criminology

CROSSES OF SAN CARLOS

"The West—promise and dream, legend and myth, the West that has not only escaped the painter, the poet and the movie makers, but because of this has escaped reality itself…"
William Eastlake

The great Sonora desert at sunrise. Two strung-out Apache kids in a stolen car. White crosses of car-wrecked Indians lining the two lane roads. Names of dead warrior kids on highway signs. A Mexican jaguar crossing over the border. *Endangered.* Looking for food. Casino lights in the distance. Parking lots littered with empty Cobra malt liquor cans. Saguaro. Ocotillo. Agave. Blood red sunsets. High beam lights. Oblivion. Reincarnation. The circle. This is on *Blood and Candle Smoke*.

CHORDS

Key of B. Capo on 4th fret in G chord positions.

Verse	*Chorus*	Bridge:
G	G-D-C	(One night when the moon…)
G	D-C	
F-C	G-F-G	Em-Bm
G (form repeats 4x)		C-G
		Em-Bm
		C-D

CROSSES OF SAN CARLOS

Two Apache kids in a stolen car,
Navigating by a falling star.
    Where are they going?
Toward Jerusalem Mountain, red amphetamine sunrise,
Mesquite, Saguaro, great mystical agave, tell 'em please,
    Where are they going?
Past the little white crosses, the highway signs,
"Stay away from that double yellow line, Jimmy Yellow Eye,
    Take care where you're going"
Ain't no alcohol allowed on the reservation,
They're headed out in search of strong libation, Ai Yi!
    They know where they're going!

  Out where the crosses of San Carlos, shine 'neath the desert moon
  Near the canyons where Geronimo rode, and the Ocotillo blooms
    Where's it all going?

Old Mexican jaguar crossed over last night,
Near the Agua Prieta border town lights
  Where's the old man going?
He's on the track of a deer or a javelina hog,
He ain't afraid of your huntin' dogs
  He knows where he's going.
He disdains your greed and your ignorance
Your razor wire, your chain link fence
  He knows where he's going.

Out where the crosses of San Carlos...

    And one night when the moon is down,
    We'll come back on you stronger
    Out on this Lordsburg Highway,
    We'll be crucified no longer

"We've seen it come and we'll watch it go,
The beer is gone, the gasoline's low,"
  Says Jimmy Yellow Eye, "Where in hell are we going?"
"Look up ahead in our high beam lights,
Some kind of leopard coming at us through the night,
  Where's the old man going?
Maybe he's takin' back his ancient hunting ground,
Blood on the streets of the cowboy towns! Yi Yi
  He knows where he's going!"
Then the scream of the tires, the curse and the swerve,
The final war cry on the final curve,
  Where in hell were they going?

  Out where the crosses of San Carlos, shine 'neath the desert moon
  Near the canyons where Geronimo rode, and the Ocotillo blooms
    Where's it all going?
    Where is it going?

MISSISSIPPI RIVER RUNNIN' BACKWARDS

"On this day in 1812, the most violent of a series of earthquakes near Missouri causes a so-called fluvial tsunami in the Mississippi River, actually making the river run backward for several hours..."

"This Day in History"
February 7

I used to see these fanatical religious pamphlets on the coming of *The Rapture*, where Christ was descending from heaven right onto what looked like the Hollywood Freeway. Cars were smashing against each other and dead people were rising up out of the ground, etc. Bad news. It's the Old Testament vision of those slick-hair evangelists. In the case of this song—it's all a backdrop for God punishing greedy bank presidents—*or something*. Maybe that's an easy shot. I like the image of the river running backwards. It's fun to sing. I dreamed I heard Levon Helm and The Band singing this one...that's the sound I had in mind. Or Dan Penn and Spooner Oldham. Funky. With horns.

CHORDS

Key of G. Like The Band—"Up on Cripple Creek."

Verse	*Chorus*	*Bridge*
G-Am	G-Am	(Steamboat whistle...)
D-C	Bm-Em-F-C-G	B flat-Am
G-Am		G
D-C-G		B flat-Am
		D

MISSISSIPPI RIVER RUNNIN' BACKWARDS

Mississippi river runnin' backwards, earthquakes shook the land
It happened down here in 1812, it's happenin' here again
Feast and famine, y'all, fire and flood—abominations, you understand?
Don't need no Old Testament prophet to tell me, we're livin' in the Promised Land

    Everybody sing, blow Gabriel, blow—blow that ragtime jazz
    Judgment day is comin' down on the land of the razz-ma-tazz

I saw carpet sweepers and microwave ovens, I saw busted out television screens
Empty of TV evangelist cats, with their hair all slicked down with Brill Cream
Now the gospel news is really real bad news, no need to invent all that doom and gloom
It's a one-legged race to the liquor store, then a hop, skip and jump into the tomb

    Everybody sing, blow Gabriel, blow….

        Steam boat whistles blowin' underwater
        Everything backwards and upside down
        Baby Moses in the bulrushes
        Paddling sideways to higher ground

Old ladies gamblin' in riverboat casinos, whirlpools swallowed 'em down
Insurance executives and banking presidents, bushwhacked tryin' to leave town
But their lifeboats went backwards up the Mississippi river, into the ancient
        old Missouri sod
Up through Iowa and Minnesota, into the hands of a righteous God

THE MOST DANGEROUS WOMAN IN AMERICA

"Pray for the dead and fight like hell for the living."
Mother Jones

My friend Ed Becker is a third generation funeral director in Mount Olive, Illinois. Mount Olive is the site of the Mother Jones monument, near old Route 66. Mother Jones (1837 to 1930) was a prominent fighter for miner rights, co-founded the IWW, and also fought for children's rights. One district attorney called her "The most dangerous woman in America," because when she lifted her hand, two hundred men would go out on strike. She was also called "The grandmother of all agitators" on the Senate floor, and she retorted, "I hope to become the great-grandmother of all agitators." In his folk song collection, *The American Songbag*, Carl Sandburg implied that Mother Jones was the "*she*" in the song "She'll Be Coming Round the Mountain When She Comes." Gene Autry also recorded a song in 1931 called "The Death of Mother Jones."

Ed Becker is collecting a series of songs about Mother Jones for a record that will benefit keeping her monument maintained. I wrote this for Ed. There used to be a bar in Mount Olive called Pee Wee's House of Knowledge. Cool, eh? This song has echoes of Merle Travis's mining songs and the atmosphere of Bruce Springsteen's *Nebraska* record.

CHORDS

Drop D tuning. Low E string dropped to D. Key of D. Finger picked.

Verse	*Chorus*	*Bridge*
D	G-Bm	(That night
D-Bm	G-D	in the House…)
D		G-F#m
D-Bm		Em-D
		G-F#m
		Em-A

THE MOST DANGEROUS WOMAN IN AMERICA

Three weeks out of prison, he drives the cold Missouri night
Strip malls and abandoned mines out on the left and the right
He drives into Mount Olive and the Becker Funeral Home
Where his daddy's lyin' with a cold hard stare, black lung and broken bones

    The most dangerous woman in America, is buried on the edge of town
    Look out, Ma, another miner's goin' down

It's darker than a dungeon down in those abandoned mines
He's drunk in the *The House of Knowledge*, plays "Sixteen Tons" a thousand times
It's colder that a witch's tit when the wind blows through these streets
Old minin' men in the Legion Bar, they're starin' at their feet

    The most dangerous woman in America is buried on the edge of town
    Look out, Ma, another miner's goin' down

The wind blows through the empty rooms of a corporation farm
There's a little blue man on the kitchen floor shootin' sparks into his arm
Three car funeral rollin' by out on the county line
"Bye bye, Daddy you're heaven bound, but right now so am I."

    The most dangerous woman in America is buried on the edge of town
    Next to the grave where they laid his daddy down

        That night in *The House of Knowledge*, he buys him a '38
        And drives out to the Discount Liquor store on the Interstate
        The Most Dangerous Woman in America has a tear froze in her eye
        For the sons and daughters of minin' men who've lost their way tonight

Bullets fly and one man dies, and one drives off alone
To the cemetery midnight and the grave of Mother Jones
He whispers low his daddy's name and then, "Mother I've come to pray…and pay
For all you done for the minin' men back in the violent days."

    The Most Dangerous Woman in American, smiles deep in the frozen ground
    And there's sirens comin' through a dead end minin' town

    The Most Dangerous Woman in America is buried on the edge of town
    Look out, Ma, another man is goin' down

DON'T LOOK DOWN

"Everything being a constant carnival, there is no carnival left."

Victor Hugo
Les Misérables

I am reminded of Ray Bradbury's carnival story, *Something Wicked this Way Comes*. It's also a film. I've always been drawn to carnivals and circuses. One of our best friends in Switzerland is Freddy Nock, the greatest wire walker in the world. I've been on a wire with him (three feet off the ground) and inside his *wall of death* motorcycle cage. The circus metaphor fits with the troubadour life. And Ferris wheels and roller coasters! Coney Island. There was a remark that I loved—made by an old heavy metal rocker—he was talking about the band he was in, and their fall from the big time: "I knew we were headed in the wrong direction when I looked up from the stage every night and saw a Ferris wheel…" Indeed. This is a song about forgiveness. Rising above the carnival, and the virtual reality of the past. The last verse references meeting my wife, who was a good friend of Doug Sahm's—*Sir Douglas*. Don't look down. Don't look back. We named our latest DVD *Don't Look Down,* and Freddy Nock uses the song in one of his wire-walking films. The song is on *Blood and Candle Smoke*.

CHORDS

Key of F. Capo on 3rd fret in D chord positions. Circus waltz.

Verse:	Chorus:	Bridge:
D-G-D-G-D	Same as verse	(St. Mary…)
D-A-G-D		Cmaj7-Bm
G-D-G-D		Cmaj7-G
D-A-G-D		D

DON'T LOOK DOWN

Have I been too far? Have I seen too much?
Working in the shadows of your big Ferris wheel
It's been ten thousand nights in these sawdust and mud shows
Walking the tightrope for a room and a meal

    Don't look down, the ground might be burning
    We're turning the corner now, we might run into God
    From the Plains of the Buffalo, to the wild dogs of Mexico
    To the loves that have laid us low, we got to leave that behind

    Oh, the rhymes of the ranges, and the kindness of strangers
    I have run all the changes of the Chickasaw waltz
    Tasted lipstick and nylons, seen your mental asylums
    Turned my back on that violence, before I turned into salt

        Saint Mary, mother of patience
        Saint Joseph of the hammer and the nail
        Come build me a ladder, to the heart of the matter
        High above the moon that shines tonight
        On this carnival trail

She stood in the corner, right next to her mother
Sir Douglas her brother, since she was a child
And the difference in years, and people's cheap fears
And their magazine tears, drove us into the wild

    Don't look down....

GUADALUPE

"Let not your heart be disturbed...Am I not here, who is your mother? Are you not under my protection? Do not grieve nor be disturbed by anything."
                                        Our Lady of Guadalupe

I was the one in the back pew, sitting for hours, watching the pilgrims, tourists and Indians file past that image—Our Lady of Guadalupe. The image on the cape of Juan Diego. The Mother of the Americas. Mexico City. Outside, *on that hill*, the older shrines sank into the Mexican earth. When I thought of the experience, years later, in my house in El Paso...the Franklin Mountains were turning pink outside my window, then blood red with the sundown. The color of old mission wine. I couldn't get the Guadalupe image out of my head, and it merged with those magic red mountains. The original story? A woman, a spirit, appeared to a poor Indian on a hill in Mexico. Five hundred years ago. She spoke in his Indian tongue, *Nahuatl*. He gathered Castilian roses in his cape—as she'd instructed—and when he opened the cape, later, her image was there. And a beautiful and powerful image it is—whether it's in a picture print, on a candle glass, or tattooed on the back on a convict. It's *haunting*. This song has nothing to do with Catholicism, or any other form of religion or black magic. It has to do with hope and belief and spirits and images and Indians. Take from it what you wish. It's my favorite song that I've written. Gretchen Peters does a powerful version on our record, *One to the Heart, One to the Head*. My version appears on the record, *Blood and Candle Smoke*.

CHORDS

Key of B, Capo on 4th Fret, played in G chord positions. Finger picked.

Verse
G-G-Am
Am-D-D7-G
G-G-Am
Am-D-D7-G

Chorus
G-C-G
G-Am-D7-G
G-C-C-G
G-Am-D-G

GUADALUPE

There are ghosts out in the rain tonight, high up in those ancient trees
 Lord, I've given up without a fight, another blind fool on his knees
And all the Gods that I'd abandoned, begin to speak in simple tongue
And suddenly I've come to know, there are no roads left to run

Now it's the hour of dogs a barking, that's what the old ones used to say
It's first light or it's sundown, before the children cease their play
When the mountains glow like mission wine, then turn grey like a Spanish roan
Ten thousand eyes will stop to worship, then turn away and head on home

    She is reaching out her arms tonight, Lord, my poverty is real
    I pray roses shall rain down again, from Guadalupe on her hill
    And who am I to doubt these mysteries? Cured in centuries of blood and candle smoke
    I am the least of all your children here, but I am most in need of hope

She appeared to Juan Diego, she left her image on his cape
Five hundred years of sorrow, cannot destroy their deepest faith
So here I am, your ragged disbeliever, old doubting Thomas drowns in tears
As I watch your church sink through the earth, like a heart worn down through fear

    She is reaching out her arms tonight…

MESABI

> *"Where I grew up was as far from the cultural center as you could get. It was way out of the beaten path...the culture was mainly circuses and carnivals, preachers and barnstorming pilots, hillbilly shows and comedians..."*
> Bob Dylan
> *Rolling Stone*

A few years ago I played a concert in Duluth and we drove by Bob Dylan's childhood home, where he lived his first few years before his family moved up to Hibbing on the Mesabi iron ore range. (Mesabi means *Sleeping Giant* in Ojibwa.) I looked out at the view this kid had from his bedroom window in Duluth. Lake Superior and the old rusty barges in dead of winter. I imagined him listening to Hank Williams on the radio and he looked out on the frozen lake. Dreaming. The Masonic Temple where he saw Buddy Holly was just down the hill. Next day we drove up to Hibbing, where he was raised. It was haunting. Looked like a movie set from a small town in 1950. Closed down theaters. Polish dance halls. Somewhere there was the storefront where his father once had a hardware store. My main thought was, *This kid came out of here and did what he did?* He didn't come from New York, or Dublin, or Paris. Then I thought of myself in that room in Inglewood, California, listening to Joan Baez sing Dylan's "Don't Think Twice It's All Right," on my uncle George's LP record player. I wanted to be a songwriter, but I didn't have the guts to step outside my room, yet, with that old Spanish guitar.

This is the title song to the record: *Mesabi*.

CHORDS

Key of D. Capo on 2nd fret in C chord positions. Rock.

Verse	*Bridge*	*Chorus*
(Guitar Figure:	(The kid heard...)	(Some things
C-G-F vamped between phrases)	Am-F	never change...)
	Am-Em	G-C-*(C-G-F)*-F-C-*(C-G-F)*
C-*(C-G-F)*-F-C *(C-G-F)*	Am-G	
F-Am-G	F-C-D-G	F-Am
C-F-C		Am-G
F-Am-G		G-F

MESABI

Have you ever seen Duluth? When the Great Lake waves are pounding?
There must be some way out of there, kid, you might end up lost or drowning
And the polkas at the Polish dance hall, and the carnivals of spring
And the rock and roll on an upright piano, didn't the kid make the high school rafters ring?

    The kid who heard Howlin' Wolf, every night on the radio
    From those air waves blasting all the way up from Nogales, Mexico
    And the ducktail boys in Saint Cloud polished up their chords of fame
    And the armory show where Buddy Holly sang, "The Learning of the Game."

        Some things never change, on the Mesabi Iron Range
        Where that wild north country rain, screams,
        "Please don't make me do the work my father did"
        Bethlehem of the troubadour kid

Have you ever heard that desert wind blow? 'Cross the City of the Angels?
I was the kid playin' football, in that Catholic school deep down in Mexican town
Richie Valens sang, "La Bamba," it's eighty miles to Tijuana
I stole my parent's car one night—never found the dark-eyed ladies in the cowboy songs

    Just a kid listening to my uncle George's record player
    While the great vinyl wheel spun round its holy prayer
    And steel guitars in the Telecaster bars of the San Joaquin towns
    And "Don't Think Twice It's All Right," from the wild Mesabi Holy Ground

        Some things never change, it's still the learning of the game
        You might end up on Fifth and Main, kid
        Please don't make me go out like my father did,
        I wanna sing like the Troubadour kid

FAREWELL NEVER NEVER LAND

Tinker Bell: *You know that place between sleep and awake, the place where you can still remember dreaming? That's where I'll always love you...That's where I'll be waiting."*
                J.M. Barrie
                Peter Pan

It's hard to erase that Disney vision in my mind—Peter Pan flying out the window, in London, with Wendy and her little brother, and their stuffed bear, in tow. Off to *Never, Never Land*—an island near *the second star on the right*...a dreamland of pirates, crocodiles and Native Americans. The recorded voice of Peter Pan was Bobby Driscoll—a great kid actor in the 1940s and '50s. Peter Pan was the boy who never grew up. Then a few years ago I picked up a book called *The Semina Scene*, about a beat-jazz-junkie scene centered around Venice, California in the 1940s and '50s. Bobby Driscoll's rise and fall was detailed in the book—he was a collage artist, post Disney, and a junkie who did prison time. He died in a vacant lot in New York and was buried in a pauper's grave. Be careful when you wish upon a star. Can you imagine this American life? A kid from Cedar Rapids, Iowa. My family rented a small ranch in Topanga Canyon (near Malibu) in the late 1950s, and it was there I think I ran into what was left of Bobby. My father has just bought me a bone-spavined racehorse named My Chief. Broke down gelding racehorses were considered discardable. We paid one silver dollar for it. The horse hung himself in barbed wire...sort of like Bobby Driscoll and the entire age, don't ya think? This song is on *Mesabi*.

CHORDS

Key of G. Broadway Musical—Rock and Roll.

Opening Refrain
(*Second Star...*)
F-Bflat-F-Bflat-F-C
Bflat-F-Bflat-F-D
Em-A-Em-A-Em-D

Verse
G-D-C-D-G-D-C-D
(All 4 lines)
Tag line: Am-D

Chorus
G-D-C-D
(Same...First three lines)
Tag: Farewell....
Em-A Em-A, Em-D

FAREWELL NEVER NEVER LAND

Second star to the right, straight on 'til morning, my little friend
There's an Island called Never Land, where childhood dreams never end
Farewell, Never Never Land, Farewell, Never Never land...

Some kids playing baseball in a vacant lot in New York City, found a body
    lyin' in the weeds
The voice of Peter Pan, the cabin boy in *Treasure Island*—Mommy didn't tell me
    Peter Pan could bleed.

No one identified the body, he was buried in an unmarked Potter's Field grave
From Cedar Rapids Iowa to Chino State Prison, oh! what a holy noise Bobby Driscoll made
    Adventures in the Hollywood skin trade

    Whatever happened to Bobby Driscoll?
    Whatever happened to Peter Pan?
    Whatever happened to the cabin boy, young Jim Hawkins?
        Farewell Never Never Land, Farewell Never Never land.

When Walt Disney terminated Bobby Driscoll's contract, little Bobby got the blues
He screamed, "Nobody terminates Peter Pan, Uncle Walt," then he started walkin'
    backwards in a junkie's shoes
Song of the South, *The Happy Time*, *Treasure Island*, *When I Grow Up*—Bobby Driscoll
    played hell out of 'em all
He was the first child actor to move to Topanga Canyon—the first one to take a fall
    Yeah Bobby really hit the wall

    Whatever happened to Bobby Driscoll...?

    Second star to the right...

CONTINUED

My old man got us a ranch in Topanga Canyon, bought me a broke down thoroughbred
    named, My Chief
That crazy old racehorse died all tangled-up in barbed wire, sort of like Bobby Driscoll
    and the entire age, don't ya' think?
I saw Bobby hangin' out near the Topanga Canyon Market—to tell ya the truth,
    he looked a trifle stoned
I walked up to him and said, "Gee, Bobby, I thought you were great in *Treasure Island…*"
He snarled, "Go away kid, and leave me the hell alone." Like a dog and I was gonna
    take away his bone

    Whatever happened to Bobby Driscoll?...

THE TRAIN OF LIFE
Woodcut by Tom Russell
2012

THE LONESOME DEATH OF UKULELE IKE

Jiminy Crickett: *Well, guess he won't need me any more. What does an actor want with a conscience anyway?*
                      Pinocchio, 1940

Every Sunday evening at six the *Walt Disney Show* came on the TV. It started with that high, creepy little voice singing "When You Wish Upon a Star." "When your heart is in your dreams, no request is too extreme..." Indeed. The singer was Jiminy Cricket, alias Cliff Edwards, alias Ukulele Ike. Ike was a vaudeville star in the 1920s and '30s—he brought the ukulele to prominence. My mother played one. She even sang some of his songs. "California, Here I Come," and others. Cliff was a funny little jazz cat. Later in his life he developed drug and alcohol problems, and used to hang around the Disney studio looking for work. He died in a charity ward in Hollywood, and the body was unclaimed (just like Bobby Driscoll). The Disney studio later found out and provided a grave. I can't get over the brutal American fact that the voices of Peter Pan and Jiminy Cricket, *the voices of my childhood*, died in the gutter and were buried in pauper's graves. It's an Old Testament thing, I suppose. Ashes to ashes. This song is on *Mesabi*. Fats Kaplin plays the ukulele.

CHORDS

Key of F. Ukulele Jazz.

Verse
F-Fdim7-Gm-C
F-Fdim7-Gm-C
Bflat-F-C-F-Bflat-F-C-F
Bflat-F-C-Dm-Gm-C

Chorus
Bflat-F-C
Bflat-F-C
Bflat-F-C
Gm-C

THE LONESOME DEATH OF UKULELE IKE

I was born in Hannibal Missouri, a funny little frog-faced man
Made my livin' singin' in the movies, on the back lots of Fantasy Land
Mark Twain came from Hannibal Missouri, and various other drunks like me
I learned to play the Ukulele, and reinvented my Destiny

    But no one really dies, do they?
    Not if they play the Ukulele
    And no one cries, baby
    Not if they're wishin' on a star, well...*maybe*

Yes, I kept Singin' in the Rain, dancin' in the Klieg Light sunshine too
I was the voice of Jiminy Cricket, wishin' on a star for you
But I died penniless and forgotten, in the motion picture old folks home
In Never Land I was in high cotton, my voice warbled out of the gramophone

    But no one really dies, do they?...

So hand me down my walkin' cane, my old vaudevillian crooner's pipes
Heh, I got one more song for you, Charley, it's called "The Lonesome Death
    of Ukulele Ike"!

    But no one really dies, do they?...

STERLING HAYDEN

"And in the worship of security we fling our lives beneath the wheels of routine—and before we know it our lives are gone. What does a man need—really need? A few pounds of food each day, heat and shelter, six feet to lie down in—and some form of working activity that will yield a sense of accomplishment. That's all—in the material sense, and we know it."
    Sterling Hayden

I used to see him on the Johnny Carson *Tonight* show. Sterling Hayden. *Actor. Sailing man. Author.* Smoking and asking the audience if anyone had a free room over the Hudson River where he could write. Then I recall a rough, black-and-white documentary on him from the 1960s, where he's sitting below decks, on his barge in Amsterdam or Paris, drunkenly talking about his life. His main hang up was ratting on people during the McCarthy hearings. He never got over it. That, and he hated the acting life. Sterling Hayden's face, his voice, and his craggy, honest-to-God character, define the image of the tough guy with a heart of gold in noir films. He was the real thing.

CHORDS

Key of D. Capo on 2nd fret, in C chord positions. Sea Shanty style.

Verse
C-F-C-G
C-F-G-C

Chorus
Same as verse.

STERLING HAYDEN

Sterling Hayden on a barge in Amsterdam, one of those backwater Dutch Canals
A bottle of Johnny Walker between his legs, drunk, but articulate as hell

He was saying, "Yeah, I ratted on people during the McCarthy hearings…Huh!
You haven't the foggiest notion of the contempt I feel for myself,
Maybe that's why we drink, eh? Some damn thing. Shipwrecks the heart. Huh? Yah!"

Sterling Hayden on a two-masted schooner, kidnapped his kids and sailed
    'round the globe
But a man can sail in one big circle, and not escape his wounded sailor's soul

> "So heave her up, my bully boys, heave her up and away we'll go
> We're bound for the bay where the white whale plays, in the midnight
>   straits of Jericho
> And if ever I return, Pretty Peggy O, All your cities I will burn…yes, I would
> With your cardboard sea and your paper moon, o'er the penny arcade
>   called Hollywood"

He ran guns through the German lines in World War Two, the Viking God
    stood six feet five
Played in *Johnny Guitar*, and *The Asphalt Jungle*, The *Killing*, and *The Long Goodbye*.

I saw him once on the Johnny Carson show, late in his troubled career
He said, "Just give me a room over lookin' the Hudson River, with a mattress
    and a typewriter,
And I'll write you a helluva novel, my dears…"

So here's to all the tough guy actors, and the false gods who made 'em
And wherever he sails tonight on the Seven Seas, may the Lord sail
    with Sterling Hayden.

FURIOUS LOVE

Martha: *Look, sweetheart, I can drink you under any god damn table you want, so don't worry about me.*
　　　　Edward Albee
　　　　Who's Afraid of Virginia Woolf?

There used to be live alligators in the fountain in the middle of the square in downtown El Paso. I believe this lasted until the mid 1960s. Too many drunks and little kids bothering the beasts. Now there's a large fiberglass sculpture in the fountain. *Alligators.* The gators are frozen in time, leaping up toward the upper floors of the old, closed down Plaza Hotel. Liz Taylor shared a penthouse on top with her first husband, Nicky Hilton. Nicky had something to do with building the joint. On the record *Mesabi*, I needed a link between Hollywood songs and Juarez songs, and Liz's presence in El Paso fit the bill. Then I read the book *Furious Love,* about Liz and Richard Burton, and I came to admire both of them. My wife's parents used to have an apartment in the Swiss Alps. Richard Burton had once owned it—moved in when he was fighting with Liz. The rooms had a pleasant, smoky odor of old Scotch, cigar smoke, and Shakespeare. Hail the Burtons! Hail their furious seasons!

CHORDS

Key of A. Capo on 2nd fret, played in G chord positions. Waltz.

Verse	*Verse*	*Chorus*
G-Bm	C-Bm-	C-G
C-D-G	Am-G	D-G
G-Bm	G-Bm	C-Bm
C-G	C-D	Am-D-G

FURIOUS LOVE

There's a penthouse on top of the old Plaza Hotel,
 In El Paso, looking out on Juarez
Liz Taylor lived there once, with her husband Nicky Hilton,
At least that's what the newspaper said

But now the Plaza's closed down and Juarez is on fire
And the news came tonight that Liz died
And one old alligator, in the Plaza Square fountain
Looked up at that penthouse and cried

>   She chased furious love, through her furious seasons
>   Always dancing between the rhyme and the reason
>   Tonight in El Paso, I'll raise a double gin fizz,
>   For the loves and the legend of Liz

ROLL THE CREDITS, JOHNNY

"The problem with the world is that everyone is a few drinks behind."

Humphrey Bogart

I ran into two old Irish bachelors on a street in Belfast who had just come out of a cinema. They were vowing to spend the rest of their lives at the movies. That's all I overheard. They disappeared into a pub for a pint. *Ah, those old films and love songs.* My wife kept saying I should write a song that could be used in a movie. I went out to my office one day and wrote this one. For the celluloid dreamers. Monte Hellman used it in his fine film, *The Road to Nowhere*. This song appears as a demo on *Veteran's Day: The Tom Russell Anthology,* and a newer version is on *Mesabi*.

CHORDS

Key of Bflat. Capo on 3rd fret, played in G chord positions.

Verse	*Chorus*
G-C	C-G
C-G-G-D	C-G-C-G
D-G-C	G-D
C-G-G-D	D-C-D-G

ROLL THE CREDITS, JOHNNY

Roll the credits, Johnny, you up there in the projection booth
Dreamtime is over now, time to put our shoes on, and hit the street
But wasn't it beautiful? Didn't we forget about the sad times for awhile?
The good guys won, the bad guys tasted bitterness and defeat

We kissed the leading ladies. Felt the warmth of their deep caress
Drank with kings and prophets, we rode rocket ships to the stars
But it's dark now on the streets of life. Christ, I think I lost my pocket knife in there,
Goddamnit, Johnny, I can't even remember where in hell we parked the car…

    But singin' keeps the fear away, and whistlin' keeps the wolves at bay
    Remember'n all we might have been, all the love that could have been
    Let's storm the old ramparts!
    Let's sing those love songs from old movies in our heart

The way she brushed her hair back with her hand
Christ, I wish I was her leading man
She knows more than you'll ever know, Johnny,
She talks to birds and animals, why won't she talk to me?

Wish she could just step down off the screen,
That little blonde in tight black jeans
Christ, I'm losing my mind now, Johnny,
The crows are laughing at us, up in the trees.

    But singin' keeps the fear away…

THE ROAD TO NOWHERE

> *"Voltaire's observation 'Illusion is the first of all pleasures' is the tag line of Monte Hellman's grandiloquent neo-noir,* Road to Nowhere. *The dangerous temptation to embrace impossible dreams is also addressed in Tom Russell's title song, a gloomy stylistic mash-up of Dylan, Springsteen and Cash…Mr. Russell sings in the sepulchral tone of a dour country prophet warning of inevitable doom."*
> Stephen Holden
> *The New York Times*

I was familiar with that iconic and masterful Monte Hellman road movie, *Two Lane Blacktop*, with James Taylor and Dennis Wilson, so when Monte Hellman's office called me about a soundtrack for his new film—I was honored. Monte said he had all my CDs. Would I write a theme song to his film, *Road to Nowhere*? *Surely*. Except I read the script several times and couldn't makes heads nor tails of the plot. It's a movie within a movie—for starters. But it finally soaked in. It was like one of those great old Italian films. I wrote this song and recorded it into a hand held digital recorder, as a *demo*—and that was the version and recording Monte used in the film. I was supposed to act in the movie, but that part was cut out. We attended the premier at The Egyptian Theater in Hollywood, drank Monte's margaritas, and came to love this great director. This is a bonus track on the record *Mesabi*.

CHORDS

Drop D tuning (Low E string dropped to D) Key of D.

Verse	*Chorus*
D	D-G
G	G-F#m
G-D	F#m-Em
D-A	A-D (Repeat)
D	
D-G	
G-D	
Em-A-D	

THE ROAD TO NOWHERE

Well the ditches are on fire
And there ain't no higher ground
You were a prince in the City of Angels, kid
Now you're pawning your clothes in a railroad town
Well, forgiveness is the killer of snakes, amigo
In the gardens of despair
Keep your mind in the middle, little brother
Out on the road to nowhere

From the Polo Club in Ibadan,
To an abandoned church in Rome
You keep thinking you recognize faces
The way the flesh is carved like ice over bone
You're making deals with the wrong class of people
Balanced between a curse and a prayer
But there's a thin line between power and glory
Out on that road to nowhere

    Row, row, row, you're your little dreamboat
    Silently down stream
    Bankers, Cops, and Candlestick makers
    They've all gone wise to your dirty little schemes
    You're riding backwards on a blind horse
    In a carnival tent way out there
    Where the tunnel of love was never finished
    Out on that road to nowhere

So it's ashes to ashes, dirt to dirt
You're ridin' high on Oxycontin and vodka, kid
So why in hell do you still hurt?
Now every day is the day of reckoning
Even the weather man makes you feel scared
Rise up Dead Man, keep on staggering down
That old broken road to nowhere

HEART WITHIN A HEART

> *"Knock on yourself as upon a door and walk upon yourself as on a straight road. For if you walk on the road, it is impossible for you to go astray...Open the door for yourself that you may know what is...Whatever you will open for yourself, you will open."*
>
> The Teachings of Silvanus

Another nod to the Gnostic Gospels—the secret Gospels unearthed in Egypt in 1946. An assortment of deep and odd poetry. *Dig a little deeper during the tough times, kid. Whatever you bring forth will save you...*True enough. I always thought the Gnostic Gospels shed a little more light on the *official* Old and New Testaments. Added the jazz and poetry. Jesus, in the end, was just a troubadour who never passed the hat. This was recorded at Jack Johnson's studio in Hollywood, with Van Dyke Parks on piano and the McCrary sisters, who sang with Bob Dylan, on the gospel vocals. Thad Beckman plays guitar. The song appears on *Mesabi*.

CHORDS

Key of G. Capo on 5th fret, played in D chord positions. Finger picked.

Chorus
There is a Heart…
D-G
D-A
D-G
D-A-D (2X)

Verse
A-D
E-A
G-F#m
Em-A

HEART WITHIN A HEART

There is a heart within your heart
A place to go when all the trouble starts
When your world spins upside down and falls apart
There is a heart within your heart

There is a soul within your soul
A secret room only angels know
Come on baby, leave your fear, rise up and go
To the soul within the soul

Once there was a crooked man, who walked a crooked mile
And all the people laughed at him, but the crooked man he smiled
As he took the road not taken, while others stood in line
He climbed his crooked mountains, one song at a time

There is a heart within your heart…

Jesus walked on water, then he turned it all to wine
He climbed his hill of destiny, one song at a time
He said, "Everything you bring forth, will save your troubled soul,
And all the fear you keep inside, will turn your heart to coal."

There is a heart within your heart…

AND GOD CREATED BORDER TOWNS

Vargas: *This isn't the real Mexico. You know that. All border towns bring out the worst in a country*
Orson Welles
Touch of Evil

When I first moved to El Paso I used to listen to a little A.M. radio station out of Juarez called Radio Canon (cannon in English.) After the radio I.D., they played the sound of an automatic weapon firing, then launched into another *narco-corrido* record. Those are the modern folk yarns about drug dealers and shootouts, pushed along by the sound of accordions, out of tune horns, *bajo sexto*, and maybe a tuba chugging along underneath. In the early days (1997 to 98), I almost got caught in the middle of two gun battles outside the Juarez bull ring. These were the incipient days of the drug war which has now made Juarez the murder capitol of—and the most dangerous city in—the world. Augie Meyers was playing my little grand piano at the house one day and I told him I'd never heard him play whorehouse honky-tonk. I picked out one of Augie's wild melodies and wrote these words to it. Joel Guzman plays the accordion and Jacob Valenzuela, from Calexico, plays the trumpet. I like the sound of this track. *Puro Juarez cantina music*. This song is on *Mesabi*.

CHORDS

Key of C. Talking Juarez Whorehouse Cantina Mariachi Blues.

Verse
C-F
F-C
C-G
G-C (repeats)

AND GOD CREATED BORDER TOWNS

Migrants coming up from Central America,
Riding on the top of freight trains, and dying in cattle trucks
Kidnapped and extorted by cartel gangs,
Saint Jude, your children are running out of luck

Meanwhile in a Juarez alleyway,
Another seven men gone down
Sometimes the devil wears a ski mask,
And God created border towns

Our guns go 'cross the Rio Grande,
Two thousand pieces everyday
And the coke and weed and methamphetamine
Come sliding back the other way

Narco-corridos on Radio Can-yon,
Accordions cover up the deadly human sound,
The devil talks in tongues of politics,
And God created border towns

Co-written with Augie Meyers

GOODNIGHT JUAREZ

"There are two ways to lose your sanity in Juarez. One is to believe the violence results from a cartel war. The other is to claim to understand what is behind each murder."
 Charles Bowden
 Murder City

I used to love to walk over the Santa Fe Bridge into Juarez and visit the bars and backstreets and the bullring. On Sunday afternoons I'd go to the market place and buy a few songs from the music trios and mariachis who worked the beer gardens. I filmed some of this for our documentary, *Don't Look Down*. That's all gone, now, because of the drug wars. Ten thousand people dead. Most of the bars bulldozed. The Plaza Monumental bullring torn down to build a Wal-Mart. The Kentucky Club bar is still there, with its photos of old bullfighters and boxers and Mexican baseball players…but who wants to be an innocent bystander, when every coked-up cartel soldier on the street is packing an automatic weapon? Goodnight, Juarez, goodnight. I recorded this with the band *Calexico* and guests Gretchen Peters, Barry Walsh, Thad Beckman, and Joel Guzman. It appears on *Mesabi*.

CHORDS

Key of A. Capo on 2nd fret in G chord positions.

Verse
G-C
G-D
G-C
G-D-G (Repeat)

Chorus
C-G-D-G
C-G-Am-Em-D
C-Bm
Am-D

GOODNIGHT JUAREZ

Juarez, I couldn't sleep tonight
Juarez, you made me weep tonight
Across the Rio Grande, I saw your poverty lights,
Goodnight, Juarez, good night

Juarez I used to paint the town
Now you've gone and turned it upside down
Into a dark and bloody battleground
Goodnight, Juarez, goodnight

 Our Lady of the Seven Sorrows, just caught the last bus out
 She said, "Seven sorrows used to fit the bill, boys, but I'd need ten thousand now."
 The mariachi horns are silent, the guitars don't make a sound
 The children have all disappeared, or they're hiding underground

The tourist market's empty now,
They even tore the bull ring down,
You wouldn't recognize this town
Goodnight, Juarez, good night

 Vuela, vuela, palomita, you old ragged and torn Dove of Peace
 Fly across this burning desert, where bodies lie beneath
 Bring me back one faded rose, a sign of love and hope
 And drop it down on this broken city, before it all goes up in smoke

Juarez, I had a dream today
The children danced, as the guitars played
And all the violence up and slipped away
Goodnight, Juarez, good night

SAINT FRANCIS

"While you are proclaiming peace with your lips, be careful to have it even more fully in your heart."
                                        Saint Francis of Assisi

I wrote this with Gretchen Peters and it appears on her great record, *Hello Cruel World*. I'll let Gretchen take it from here. She writes: "I co-wrote this song with Tom after receiving an email with some lyrical fragments from him, among them the line, '*Saint Francis walking on the water.*' I was sitting in my house on the Gulf of Mexico, trying to write but mostly obsessing about the thousands of gallons of oil an hour that were currently spewing into the gulf due to the *Deepwater Horizon* disaster. His words reached me like a balm. Religious zealots tell us that the earthly plane doesn't matter. That the earth is ours to use and abuse. It seemed to me the lyric was about that moment when we wake up, spiritually, to the natural world—the world that Saint Francis called *the mirror of God*. We are only capable of that kind of awareness for brief periods of time—but surely it is time."

CHORDS

Key of G. Capo on 5th fret, drop-D tuning (DADGBE)

Verse:
G^{sus9}-G^{sus9}
G^{sus9}-G^{sus9}
D-C
G^{sus9}- D (Repeat)

Bridge:
D-C
G^{sus9}-D
D-C
Em-F-F
G^{sus9}-G^{sus9}

SAINT FRANCIS

Saint Francis walking on the water
All his lambs have gone to slaughter
All the creatures who receive his grace
You can see them all in his haggard face

Saint Francis begging at your doorway
You want to let him in but what will the neighbors say?
You know you can't go on but you can't give up
And he answers you with his begging cup

Saint Francis sitting at your table
A cup of tea among the faithful
Behind a wall that's made of little lies
Much to your surprise you start to cry

>	and by these wounds you will be whole again
>	by these signs you will know
>	you'll feel a stirring in your soul again
>	'til sweet amnesia takes a hold

Saint Francis sleeping in the meadow
His halo is a raven's shadow
He's been sleeping for eight hundred years
In a potter's field full of sparrow's tears

And while we sleep and dream of heaven's gates
Down here on earth the old man waits

CO-WRITTEN WITH GRETCHEN PETERS

300

APPENDIX A: CO-WRITE INFORMATION

All Tom Russell Songs:
Thomas George Russell, Frontera Music (ASCAP)
Administered by Bug Music/BMG

Tom Russell/Ian Tyson co-writes:
"Navajo Rug," "The Banks of the Musselshell," "The Rose of the San Joaquin," and "Claude Dallas." Copyright: End of the Trail Music (Socan), Frontera Music (ASCAP), Slick Fork Music (SOCAN)

Tom Russell/Dave Alvin co-writes:
"Out in California," "Between the Cracks," "Down the Rio Grande," "California Snow," and "Haley's Comet." Copyright: Frontera Music (ASCAP), Blue Horned Toad Music (BMI)

Tom Russell/Katy Moffatt co-writes:
"Walkin' on the Moon," "Sparrow of Swansea," "Wings of a Blackbird," "Half Moon Boulevard," and "The Dreamin'." Copyright: Frontera Music (ASCAP) Red Moon Music (BMI)

Tom Russell/Sylvia Tyson co-writes:
"Chocolate Cigarettes," "The Sound of One Heart Breaking," and "Saint Lily of the Mohawks." Copyright: Frontera Music (ASCAP), Salt Music (ASCAP)

Tom Russell/Nanci Griffith co-writes:
"Outbound Plane." Copyright: Universal Music Publishing

Tom Russell/Greg Trooper co-writes:
"Hong Kong Boy," and "The Heart." Copyright: Frontera Music (ASCAP) Door Number One Music (BMI), and Sony/ATV, Songs of Welk, Peg Music (BMI)

Tom Russell/Bob Neuwirth co-writes:
"The Biggest Border Town in the World," and "Beyond the Blues." Copyright: Frontera Music (ASCAP), Dry Clam Music (ASCAP)

Tom Russell/Gretchen Peters co-writes:
"Saint Francis." Copyright: Frontera Music (ASCAP), 2011 Circus Girl Music, administered by Carnival Music

Tom Russell/Steve Young co-writes:
"The Angel of Lyon." Copyright: Frontera Music (ASCAP), Golden Chain Music (BMI), H Two O Music (BMI)

Tom Russell/Paul Zarzyski co-writes:
"All This Way for the Short Ride," "Bucking Horse Moon," and "The Heart of a Bucking Horse." Copyright: Frontera Music (ASCAP), Bucking Horse Moon Music (ASCAP)

Tom Russell/Augie Meyer co-writes:
"And God Created Border Towns." Copyright: Frontera Music (ASCAP), Magnifico-Meyers Music

Tom Russell/Andrew Hardin co-writes:
"Racehorse Haynes." Copyright: Frontera Music (ASCAP), Alligator Farm Music (BMI)

Tom Russell/Peter Case co-writes:
"Beyond the Blues." Frontera Music (ASCAP), Trumpet Blast (BMI)

Tom Russell/Alan Rhody co-write:
"Ten Cent Lemonade." Copyright: Frontera Music (ASCAP), Headless Horseman Music/ Universal Music Group

APPENDIX B: TOM RUSSELL DISCOGRAPHY

Hardin & Russell
Ring of Bone (1976)
Wax Museum (1978) reissued as *The Early Years* (1994) – Dark Angel

The Tom Russell Band
Road To Bayamon (1987) – Philo
Poor Man's Dream (1989) – Philo
Hurricane Season (1991) – Philo
All Around These Northern Towns (2001) – Norske Gram
Raw Vision: 1984-1994 (2005) – Philo

Tom Russell
Heart On A Sleeve (1984) – Frontera
Cowboy Real (1991) – Philo
Beyond St. Olav's Gate: 1979-1992 (1992) – Roundtower
Box of Visions (1993) – Philo
The Rose of the San Joaquin (1995) – Hightone
The Long Way Around (1997) – Hightone
Song of the West (1997) – Hightone
The Man From God Knows Where (1999) – Hightone
Borderland (2001) – Hightone
Museum of Memories (2002) – Dark Angel
Modern Art (2003) – Hightone
Indians Cowboys Horses Dogs (2004) – Shout! Factory
Hotwalker (2005) – Hightone
Love and Fear (2006) – Hightone
The Wounded Heart of America (Tom Russell Songs) (2007)
Veteran's Day: The Tom Russell Anthology (2008) – Shout! Factory
Blood and Candle Smoke (2009) – Shout! Factory
Cowboy'd All To Hell (2010) – Frontera
Mesabi (2011) – Shout! Factory

With Gretchen Peters
One To The Heart, One To The Head (2009) – Scarlet Letter/Frontera

With Barrence Whitfield
Hillbilly Voodoo (1993) – East Side Digital
Cowboy Mambo (1994) – East Side Digital

DVDs
Hearts On The Line (2005) – Hightone
Don't Look Down (2011) – Frontera

With Ian Tyson
Mano A Mano (2008) – Canyon

Compiled by John Yuelkenbeck

APPENDIX C: TITLE INDEX

A
Acres of Corn	188
Alkali	26
All This Way for the Short Ride	162
Ambrose Larsen	184
Amelia's Railroad Flat	95
The Angel of Lyon	110
Ash Wednesday	246

B
Bacon Rind and Chief Seattle	166
The Ballad of Edward Abbey	168
The Banks of the Musselshell	148
The Basque	172
Between the Cracks	138
Beautiful Trouble	236
Beyond the Blues	56
The Biggest Border Town in the World	61
Billy Collins	128
Blood Oranges	108
Blue Wing	46
Box of Visions	106
The Boy Who Cried Wolf	220
Bucking Horse Moon	164

C
California Snow	213
Canadian Whiskey	38
Chinatown in the Rain	58
Chocolate Cigarettes	65
Claude Dallas	153
Criminology	264
Cropduster	24
Crosses of San Carlos	266
The Cuban Sandwich	68

D
The Death of Jimmy Martin	252
Denver Wind	120
Don't Look Down	272
Down the Rio Grande	204
The Dreamin'	186

E
East of Woodstock, West of Viet Nam	256
The End of the Trail	22
The Evangeline Hotel	102
The Eyes of Roberto Duran	112

F
Farewell Never Never Land	278
Finding You	263
Four Chambered Heart	239
Furious Love	286

G
Gallo del Cielo	83
And God Created Border Towns	294
Goodnight, Juarez	296
Grapevine	229
La Goulue	92
Guadalupe	274

H
Haley's Comet	90
Half Moon Boulevard	126
Hallie Lonnigan	151
Hand Carved Heart	132
The Heart	76
The Heart of a Bucking Horse	174
Heart within a Heart	292
Hong Kong Boy	74
Home Before Dark	124
Hurricane Season	98

I
Isaac Lewis	226
It Goes Away	248

J
Jack Johnson 72
Joshua Tree 30

K
The Kid From Spavinaw 218

L
Little Blue Horse 170
The Lonesome Death of Ukulele Ike 282
Love Abides 198

M
The Man From God Knows Where 178
Manzanar 104
Mesabi 276
Mineral Wells 63
Mississippi River Runnin'... 268
The Most Dangerous Woman... 270
Muhammad Ali 222

N
Nazareth to Bethlehem 70
Navajo Rug 142
Nina Simone 261

O
Oil Field Girls 54
Old Heart 250
Out in California 136
Outbound Plane 52
The Outcast 182
The Outcast (Revisited) 196

P
Patrick Russell 180
The Pugilist at Fifty-Nine 234

R
Racehorse Haynes 224
Rayburn Crane 32
The Road to Bayamon 44
The Road to Nowhere 290
Roanie 156
Roll the Credits, Johnny 288
The Rose of the San Joaquin 130

S
Saint Francis 298
Saint Lily of the Mohawks 78
Saint Olav's Gate 36
Santa Ana Wind 258
Sitting Bull in Venice 190
The Sky Above, The Mud Below 144
The Sound of One Heart Breaking 244
Spanish Burgundy 40
Sparrow of Swansea 116
Stealing Electricity 242
Sterling Hayden 284

T
Ten Cent Lemonade 122
They're Closin' Sunny's Diner 114
Throwin' Horseshoes At The Moon 194
Tonight We Ride 159
Touch of Evil 202

U, V
U.S. Steel 42
Veteran's Day 48

W
Walkin' on the Moon 50
What Work Is 215
What Do You Want 134
When Irish Girls Grow Up 192
When Sinatra Played Juarez 208
Where the Dream Begins 210
Wings of a Blackbird 118
Winnipeg 100
Woodrow 231

Z
Zane Grey 28

PANCHO VILLA
Woodcut by Tom Russell
2012

Tom Russell's records are available from
www.villagerecords.com and *www.tomrussell.com*.

Tom Russell's artwork is available from
www.rainbowman.com, www.yarddog.com
and Bishop Gallery in Scottsdale, Arizona.

Lightning Source UK Ltd.
Milton Keynes UK
UKHW05f0021240618
324670UK00010B/237/P